On NATURAL
and REVEALED
THEOLOGY

Other works by Dr. Surrendra Gangadean & The Logos Foundation:

Philosophical Foundation: A Critical Analysis of Basic Beliefs

History of Philosophy: A Critical Analysis of Unresolved Disputes

Theological Foundation: A Critical Analysis of Christian Belief

Philosophical Foundation: Trivium Study Guide

The Logos Papers: To Make the Logos Known

*The Westminster Shorter and Larger Catechisms:
A Doxological Understanding*

*The Westminster Confession of Faith:
A Doxological Understanding*

*The Logos Curriculum:
Grammar Catechisms: Philosophical, Theological, and
Historical Foundations*

Fundación Filosófica: Un Análisis Crítico de Creencias Básicas

DOXOLOGICAL REFORMED COMMENTARY SERIES:

*The Book of Revelation: What Must Soon Take Place
Doxological Postmillennialism*

*The Book of Job: Deepening the Revelation of God's Glory for All Time
An Ironic Theodicy*

*The Epistle to the Romans:
The Righteousness of God Revealed from Faith to Faith
The Gospel According to St. Paul*

*The Biblical Worldview: Creation, Fall, Redemption
Genesis 1–3: Scripture in Organic Seed Form*

On NATURAL *and* REVEALED THEOLOGY

Collected Essays of Surrendra Gangadean

SURRENDRA GANGADEAN

LOGOS PRESS PAPERS ◆ λ LOGOS

A DIVISION OF THE LOGOS FOUNDATION

Phoenix, Arizona

On Natural and Revealed Theology: Collected Essays of Surrendra Gangadean

Copyright © 2023 Surrendra Gangadean

Logos Papers Press 2023
Phoenix, Arizona
logospaperspress.com
thelogosfoundation.org

Printed in the United States of America

Cover design: Brian J. Phelps
Typesetting: Matthew P. Hicks & Brian J. Phelps
Back cover image: Don Fitzsimmons

Library of Congress Cataloging-in-Publication Data pending

Gangadean, Surrendra, 1943–2022.
    On natural and revealed theology: collected essays of Surrendra
    Gangadean
    Includes bibliographical references, footnotes, and index.
    ISBN 979-8-9880399-7-6 (hardcover)
    ISBN 979-8-9880399-8-3 (paperback)
    ISBN 979-8-9880399-9-0 (e-book)

1. Natural Theology 2. Revealed Theology 3. General Revelation
4. Special Revelation 5. Philosophical Foundation 6. Theological
Foundation I. Title

To

A wise master builder,
who laid the foundation.

A Defender of the Faith,
who demolished arguments and pretensions
raised against the knowledge of God.

A faithful servant,
who showed what is clear.

Our spiritual father,
who led us in the way everlasting.

CONTENTS

EDITOR'S PREFACE

D R. SURRENDRA GANGADEAN (1943–2022), professor, pastor, husband, father, mentor, friend, and builder, was a giant in the faith, a Philosopher among philosophers, and a Theologian among theologians. He spent a lifetime refining the foundation for philosophy, theology, and Historic Christianity. The main focus of Dr. Gangadean's work is the good as the knowledge of God and the goal of the earth being filled with the knowledge of the glory of God.[1] He argues that for this goal to be achieved, there must first be unity in the Church, that the world might believe.[2] But, for unity in the Church, there must be a shared foundation. Dr. Gangadean has paved the way in showing the philosophical, theological, and historical foundations for the Christian faith with the hope that others, by the grace of God, might build a lasting culture, a City with foundations.

Natural theology (general revelation) provides the philosophical foundation, while revealed theology (special revelation) provides the theological. Theological foundation and the work of the Holy Spirit leading the Church into all truth provide the historical foundation. Philosophical foundation argues that the basic things about God and man and good and evil are clear to reason, so that unbelief is without excuse. Dr. Gangadean seeks to establish clarity and inexcusability in a step-by-step process from foundation to fullness of life in Christ. He begins with the most basic—the cornerstone—and proceeds to the less basic, starting with Common Ground, then the argument that at least something must be eternal, that only some is eternal (matter exists and is not eternal, and the soul exists and is not eternal), for special creation (vs. naturalistic and theistic evolution), natural evil is due to moral evil (the problem of evil), the necessity for special revelation

---

1. *Isaiah 11:9; Habakkuk 2:14.*

2. *John 17:21.*

(scripture) based on the existence of natural evil, and the moral law that is written on the hearts of all men.[3]

Theological foundation builds upon these first steps, going on to show that only Genesis 1–3, and what builds on the biblical worldview of creation–fall–redemption, is consistent with clear general revelation. Dr. Gangadean has developed the biblical worldview in both narrative and theological forms, drawing out the meaning and implications of creation as revelation, sin and death, curse and promise, repentance and faith, justification and sanctification, baptism and calling, resurrection and reward. These themes are present throughout the *Collected Essays* but became crystalized in Dr. Gangadean's later work.[4]

The Historic Christian Faith is the work of the pastor-teachers, after much discussion in Church councils, summed up in the great creeds and confessions/councils of the faith. Dr. Gangadean argues that Historic Christianity builds upon what was agreed upon in The Jerusalem Council (A.D. 51), The Apostles' Creed (*ca.* 180), The Council of Nicaea (325), The Council of Carthage (397), The Council of Chalcedon (451), The Council of Orange (529), and the several creeds of the Reformation period leading up to the Westminster Confession of Faith (1648), which he considers the high-water mark of the Christian faith, meaning that it is the most conscious and consistent expression of Christian doctrine up to that time. Yet, Dr. Gangadean emphasizes that there have been serious challenges to the Christian faith, both internal and external, since the Reformation that have not yet been addressed, and that must be addressed if we are to have unity of the faith and that the world might believe. His work paves the way for addressing these challenges.[5]

---

3. These arguments are fully developed in: Surrendra Gangadean, *Philosophical Foundation: A Critical Analysis of Basic Beliefs*, Second Edition (Phoenix: Public Philosophy Press, 2022).

4. Surrendra Gangadean, *Theological Foundation: A Critical Analysis of Christian Belief* (Phoenix: Logos Papers Press, 2023).

5. For internal challenges to the Christian faith, see: Surrendra Gangadean, *The Westminster Shorter and Larger Catechisms: A Doxological Focus* (Phoenix: Logos Papers Press, 2023) and *The Westminster Confession of Faith: A Doxological Focus* (Phoenix: Logos Papers Press, 2023). For external challenges to the Christian faith, see: Gangadean, *Philosophical Foundation* and *History of Philosophy: A Critical Analysis of Unresolved Disputes* (Phoenix: Public Philosophy Press, 2022). For both internal and external challenges, see: Surrendra Gangadean, *The Logos Papers: To Make the Logos Known* (Phoenix: Logos Papers Press, 2022).

Dr. Gangadean was born in Trinidad, West Indies, on April 26, 1943. He immigrated to the United States with his family in 1957. He had a family background of Hinduism, seriously contemplated Buddhism and Existentialism, and ultimately converted to Christianity in 1961. We include his testimony in this work to show the meaning of his conversion in his own words. He graduated with an M.A. in English from Arizona State University and an M.A. in Philosophy from the University of Arizona. He started teaching within the Maricopa County Community College District in 1968, teaching for forty-five years before retiring in 2013. Dr. Gangadean developed much of his thinking about philosophical foundation in the context of teaching in the secular academy. He was pastor of Westminster Fellowship church from 2000 until 2022 and was the founder of Logos Theological Seminary. He developed much of his thinking about theological foundation in the context of pastoral ministry and preparing those who would teach in the church.

His early church background included time in the Baptist Church and then in the Charismatic movement before discovering the Reformed Faith and the Westminster Standards, which he held to for the rest of his life. Dr. Gangadean diligently sought the Lord by the ordinary means of daily searching of the Scriptures, family devotions, regular church attendance, fellowship with believers, and witness to others. His life was a witness to many who came to the faith and who continue with the hope of the teaching that he shared. His entire Christian life was focused continually on the clarity of general revelation and the inexcusability of unbelief. He brought many to faith and is now with the Lord he loved, patiently waiting and watching for us to help complete the work of the Kingdom of God on earth. Dr. Gangadean entered into rest on February 12, 2022. The Logos Foundation, the educational ministry that he founded, continues the work that he began through publications and educational outreach.

On Natural and Revealed Theology: Collected Essays of Surrendra Gangadean is a collection of published papers and public lectures presented by Dr. Gangadean and edited into essay form. We have presented the papers from the most recently presented or published to those given earlier in his life, except for the first essay, "Rational Presuppositionalism: Critically Examining Assumptions for Meaning," which we include as prolegomena to the rest of the essays. Reading backward helps the reader see his ideas' fuller expressions first and then go back to see their earlier forms. We include topics that may be repeated, such as the moral law and the unity of the faith, because, though similar, they address different aspects of the subject and are like facets of a diamond, which, when brought together, shine more brilliantly.

Dr. Gangadean's earlier essays (1975–1977) show his getting the idea of foundation into focus, deepening his understanding of the faith, and his movement to Historic Christianity. Much of his thinking during this stage stems from meditation on the Word of God and thinking through the implications of the Westminster Standards.

His mid to late career essays (1996–2013) are developed in the context of teaching within the academy, seeing the challenges of the Modern and Postmodern periods, and developing of philosophical foundation—what is clear to reason about God, man, good, and evil, including the moral law and its applications. The seeds of philosophical foundation are present in his early thinking but come to full expression during these years. His conversations within Christian philosophical circles also spurred his development of an apology for natural theology during this time.

The later post-retirement essays (2014–2020) are developed in the context of his pastoral ministry, teaching in the seminary, and outreach by seeking unity in the Church. These contexts help further develop the theological foundation, including the biblical worldview in narrative and theological form, the historical foundation, and the focus on the goal of unity of the faith and completing the work. Each essay in this work paved the way for his books on philosophical foundation, theological foundation, and the Historic Christian Faith.

Dr. Gangadean's works are to be read together as part of a systematic whole. He believed that the Christian worldview is a system of Truth and that the Logos, in its fullness, provides a way of life for the Church. His teaching is nothing less than the foundation for the City of God. We have provided footnotes to other sources for the ideas expressed in these essays and encourage those who are seeking to advance their understanding by making appropriate connections between the different texts to see the whole of Dr. Gangadean's vision.

Because these papers were delivered as public lectures or were submitted as journal articles, they are addressed to a particular audience at a specific time in Dr. Gangadean's thinking. As such, they have a more personal tone than some of his other work. We hope the reader gets a sense of Dr. Gangadean's focus and drive, passion for the good, love for others, and tireless witness to the truth from these essays. May you meditate on the words in this book as Dr. Gangadean meditated on these ideas for a lifetime. May your understanding and faith be deepened. And may you be spurred on to seek the unity of the faith, that we might be one, that the world might believe, and that the earth be filled with the knowledge of the Lord as the waters cover the sea. Amen.

—KELLY FITZSIMMONS BURTON,
for THE LOGOS FOUNDATION
EDITORIAL BOARD
Young, Arizona
June 2023

THE TESTIMONY OF
SURRENDRA GANGADEAN

December 12, 1961

PREDOMINANT IN THE MINDS OF MOST MEN TODAY is an unspoken resignation that conflicting ideas should exist and still be compatible. Indifference to the singleness of truth is their plan for peace, but to no avail because purpose is omitted. Therefore, I dedicated myself to a serious search for the truth. Though I was a philosophy major, I dropped out of classes so that my mind would not be bothered by the history of trivialities.

An unplanned encounter with a Campus Crusade member precipitated into my thoughts the possibility of a living God who loved me. That I could know Christ personally was the crux of his message. How I laughed inside. How ridiculous! How impossible! In my stubborn ignorance, I had already decided Jesus Christ was only a suitable, subtle myth to help enforce social norms and morals. But my yearning to know was strong and I doubted my ability to reason about unfamiliar things. Therefore, I reasoned if there were a God and I sought earnestly and honestly, He would allow me to find Him. An accepted challenge to read the Gospel of John removed my ignorance. To know Him, if He is, and the motives for His actions became tantalizing. Again, a student active in Campus Crusade brought the Bible before me to show me "For by grace are you saved through faith and that not of your own doing. It is the gift of God, not because of works, lest any man should boast." This penetrated the cloud of unconscious egotism that surrounded my soul. I was robbing God by claiming for myself the applause for whatever I did. It was robbery because it was He who had created me (with all my faculties to do good) and not I myself. The necessary punishment to accomplish justice was eternal separation from my creator. But the magnificence of God's love was revealed in Christ who died in taking my punishment upon Himself. Now I could only believe Christ was real and accept what He did for me.

The genuine peace instilled in my heart by faith in God increased when I recognized that in all this God had a purpose and plan for my life. Submitting to His will now becomes my constant purpose and delight.

THE ESSAYS

1

———

PROLEGOMENA:

RATIONAL

PRESUPPOSITIONALISM

Critically Examining Assumptions for Meaning

Westminster Fellowship Distinctives

April 2000

R ATIONAL PRESUPPOSITIONALISM IS AN epistemological method used to settle philosophical disputes by critically analyzing assumptions for meaning. It applies reason as a test for meaning to what is presupposed in a dispute.

Rational Presuppositionalism (RP) affirms that: some things are clear, the basic things are clear, the basic things about God and man and good and evil are clear to reason.[1] RP is an answer to skepticism and fideism. It is an alternative to rationalism and to empiricism, both of which make uncritically held assumptions.[2]

Thinking is presuppositional. We think of the less basic in light of the more basic. We think of truth in light of meaning, experience in light of basic belief, conclusions in light of premises, and the finite and temporal in light of the infinite and eternal. If we understand what is

———

1. Gangadean, *Philosophical Foundation*, 287-292.

2. Gangadean, *History of Philosophy*, 131-149.

more basic, we can understand what is less basic; if we agree on what is more basic, we can agree on what is less basic.

RP seeks to avoid needless disputes by examining if there is agreement on what is more basic. It seeks to avoid straining at gnats while swallowing camels. It looks at both the objective and the subjective aspects of knowledge and dialogue. Dialogue presupposes a commitment to reason along with an understanding of the nature of reason.

Having knowledge presupposes a concern to know, which presupposes integrity as a concern for consistency, both theoretically and personally. If there is commitment to reason, with integrity, disputes can be settled.[3]

Skepticism claims that knowledge is not possible. It is rooted in uncritically held assumptions, that if rationalism (for example, Descartes) and empiricism (for example, Hume) cannot give knowledge, then no knowledge is possible.[4] Consistently held, skepticism leads to nihilism, in which no distinction is clear, including the distinction of *a* and *non-a*, being and non-being, true and false, and good and evil.

Skepticism denies reason, makes dialogue impossible, and leads to silence as well as a cessation of all thought. It dissolves the meaning of its terms—*knowledge* and *possible*. Pragmatism cannot overcome the meaninglessness of skepticism.[5] And fideism (appeal to faith apart from proof based on understanding) becomes an arbitrary affirmation of one view from among many.

RP affirms that sense experience gives knowledge of appearance but not of reality, and that the data of experience (common sense, scientific, or mystical) must be interpreted in order to be meaningful. RP does not allow the postmodern skeptical view that "it is all a matter of interpretation." Philosophy does not end with interpretation but begins here.

Every interpretation can be, and must be, tested for coherence and meaning. RP affirms that the self-evident truths of rationalism (Descartes' *cogito* or Jefferson's self-evident truths) are not logically basic, even though they are taken as properly basic. The alternatives of absolute idealism and naturalism require a response.

---

3. Gangadean, *Philosophical Foundation*, 287-292.

4. Gangadean, *History of Philosophy*, 9-12.

5. Gangadean, *Philosophical Foundation*, 117-118.

Rational Presuppositionalism is to be distinguished from fideistic presuppositionalism, in which one moves from Scripture (the Triune God of the Bible) to reason. RP is to be distinguished from axiomatic presuppositionalism, in which one begins with the Scripture as one's set of axioms.

RP is to be distinguished from reformed epistemology, in which one begins with what is taken as properly basic beliefs.[6] RP is to be distinguished from evidentialism, in which one seeks to argue from miracles to God. RP is to be distinguished from common sense realism, in which the objective existence of the external world is assumed.[7]

RP affirms that the clarity of general revelation is necessary for the inexcusability of unbelief and undertakes to show what is clear from general revelation by showing that the alternatives of unbelief are contrary to reason.[8] It is to be distinguished from all attempts to answer historical criticism of the Scriptures without first establishing the clarity of general revelation.

RP begins with an affirmation of the nature of reason based on the reality of thought. Reason is to be defined in itself, in its use, and in us.[9] Reason in itself is the laws of thought. Most basically, these are the law of identity: *a* is *a*; the law of non-contradiction: not both *a* and *non-a*, at the same time and in the same respect; and the law of excluded middle: either *a* or *non-a*. Other laws of thought are based on these laws. To doubt these laws is to lose all distinctions and to cease to think.

Reason in its use is formative, critical, interpretive, and constructive. Reason is used to form concepts, judgments, and arguments, which are the forms of all thought. Whenever there are thoughts, reason is being used formatively. Reason is used critically as a test for meaning. It is applied especially to basic beliefs as a test for meaning. If a belief, upon analysis, violates a law of thought, it lacks meaning and cannot be true. Reason is used to interpret experience in light of one's basic beliefs. No experience is meaningful without interpretation, and every interpretation can and must be tested for meaning. And lastly, reason

---

6. Gangadean, *History of Philosophy*, 175-179.

7. Gangadean, "Paper No. 3: The Principle of Clarity, Rational Presuppositionalism, and Proof," in *The Logos Papers*.

8. Gangadean, "Paper No. 3" in *The Logos Papers*; Gangadean, *Philosophical Foundation*, 71-161.

9. Gangadean, *Philosophical Foundation*, 10-15.

is used to construct a coherent world and life view upon one's basic belief. Worldviews are manifest in cultures. They are held more or less consciously and more or less consistently and, therefore, continually face the internal and external challenges of reason.[10]

Reason is always being used formatively. It is often used constructively, without first being used critically. It is sometimes used interpretively without realizing it. Reason in itself is not fallible, but a person may fail to use reason critically and fully.

Reason does not succeed only if it persuades subjectively, but if it answers objections with an objectively sound argument. Many objections against reason and rationalism are really against what amounts to a failure to use reason.[11] Reason in itself must therefore be distinguished from reason in its use.

Reason in us is natural, ontological, transcendental, and fundamental. Reason is natural, not conventional. It is universal, the same in all persons. Reason as the laws of thought is common ground among all thinkers. What distinguishes us is not reason, but the willingness to use reason. What distinguishes us is not our assumption, but the willingness to critically examine our assumption for meaning.

Reason is ontological. It applies to being as well as to thought. There are no square-circles, no uncaused events, no being from non-being. It applies to all being, including the highest being. God is not both eternal and not eternal, at the same time and in the same respect. Matter is not both extended and not extended, at the same time and in the same respect.[12] There is no noumenal realm or dimension in which reason does not apply, but to which faith gives access.[13] While the mysteries of faith do not originate in reason, they do not go against reason. Miracles are not against the laws of reason, but against a law of nature. Reason, as an aspect of God's being, is eternal. The laws of nature are created. Paradoxes are puzzling to reason insofar as assumptions present and at work are not yet critically examined and corrected. Finite

---

10. Gangadean, "Paper No. 19: Foundation for Philosophy of History," in *The Logos Papers*.

11. Gangadean, *History of Philosophy*, 131-137.

12. Gangadean, *History of Philosophy*, 38.

13. Gangadean, *History of Philosophy*, 151-153; Gangadean, *Philosophical Foundation*, 109-110.

beings cannot have exhaustive or comprehensive knowledge of anything, but the unknown is not against the laws of reason.

Reason is transcendental. It is authoritative and self-attesting. It is transcendental in that it stands above thought and makes thought possible. It cannot be questioned but makes questioning possible. Statements about general and special revelation (Scripture) can and must be questioned, by reason, but reason itself as the laws of thought cannot be questioned. As transcendental, it cannot be argued for, even in a circular manner. In thought, what is of highest authority is self-attesting, and only reason is self-attesting.[14] Scripture assumes reason as that by which Scripture is to be understood. Scripture, if it is to be received, must be spoken in the name of God; that is, it must be consistent with the nature of God known from general revelation. There is not and cannot be any conflict between reason, general revelation, and Scripture. Scripture is set against all other forms of special revelation, not against reason and general revelation.

Reason is fundamental. It is fundamental to other aspects of human personality. Feelings are directed by belief about the good and thought and feeling move the will to act. Feeling and will are not independent of or contrary to belief. Conflicts within the understanding are manifest in conflicts in feeling and will. Unnoticed, these misunderstandings—as conflicts within our thoughts—lead to apparent conflict between thought and feeling, etc. Our deepest need is for meaning. Our deepest misery is in the awareness of the lack of meaning. Meaninglessness is a fundamental aspect of spiritual death and, sometimes, physical death is sought as an escape from spiritual death. Boredom comes from meaninglessness, in which the creation, apart from or in place of the Creator, cannot satisfy. Failure to be rational is experienced as guilt, from which escape is sought in the unending rationalizations of self-justification. Our greatest happiness is from the use of reason in understanding the creation, when this understanding leads to the knowledge of God.

The first application of RP is to the question, what is real? It clarifies the subjective factors of integrity and commitment to reason as preconditions to knowledge. It prevents further discussion, which would be fruitless if these preconditions are not in place.

---

14. Gangadean, *Philosophical Foundation*, 298-299.

We begin with the question what is real? because existence is our most basic concept, and eternal existence (without beginning) is more basic than temporal existence (with beginning).

To show that "some is eternal" is true, we show that the contradiction "none is eternal" cannot be true. "None is eternal" implies that all is temporal, all had a beginning, all came into being. If all came into being, it would have come into being from non-being, which is impossible. Hence, "none is eternal" cannot be true, and its contradiction "some is eternal" must be true. All came into being from non-being is not the same as creation *ex nihilo*, in which God is eternal and acted to create.[15]

By non-being is meant the absence of all being whatsoever, not just the absence of all visible being. An unending series of finite and temporal beings having the power to create *ex nihilo* is not an objection that has been (or, upon analysis, can be) made.

If it is agreed that it is clear to reason that there must be something eternal, we can go on to the next step in showing what is clear.[16]

---

15. Gangadean, *Philosophical Foundation*, 61-68.

16. "Paper No. 102: The Clarity of General Revelation," in *The Logos Papers*; Gangadean, *Philosophical Foundation*, 71-284.

2

THE GOOD AND THE BEATIFIC VISION

Logos Theological Seminary, Summer Seminar

July 2020

THE GOOD IN THE BIBLICAL WORLDVIEW:
Creation–Fall–Redemption

THE GOOD IS THE CHIEF END OF MAN, the highest value, eternal life. The chief end is to glorify God and to enjoy him forever. Moral evil is sin. All have sinned and come short of the glory of God. Understanding good and evil is central to understanding the human drama. Two trees were planted in the middle of the Garden of Eden, the tree of life and the tree of the knowledge of good and evil. The tree of life represented life—man's highest value. Eating of the tree of the knowledge of good and evil represented the way of sin and death: "In the day you eat you will surely die." Man sinned, and died, first spiritually, and then physically also. The original sin, concerning the knowledge of good and evil, is the original sin of all men and directs the course of all history and of every life. How then was good and evil understood, under sin and death, and how should it be understood now, in the way of life?

The beginning of Scripture (Genesis 1–3) reveals the biblical worldview of creation–fall–redemption. The fall of man presupposes the order of creation, and redemption presupposes both creation and the Fall. In the Fall, man turns away from God's order in creation under Adam. In redemption, man is restored to the order of creation through repentance and faith in Jesus Christ, the new covenant head in the place of Adam. Christ came to undo what Adam did, and do what Adam failed to do. Christ is the Logos, the eternal Word of God incarnate, who makes God fully known. He is the Son of God by whom all things were made. Man is made in the image of God, with the moral law written on his heart, with the ability and responsibility to know and to acknowledge God as the only true God. Man is crowned with light and honor, to rule (have dominion over) the creation under God. The life of the logos is in all men as light, by which he can understand God's self-revelation in creation and providence. By this light of reason, man is to name the creation and develop all the powers latent in himself and the creation. To have dominion, man must be fruitful and multiply and fill the earth. It will take all of mankind all of history to accomplish the work of dominion, to move from the Garden of Eden to the City of God. As God completed his work of creation, man, the image of God, will complete his work of dominion. As God completed and rested from his work, man also will complete and rest from his work. The Sabbath day of rest, every seventh day reminds man of his work and calling, and the hope of completing it. By the work of dominion, man is to glorify God, the end of which is to fill the earth with the knowledge of God as the waters cover the sea. The good, the chief end of man, is to glorify God and to enjoy him forever.

At the beginning of his work, man is tested for his understanding of good and evil and for his obedience to God's command not to eat of the tree of the knowledge of good and evil. Man's understanding/ faith is tested by an argument, the conclusion of which is the denial of God's Word: "you shall not surely die." The reason or premise is: "God knows that when you eat you shall be like God knowing good and evil." The premise raises three questions: 1) What is good and evil? 2) How does God know good and evil? And, 3) can man be like God in knowing good and evil? Adam had already been naming the animals and his wife as his helpmeet. He grasped the nature of animals and of his own nature distinct from the animals, and his own origin and work in naming his helpmeet "woman," for he saw that she was taken out of man by God. In understanding the nature of things created, in anticipation of dominion, he could and should know that the good for a being is according to the nature of that being and that God, by creation of the nature of beings, determines the good for each being. He could and should know that he cannot create but only discover the nature of things. Man can never be like the infinite Creator God. He could and should have communicated this to his helpmeet in the work of dominion. And he was with her at the time of temptation, to make this clear if needed. His desire for her led him to listen to her voice rather than the voice of God. Judging by sense experience and appearances, she ate, gave it to her husband, and he ate also. So, man fell into sin, and all mankind fell in and with him.

Had man been pursuing the knowledge of God as the good, he would have seen and kept in mind what is clear about God and man and good and evil. At some point, prior to the temptation, left to himself, man ceased to diligently seek God and therefore ceased to understand the meaning of things. Spiritual death—not understanding meaning, or meaninglessness, was inherent in not diligently seeking God. He believed what was absurd, neglecting and collapsing the distinction between the finite (creature) and infinite (Creator). Man put himself in the place of God to determine good and evil. Without understanding, which is the reward of diligently seeking God, there is no enjoyment of God. Enjoyment of the creation without meaning was empty (boring), leading to all kinds of excess and unrighteousness. Man fell into the bottomless pit of spiritual death.

Sin is permitted by God and made to serve God's purpose in creation. Creation is revelation—necessarily, intentionally, and exclusively. There is no direct knowledge of God by the creature apart from God's self-revelation in his acts of creation and providence. Sin serves to deepen the divine revelation, especially of God's justice and mercy in redemption. Death in sin shows the divine justice. Being brought from death to life shows God's mercy. If evil (unbelief) is removed abruptly, the revelation is not deepened. If evil/unbelief is not removed, the revelation will not be seen. Evil, therefore, is removed gradually. Unbelief, in every kind and degree, and in combination with belief, is allowed to work itself out in world history. The spiritual war, between the understanding and misunderstanding of good and evil, is age-long and agonizing. In the end, good will overcome evil. Through the rule of Christ in the place of Adam, the earth shall be full of the knowledge of the Lord as the waters cover the sea. Christ, through the Church—his body—makes disciples of all nations. Only when all is subdued to Christ is the work of dominion completed. Redemptive history ends with the resurrection of all who have died physically. Only then do all believers, together, inherit their reward of the kingdom of God in everlasting joy.

In redemption, Adam is called back through his sense of shame in the awareness of his nakedness. Man's physical nakedness, now, under sin, reminds him of his spiritual nakedness (lack of righteousness in disobedience). He avoids shame through self-deception by a covering of leaves. The covering itself cannot be covered and can be seen for what it is. He is called back a second time, to self-examination, by the question "Where are you?" He resists this call by self-justification, blaming his wife and God. In light of his neglect of seeking and understanding what is clear about God and man and good and evil, and his self-deception, and his self-justification, God calls man back a third and final time through the curse and promise. The curse consists of toil and strife, and old age, sickness, and death. The promise is given in terms of a spiritual war: "I will put enmity between you (Satan) and the woman." The war will be age-long (through the seed/generations) and agonizing, and asymmetrical (truth vs. force and falsehood), but will result in good vanquishing evil. Adam now repents and obeys—he will be fruitful even under the curse. He calls his wife's name Eve, for she will be the mother of all the living and of a seed, through whom the promise will be fulfilled, and the work of dominion completed: "He (the seed of the woman) will crush your head," that is, he will crush the head of Satan, the father of lies, speaking through the guise of the serpent.

Then comes the expulsion. Based on repentance and faith in the promise, man is forgiven and covered in coats of skin, signifying a covering of righteousness through the death of another. They must yet be cleansed. Through suffering under the curse, they must learn the Truth, through which they are sanctified, that is, made wholly devoted to the good.

HOW WE CAN KNOW GOOD AND EVIL

The age-long and agonizing history of redemption begins—good versus evil, belief versus unbelief, misunderstanding good and evil versus understanding good and evil. There are many ways the good has been misunderstood, but only one way in which it should be understood. The most common view of the good in Christianity has been that after a believer dies, that person goes to heaven and there they receive the fullness of blessing, usually through a direct, immediate, mystical vision of God, often referred to as the beatific vision. The alternative view is that the good is the knowledge of God through the work of dominion so that the earth is filled with the knowledge of the Lord as the waters cover the sea. These two views of the good are starkly different. Can we have knowledge (that is, rational justification) for the answer to the question, "what is the good?" Is the good the knowledge of God? Must that knowledge be through the work of dominion? The answer will be approached first through the clarity of general revelation, then through Scripture, then through the creeds of the Historic Christian Faith.

The Good from General Revelation

The good is the moral absolute, the end in itself, sought for its own sake and not for anything else, the *summum bonum*. All else in ethics is relative to the moral absolute, the highest value. Ethics assumes choice. Choice assumes values. Values assume the highest value, the end in itself, the good. Ethics assumes metaphysics, and metaphysics assumes epistemology. Metaphysics addresses the question of the existence of God and the nature of man. If there is no metaphysical absolute, there can be no rational justification of moral absolutes. If there is no God, if all is one, or, if all is eternal (material or spiritual monism, or dualism), then either all is one and the same, or equal, and one thing cannot be said to be better than another. And, without personal immortality, man cannot attain to the good in any lasting sense and there is no rational justification to pursue what is unattainable. And if freedom is only apparent, and not real, then choice and morality are an illusion. And if there is no clarity, then meaning and morality are not possible. And if reason as the laws of thought is not self-attesting and not the test for meaning, then we cannot speak of any clarity.

There are two common errors concerning the good, which are antinomies (contraries that can both be false) that have dominated the discourse in ethics on both a personal and academic level. If the good is the end in itself, then it is not the means to the good. Virtue, of every kind, is the means to the good, not the good. Again, the good is not the effect of possessing what one believes to be good, that is, happiness.

Ethics is teleological (aimed at the good), not deontological (aimed at virtue) or consequential (aimed at happiness).

The good must be objectively clear to all, that is, objectively easily knowable to any seeking to understand. It is axiomatic that good for a being is based on the nature of that being. The good for a human being is based on human nature, which is immediately knowable to human beings. If we cannot know our own nature, how can we know the nature of the world or the origin of the world? Those metaphysical positions which deny essences or the knowability of essences are, in the end, moved to silence.

Human nature is a unity of diversity. The diversity, and the virtue of each part, serve the good of the whole person. The end in itself binds all the virtues into a perfect unity. Virtues, without the good, become vices by excess. The reward of virtue is not happiness but the good. Happiness is the intrinsic effect of the good. Happiness without the good is not lasting. When sought in itself, happiness cannot satisfy and soon becomes boring, leading to excess and what is contrary to human nature.

As the end in itself and the end of all ends, the good is one and the source of unity. It must be one in each and the same for all, the source of unity in each and for all. Man, by nature, is rational. If human nature as such is universal and fundamental, then the good must be rational and therefore cognitive, not a non-cognitive mystical state.

It is self-evident we think: we form concepts, judgments, and arguments. These three are the forms of all thought. Concepts are universal; they grasp the essence of a thing. The essence is a set of all qualities that all members of that class of things have, that they always have, and what distinguishes that class from all others. Man is a rational animal, distinct from angels and animals. A concept, grasping a universal, is the first act of reason, not of the senses, which perceive images that are always particular. Reason in man distinguishes man from animals. Animals, like man, perceive, but perceiving is not thinking. An image is not a concept. The word "man" expresses the concept man, what all men have in common. A judgment joins or separates two concepts, as in "man is mortal." An argument infers a conclusion from two judgments or premises: All men are mortal. Socrates is a man. Therefore, Socrates is mortal.

It is self-evident that there are laws of thought: the law of identity—*a* is *a*; the law of non-contradiction—not both *a* and *non-a*, at the same time and in the same respect; and the law of excluded middle—either *a* or *non-a*. These laws of thought are called the laws of reason, or reason in itself. By nature, we think. We think of the less basic in light of the more basic. We ask and answer basic questions about knowledge: how do we know? About being: what is real/eternal? About the good: what ought I to do? If we agree on the more basic, we can and will agree on the less basic. One's view of ethics depends on one's view of metaphysics, which depends on one's view of epistemology.

Actions are guided by desires, which depend on one's beliefs. Thinking, therefore, is fundamental in man. To be is to act, grounded in desires, which are grounded in thought as determined by reason. Good for man as a rational being is the use of reason to the fullest. We use reason to grasp the nature of things. The nature of things, as created, reveal the nature of God. Good for man as a rational being is, therefore, the knowledge of God. The nature of things is known by dominion, which is to name and develop the powers latent in the nature of things. Dominion, therefore, requires the work of all men through history. The good, therefore, is corporate, cumulative, and communal (increased by sharing). The fullness of man's rule over all on earth (land, sea, and air) results in the earth being filled with the knowledge of God as the waters cover the sea.

Is There Hope That the Good Can Be Achieved?

Man is fallen. Left to oneself, no one seeks God, no one understands what is clear to reason. It appears unlikely that the good in any sense of fullness will come about. Yet there is the theodicy concerning God's justice and mercy ruling in history. There is the Sabbath hope. There is the call to preach the gospel of repentance and that the kingdom of heaven is at hand, growing to fullness now, not a cataclysmic future event. There is the call to disciple the nations. There is redemptive history, the promise preserved through ages of apostasy. There is redemption accomplished through the Incarnation, crucifixion, and resurrection. There is the work of the Holy Spirit leading the Church into all truth through the pastor-teachers, and councils, and creeds, and there is the Lord's Prayer, to teach us to pray.

The Church is divided and in captivity to unbelief in the spiritual war between belief and unbelief. Its foundations (first principles) must be laid again. The Church must recover from the original sin of misunderstanding good and evil. In response to the preaching of the gospel, the Church must open its doors to those who repent of root sin; the Church's doors are not open to the unrepentant, who put themselves in the place of God to determine good and evil. It is not open to those failing to seek and to understand what is clear to reason about God and man and good and evil.

Is there hope that the good can be achieved? There are two ways before man: good and evil, life and death, both of which are objectively clear to reason but subjectively unclear due to every degree of admixture in misunderstanding. Moral evil is an act against one's human nature. Man neglects, avoids, resists, and denies reason regarding what is clear about God. Man progressively denies Common Ground, which makes thought and discourse possible.[1] Yet man does not and cannot cease to be human, made in the image of God. The light of reason shines in the darkness of unbelief. Man still gives meaning to experience, even mystical experience, that seeks to leave reason behind. He still seeks to justify himself against the alternative way and maintain autonomy against God's law. Without grace, man remains in the state of spiritual death. The enduring contradiction in fallen man of the need for meaning, with the denial of reason, of any possibility of meaning, is the essence of spiritual death. Only conviction of sin and death, of not seeking and therefore not understanding meaning, can bring a change of mind. That change is repentance.

THE NEED FOR REPENTANCE FROM
FALSE VIEWS OF GOOD AND EVIL

In redemption, by a spiritual war between belief and unbelief, between meaninglessness and meaningfulness, believers too must repent of remaining sin and guilt. The incoherence of false views of good and evil must be seen existentially through a penetrating conviction. Failure by

---

1. Gangadean, "Paper No. 2: Common Ground: The Necessary Condition for Thought and Discourse," in *The Logos Papers*; Gangadean, Papers No. 50–53: Common Ground (Parts I–IV) in *The Logos Papers*.

the believer to understand the clarity of general revelation will continue into the reading of Scripture and the Church creeds. It is a failure to use reason by good and necessary consequences to understand
meaning contextually. Literalism is commonly used by Christians
in place of contextualism: heaven and hell as future replace life and
death now present; fruit sin replaces root sin; fideism—belief without proof based on understanding—replaces faith. The outward visible signs of the sacraments are taken for the invisible reality signified.
Happiness—the effect, is taken for the cause—the good. When the
cornerstone of clarity and inexcusability is rejected, reason, which is
most basic in epistemology is missing. Empiricism of every kind (appeals to facts, purportedly without interpretation) claims precedence.
Tradition, common sense, intuition, and observation replace the critical use of reason. Claims of factual meaning without interpretation
require deconstruction. The Word of God as Scripture simpliciter replaces the Word of God as logos, Truth in its fullness. In the current
collapse of the culture of Christianity, "The stone which the builders
rejected [clarity and inexcusability] has become the cornerstone. This
is the Lord's doing. It is marvelous in our eyes."[2] There is no lasting
foundation without the cornerstone, and there are no walls or gates, or
City of God without foundation. Only pietism and legalism remain,
forms of godliness without the meaningful content that gives it power.

Truth is one; it is the narrow way. Errors are many; broad is the way
that leads to destruction. The good is the knowledge of God through
the work of dominion. Error is everything else, every form of heav-
en where one is supposed to receive the fullness of the blessing given
immediately in the afterlife. But the absence of sorrow is not the fullness of the blessing. The Garden of Eden, without sorrow before the
Fall, is not the City of God at the end of history. An immediate, intuitional vision of God (whom no man has seen nor can see) bypasses
the revelation of God in creation and mankind's work of dominion.
An immediate, intuitional vision of God lacks cognitive content and
is mystical, non-rational, against human nature as rational and man's
fundamental need for cognitive meaning (content with understanding). The beatific vision as non-rational is non-human and anti-human. We are not, and cannot become, like God (the original sin). The

---

2. *Psalm 89.*

finite, temporal, and changeable creature can never cross the line to become like God, who is infinite, eternal, and unchangeable (attributes that are incommunicable to the creature). There is no mystical union where we know God as God knows himself. Reduction to animal (in pleasure as happiness) or elevation to God (in mystical bliss as happiness) are both denials of rational human nature, the denial of which is the essence of moral evil.

Literalism

There are many ways in which literalism denies the contextual meaning of the Word of God. The visible creation reveals the invisible God, who is spirit, without body and parts and changeable passions. Anthropomorphism takes the visible literally. Seeing God face to face, contextually understood, is either seeing him without a veil of sin or understanding the invisible attributes of God without type and shadow. Near to God, in space, literally, is to be contrasted with spiritual nearness to God by God's indwelling presence, by his Word and Spirit. Angels in heaven, who did not understand the revelation of God given in their own being, fell into the pit of darkness/meaninglessness. The angel of light deception in the Garden was based on an absurd (meaningless) lie. Even in the most intimate of human relations, we know the depth of the being of others through their words and actions (not by gazing deeply and directly into their souls).

Popular eschatology abounds with literalism, which vanishes like shadows in the light of contextualism. Literalism often opposes allegoricalism without being aware of the alternative of contextualism. The lake of fire is called the second death, which is spiritual, present, and inherent in sin, not future, external, and imposed. There are two deaths, physical and spiritual. Which is meant by the common term "death" is to be determined by the context throughout all of Scripture. This is manifest pointedly in Jesus' statement: "I am the resurrection and the life," both physical and spiritual. The one who believes will never die—spiritually. The first resurrection is spiritual.[3] The second resurrection is physical. There is only one physical resurrection of all the dead, at the same time, at the one visible, bodily return of Christ at the

---

3. *Ephesians 2:1.*

end of history. To claim that there are two physical resurrections, separated by 1000 years, has led to utter confusion in the name of literalism on the principle of one word, one meaning. Heaven, when taken as a literal place, with mansions and streets of gold, becomes a caricature (like any sensual paradise). It is not the City of God now coming upon the earth, according to the Lord's Prayer: "Thy kingdom come." The new heavens and the new earth are renewed by redemption, not replaced by another creation. There is continuity in the resurrection of the body and the regeneration of the soul, not a replacement. There is continuity from the old administration of the covenant of grace in the Old Testament to the New Testament, in which the sacraments of circumcision and baptism signify the same reality (being born again or having a new heart). So, also, there is continuity from the Passover to the Lord's Supper in the spiritual reality signified.

The destruction of Jerusalem, foretold by Christ, came to pass in A.D. 70. The sun does not literally turn to darkness and the moon to blood before the destruction of the temple comes. The temple does not have to be rebuilt today in order to be destroyed according to Christ's prophecy. The antichrist is anyone who denies Jesus as the Son of God incarnate, not a future sinister figure. The mark of the beast is any totalitarian government that puts man's law—the 666—in the place where God's law was to be placed, symbolically on the forehead (a reminder to meditate on God's law day and night) and on the hand (a reminder to always do God's law). Armageddon is not a cataclysmic physical war fought in the future, but a spiritual war—pictured physically—fought with a sword coming out of the mouth, that is, a spiritual sword, which is by speaking the Word of God. The harlot pictures man's economic system of values without God. The false prophet is man's educational system without God. The kingdom of darkness opposes Christ's rule over his kingdom as the true prophet, priest, and king. During Christ's thousand-year rule, believers, by spiritual rebirth—which is the first resurrection—rule during their lifetime with Christ by making disciples of all nations. The millennium ends with the second, that is, the physical resurrection of the body, at the end of history. The bottomless pit is a picture of spiritual death: meaninglessness (darkness of mind), and boredom (the burning of unquenchable desire), and guilt (the torment of the worm of conscience), increasing without end—bottomless.

It is in light of the propensity of the unreflecting mind toward literalism, based on sense experience—seeing is believing—that the lack of understanding of good and evil, and life and death, and heaven and hell, can best be explained. Speaking against literalism, the first Council of Jerusalem in A.D. 51 ruled against the teaching that you must be circumcised to be saved. As a literalist interpretation opposed Christ then, it continues to oppose the Word of God today.

Allegoricalism

After the error of literalism, the Church in the Apostles' Creed opposed Greek gnosticism and allegoricalism. Gnosticism rejects the clarity of general revelation for a hierarchy of beings above humans that give special hidden revelation that is necessary for salvation in a dualist worldview, which affirms that both the material world and souls are eternal. Scriptures interpreted allegorically from a foreign dualist framework affirmed that spirit is good, evil originates from the body, and the material world, which was formed by a finite god (the Demiurge). Dualism, from the school of Athens (Plato and Aristotle), gained its major entry into Christianity through the influence of Augustine and Aquinas. Under its influence, the best minds withdrew from the world by celibacy and monasticism for the life of prayer and contemplation, seeking knowledge of the highest reality directly, apart from creation and the work of dominion. Greek dualism, in the belly of the beast of Greek philosophy, emerged, while the watchmen slept, to burn down Christianity to its foundations. It displaced any knowledge of God through the work of dominion with the otherworldly view of a beatific vision. Christianity, without clarity, pursued an antinomy of either a literal material heaven as the good or an allegorical, mystical, beatific vision as the good, both of which bring death by emptying good and evil of any meaning.

Clarity Is the Cornerstone

Without the use of reason to understand good and necessary consequences, all sources of revelation, from creation, Scripture, and creeds, are emptied of meaning. The assumptions and implications of the doctrine of the Trinity at Nicea, the canon of Scripture at Carthage, Christ as fully God and fully man at Chalcedon, and the sovereignty of divine grace at Orange, were not preserved and built upon for over 1000 years. Restoration in the Reformation through several creeds from 1530 to 1648 reached its highest level of consciousness and consistency at that time in the Westminster Standards of 1648. The first question of the Shorter Catechism affirmed that "Man's chief end is to glorify God and to enjoy him forever." Christians, in general, give verbal assent to this, but most fall away as the meaning is deepened. We are to glorify God in all that by which he makes himself known.[4] And God makes himself known through all his works of creation and providence.[5] The outcome of this view of glorifying God is that the earth shall be full of the knowledge of the Lord as the waters cover the sea.[6] But the doxological focus on knowing God's glory cannot be entered without repentance of root sin as described in the opening words of the Westminster Confession of Faith: "The light of nature [reason] and the works of creation and providence do so far manifest the wisdom, power, and goodness of God so as to leave men inexcusable." The doctrine of clarity and inexcusability begins the Historic Christian Faith in the Westminster Confession, as it does in Paul's understanding of man's need for the gospel of Christ,[7] and as it does for Common Ground, the necessary conditions for thought and discourse. Clarity is the cornerstone. One cannot understand good and evil without the cornerstone.

Many theologians and pastors who profess adherence to the Reformed Faith expressed in the Westminster Confession of Faith have little interest in showing how God's eternal power and divine nature are clear to reason. The common view seems to affirm the *sensus divinitatis*, that we all know that God exists by a spontaneous intuition, but suppress this knowledge. In this view, understanding is not by diligently seeking, and there is no failure to understand. Knowledge by intuition is appealed to by voluntarists who believe that the will of man can act apart from and against human knowledge in the intellect.[8] Voluntarism assumes there is no culpability without actual knowledge, but the claim

4. *Westminster Shorter Catechism Question 101.*

5. *Westminster Confession of Faith, 4.1, 5.1.*

6. *Isaiah 11:9.*

7. *Romans 1:18-20.*

8. Gangadean, "Paper No. 120: Contra Voluntarism: The Will Is Not Independent of the Intellect," in *The Logos Papers.*

that there is no culpable ignorance is opposed by the prayer, "Father, forgive them; for they know not what they do." In voluntarism, there must be an equivocation of "knowledge" to avoid saying, "You shall know the truth and the truth shall set you free." Furthermore, the content of the knowledge of God by intuition has not been agreed upon. Is God merely a higher power, a god, like Zeus? Is this knowledge by intuition the same in all? Is it knowledge of the only true God? Or is it like Satan's knowledge, or like Adam's knowledge of God at the temptation? Or like Cain's, or like the god of deism, or like the god of Islam? Or is it like the god of post-biblical Judaism? In any of these, there is no need for vicarious atonement. There is not a God of both infinite justice and infinite mercy. Aquinas maintains there is proof for God, but this is attainable only by a few trained in metaphysics. If it is not clear to all by reason, in what sense can it be said that all have sinned? And without sin, what need is there of Christ? Is the gospel, therefore, emptied of meaning before it is even preached? Without clarity, there is no inexcusability, no sin and death, no call back through the curse, no answer to the problem of evil, no need for scripture as redemptive revelation; only the inevitable drift to universalism, and irrelevance, which is where we are today in the Church.

Need for the Foundation

One can be, like Nicodemus, a master or teacher in Israel, and not know basic things. Jesus said to Nicodemus: "Except a man be born again, he cannot see the kingdom of God."[9] He heard the words "born again" literally, a pattern repeated throughout the Gospel of John. "How can a man be born when he is old? Can he enter the second time into his mother's womb, and be born?"[10] The literalism of Nicodemus blocked him from hearing and seeing, and entering the kingdom of God. Without context, words are emptied of meaning to the point of absurdity. Jesus explained: there are two kinds of births, not one, physical—of water, and spiritual—of the Spirit. Two, not one. Nicodemus is still incredulous. Jesus explains further. The work of the Spirit is like the wind, invisible, but its effect is manifest; we hear the sound

9. *John 3:3.*
10. *John 3:4.*

of it. Nicodemus cannot see how this is possible. Then he is reproved. Are you a master in Israel and do not know these things? Nicodemus did not know that circumcision signified the infant's need for a new heart—to be born again. He did not have several layers of foundational principles in place by which circumcision is to be understood. If he had faith in understanding things more basic, he would have understood the less basic. First, clarity and inexcusability, then sin and death (seen in Adam's sin), then the curse and the promise of redemption, then repentance and faith, and justification and sanctification (seen in the coats of skin and in the expulsion from the Garden), then circumcision/baptism and calling through discipleship in the Church, consummated by resurrection and reward.[11] One can be, like Nicodemus, in the Church outwardly without having faith/understanding inwardly. Without understanding the most basic concepts of good and evil, one cannot understand, like Nicodemus, what comes after.

Hindering Faith, Hope, and Love

Holding a false view of the good is more than an innocent distraction or an annoying nuisance. It is antithetical to and will hinder a person (and those near to him) from the true view of the good, and of hope, and of patiently working for it. It will hinder faith, hope, and love. Heaven as the good, individually inherited as a beatific vision, is a false hope which makes what is necessary to know and to achieve the good irrelevant. Knowledge of God by intuition makes knowledge by diligently seeking without reward. Direct knowledge of God makes knowledge from the creation a mere shadow, secondary at best to the good. A beatific vision without cognitive content does not and cannot satisfy man's deepest longing for a life full of meaning. That I can receive the fullness of blessing by mystical vision, directly and immediately in heaven, makes the work of dominion on earth by myself and all mankind irrelevant or unnecessary, or meaningless. A non-cognitive, contentless vision of God is a mystical/blissful state of consciousness, which is no different from that reported by mystics in other traditions. Whether it is nirvana in Buddhism, *moksha/samadhi/sat chit ananda* in Hinduism, or ecstasy/bliss in *Samkhya/*yoga, mystical states do not

---

11. Gangadean, "Paper No. 36: The Pillar and Ground of the Truth: Rebuilding the Church's Foundation" and "Paper No. 37: The Seven Pillars: A Brief Summary," in *The Logos Papers*.

last; they are like deep, dreamless sleep. No experience (mystical or ordinary), if recollected, is meaningful without interpretation. Any valid interpretation must be consistent with clear general revelation. At present, no such interpretation has passed scrutiny, not from al-Ghazali, or Aquinas, or theosis (in Eastern Orthodoxy), or glossolalia (in the Charismatic movement), or encounters with angels, or with extraterrestrials, or afterlife experiences, or being caught up to a third heaven. Bliss/happiness is lasting only from the knowledge of God through the work of dominion.

Inheriting the Kingdom of God

What a believer inherits in Christ is not heaven, but the kingdom/City of God, which comes by Christ's rule through his body, the Church, making disciples of all nations. In this kingdom, the will of God is done on earth as it is in heaven. Christ, in the place of Adam, subdues all things to himself. In redemption—by spiritual war—according to the words: "I will put enmity between you and the woman," believers demolish every argument raised up against the knowledge of God. They are called to overcome (have dominion) in every trial of faith, in every test of the understanding, to take every thought captive to the obedience of Christ, to show that Christ is the Logos, the Word of God incarnate, who makes God fully known. Heaven as the beatific vision is antithetical to the earth filled with the knowledge of God, to seeking first the kingdom of God in all relations of life, to building up the kingdom of God into which the kings of the earth bring their glory. The Church must hear with understanding the preaching of the gospel: "Repent, for the kingdom of heaven is at hand."

He Who Has Ears to Hear

Hearers are warned, repeatedly and continually: "Take heed how you hear,"[12] and "he that has an ear to hear, let him hear,"[13] and "whoever hears (with understanding) will be given more, and whoever lacks understanding, from him shall be taken even that which he seems to

---

12. *Luke 8:18.*
13. *Matthew 11:15.*

have."[14] The parable of the sower describes a four-fold state of hearers. Suffering in the soul is like pain in the body, of many kinds and degrees. Pain begins to get our attention that something is wrong. The vanity, the meaninglessness, the emptiness, the forlornness, the waste, the pigsty—all forms of the curse, call to self-examination and away from hypocrisy. The living feel pain, a sign of life, the first stirrings after the sleep of self-inflicted death. Only by grace is life restored to the dead. The dead die when they shut their eyes and close their ears. Repentance begins with Job by hearing and seeing: "I have heard of you with the hearing of the ears, but now my eyes see you. Wherefore I abhor myself and repent in dust and ashes."[15] What begins with neglect increases with avoidance and resistance, to finally, the denial of reason itself—the life of the logos in all men. Having forsaken God, we become God-forsaken. Christ, in man's place, bore God's wrath: "My God, my God, why have you forsaken me."[16] His soul was made an offering for sin. In Christ, in the same act, in the same cry, the justice and mercy of God are fully revealed. And in all of human history, the whole earth is full of his glory. The beatific vision bypasses all of God's self-revelation in history. Therefore, "He who has ears to hear, let him hear."

The Perspicuity of the Good

Change from a fundamental misunderstanding of good and evil begins with seeing how clear it is. Lack of understanding is without excuse, much as we try to excuse it. The perspicuity of the good is clear in every formal approach to ethics and also in every essential characteristic of the good. Formally, ethics flows out of epistemology and then metaphysics, naturally. There are necessary conditions for rational justification in ethics. As the end in itself, ethics is teleological, not deontological or consequential. The good is clear, being grounded in human nature. The good is the source of unity, one and the same in each person and for all persons. It is clear throughout human history, from the Garden of Eden to the completion of culture in the City

---

14. *Mark 4:25.*
15. *Job 42:5-6.*
16. *Matthew 27:46; Psalm 22:1.*

of God. It is clear expressly in Scripture, and no literalism in eschatology can withstand its clarity. It is clear in the doxological focus of the Westminster Confession of Faith, the high-water mark—so far—of the Historic Christian Faith. The challenges of modern and postmodern history have become a perfect storm in their present urgency. In its peal of thunder and flashes of lightning, deep calls unto deep in the recurring decay of culture worldwide. The sound of an ancient lamentation is rising again, as of a mother weeping for her children.

The good is clear in its every characteristic. The good must be continuing from this life to the next. Only knowledge can (and must) be taken from this life; therefore, only knowledge can and must be the good. The good must be inexhaustible, growing forever in the hereafter, according to the requirements of human nature. Only knowledge through ever-deepening understanding is inexhaustible. The good must be comprehensive, encompassing every choice of value in life. Only knowledge of life is as comprehensive as life. The good must be inalienable; it cannot be lost or taken away. Only knowledge is inalienable; therefore, only knowledge can be the good. Being inexhaustible and comprehensive, it must be corporate (achievable only by the efforts of many). Only knowledge, by the experience of the many, is corporate. It must be cumulative, as the increasing experiences of dominion through the generations throughout history. Only knowledge is preserved and is cumulative; all else turns to dust. If it is corporate and cumulative, it must be communal, increasing by being shared. Only knowledge is communal; lesser goods decrease with sharing.

Finally, the good must be fulfilling, ultimate, and transformative. It is fulfilling, satisfying, the most satisfying, and the only source of lasting satisfaction. Man's chief end is to glorify God and to enjoy him forever. Knowledge is satisfying in the wonders of childhood, and later, in the travel of imagination and senses, by mind and body, to the wonders of the world, in witnessing glories revealed in all kinds of human achievements and in the shouts of praise resulting. Even the sensuous in human intimacy is intensified only as it reveals the other and only in its yielding appearances of the transcendent. Only knowledge brings men to rapture. Therefore, the good must be knowledge. Rapture is lasting only if it is grounded in the ultimate. Only the infinite, the eternal, and the unchangeable is ultimate. Therefore, only the knowledge of God, revealed in creation and providence, must be the good. Lastly, the good must have power intrinsic to it. Only the knowledge of God has the power to transform and set a person free from the misunderstanding that holds a person in bondage. Only knowing the Truth sets a person free. Therefore, only the knowledge of God is the good. Knowing God is eternal life, which is continuing, inexhaustible, comprehensive, inalienable, corporate, cumulative, communal, fulfilling, ultimate, and transformative. Selah.

The Good Is Achieved Through the Moral Law

As the good is objectively clear but subjectively unclear due to moral evil, so the good is objectively easily attainable, though subjectively difficult to attain. The good is achieved through the moral law, which is clear, comprehensive, and critical—a matter of life and death. Although it is given in Scripture as the Decalogue, it is first given in human nature by creation. That the law is given in human nature, and therefore clear and easily knowable, is affirmed by both Moses and the apostle Paul.[17] The comprehensiveness of the law is accessed by meditating on the law, day and night. What follows is a brief glance at the depth and breadth of the moral law given in general revelation.

Moral Law 1

The first moral law affirms God the Creator as the ground or determiner of the good. Man is to know and acknowledge God as the only true God and not, absurdly, put himself in the place of God to determine good and evil. The curse of natural evil is God's call back to know God, who, as just and merciful, redeems man from sin and death by vicarious atonement. No other God exists.

Moral Law 2

The second moral law forbids all forms of idolatry, all thinking of the infinite God in light of the finite creature. Instead, we have to think presuppositionally, that is, think of the less basic/finite in light of the more basic/infinite. As we are not to raise self to God (ML 1), we are not to lower God to self (ML 2). Idolatrous worship of the golden calf

---

17. *Deuteronomy 30:11-14; Romans 2:14-15.*

(a prosperity gospel of pleasure as the good) sank Israel into oblivion and is true for all nations whose God is not the Lord.

Moral Law 3

The third moral law calls for integrity, a concern for consistency, both logical and existential, over and against hypocrisy in self-deception and self-justification. Hypocrisy requires a distortion of the truth to avoid the light of reason. To take God's name in vain is to empty God's self-revelation of meaning. Meaninglessness deepens over the seasons of social life, reaching to the third and fourth generations, ending in a societal winter of discontent in despair. The moral law against autonomy, idolatry, and hypocrisy protects and advances the city, the kingdom built on these laws, the foundations, walls, and gates of which will last through all generations.

Moral Law 4

Man must work. The end of all work is the good, which is corporate, cumulative, and communal. That the good will be achieved is guaranteed by the sovereignty of the divine goodness. In spite of universal human and cosmic opposition, good overcomes evil by a rugged gradual idealism, through a spiritual war between belief and unbelief, which is age-long and agonizing. Mankind has endured calamity throughout history. We are now a global village once more. And once more, man stands on the brink of annihilation by the curse of war, famine, and plague. Man can hope, beyond pure conjecture, that since the universe exists by infinite goodness, good will overcome evil. Work will be completed. The sign of the Sabbath, given from the beginning, will become reality.

Moral Law 5

Authority is based on insight into the good and the means to the good. Insight is rational, not personal, and historically cumulative, not individual. When honor is given to whom honor is due, insight will be acknowledged. Voices without insight will not be listened to. The cumulative insight of the Historic Christian Faith must be rebuilt so that the Church, which is the pillar and ground of the truth, can disciple its members in order to disciple all nations to observe the moral law.

Moral Law 6

To affirm human nature as rational is to affirm human dignity. Denying a common human nature is anti-human. Failure to see that nature first in oneself, as the image of God—with the ability and responsibility to know what is clear to reason—leads to dehumanizing oneself, then others. Anti-humanism prevents dialogue and causes one to resort to manipulation by propaganda or control by brute force. Millions have been killed by anti-humanist ideologies through the ages.

Moral Law 7

The origin of one's being, and the nurture of one's being, is from the physical union of one man and one woman. Man is a body/soul unity. The physical union is not to be separated from the reality that it signifies—a spiritual union, which is love. A full union in marriage, which is monogamous and complementary, is lasting. Love seeks the good for the other, where the other person is not the good by way of a romantic fantasy. The good is by and for persons. Love in marriage, if it is to be lasting, must be based on friendship, the effect of mutual commitment to the good.

Moral Law 8

Value is a function of supply and demand. Supply is a function of talent; demand is the function of one's view of the good. Talent is given in the origin of one's being. Each is to develop that talent for the benefit of all. Failure to do so is to steal from the commonwealth from which all benefit. Neither man, individually nor collectively, owns wealth absolutely. Only God, as the giver of talent, owns wealth absolutely. Each man is a steward only of all that he possesses. Value without the good is spiritual harlotry, subject to all moral sanctions, affecting full participation in the human community.

Moral Law 9

In justice, equals are to be treated equally. Justice is first ontological, then social. Social justice, in the courts, is a function of knowing the truth. Full justice is from knowing the whole truth. We are to pursue justice by knowing and speaking the whole truth. The logos is Truth.

Failure to know and to speak the Truth is to participate in injustice and its cumulative consequences. Since Truth is clear, failure to know and to speak the truth is without excuse and has ontological, that is, inherent consequences.

Moral Law 10

Only the good has lasting satisfaction. All discontentment with bitterness, envy, resentment, despair, and excess arises from not knowing and pursuing the good. There is no cure for discontent without the good, only deeper despair, like rottenness in the bones. The good is easily knowable by all. By nature, we are rational. The good is clear to reason. Those who forsake their own true nature and cannot assert unequivocally that *a* is *a*, in the depth of critical thinking, forsake the law and forsake their own mercies.

Meditation on the Lord's Prayer

It would be fitting then to close these reflections with a call to meditate on the preface and first three petitions of the Lord's Prayer.

"Our Father which art in heaven"

The preface of the Lord's Prayer teaches us to draw near to God with all holy reverence and confidence, as children to a father, able and ready to help us; and that we should pray with and for others.[18] "Your Father knows what you need before you ask him."[19] "How much more will your Father in heaven give good gifts to those who ask him."[20] "As a father has compassion on his children, so the Lord has compassion on those who fear him."[21] "How much more should we submit to the Father of our spirits and live."[22] Jesus called out with a loud voice, "Father, into your hands I commit my spirit."[23] We are to avoid no prayer and vain prayer. We are to pray according to the Word of God.

---

18. *SCQ. 100.*
19. *Matthew 6:8.*
20. *Matthew 7:11.*
21. *Psalm 103:13.*
22. *Hebrews 12:9.*
23. *Luke 23:46.*

"Hallowed be thy name"

In the first petition, we pray that God would enable us, and others, to glorify him in all that whereby he maketh himself known; and that he would dispose all things to his own glory.[24] "Now this is eternal life: that they may know you, the only true God, and Jesus Christ, whom you have sent."[25] "God saw all that he had made, and it was very good."[26] "The whole earth is full of his glory."[27] "Since the creation of the world God's invisible qualities, his eternal power and divine nature, have been clearly seen, being understood through what has been made, so that men are without excuse."[28] "God blessed them and said to them, 'Be fruitful and increase in number; fill the earth and subdue it.'"[29] "For the earth will be full of the knowledge of the glory of the Lord as the waters cover the sea."[30] We are to avoid worldliness and otherworldliness. God is known by creation and history.

"Thy kingdom come"

In the second petition, we pray that Satan's kingdom may be destroyed; and that the kingdom of grace may be advanced, ourselves and others brought into it and kept in it; and that the kingdom of glory may be hastened.[31] "Seek first the kingdom of God and his righteousness."[32] "Go and make disciples of all nations."[33] "We demolish arguments and every pretension that sets itself up against the knowledge of God."[34] "The kingdom of heaven is like a mustard seed."[35] "The kingdom of heaven is like yeast."[36] "He must reign until he has put all his enemies

---

24. *SCQ. 101.*
25. *John 17:3.*
26. *Genesis 1:32.*
27. *Isaiah 6:3.*
28. *Romans 1:20.*
29. *Genesis 1:28.*
30. *Isaiah 11:9; Habakkuk 2:14.*
31. *SCQ. 102.*
32. *Matthew 6:33.*
33. *Matthew 28:19.*
34. *2 Corinthians 10:4.*
35. *Matthew 13:31.*
36. *Matthew 13:33.*

under his feet."[37] We are to avoid no hope and false hope. The kingdom of God grows gradually to its fullness.

"Thy will be done on earth as it is in heaven"

In the third petition, we pray that God, by his grace, would make us able and willing to know, obey, and submit to his will in all things, as the angels do in heaven.[38] "Do not turn from the law to the right or left; meditate on it day and night."[39] "The law of the Lord is perfect, restoring the soul."[40] "These laws are to be on your hearts. Impress them on your children."[41] "The nations show the work of the law is written in their hearts."[42] "Teach the nations to observe all that I have commanded."[43] "Love the Lord your God with all your heart and with all your soul and with all your mind. And love your neighbor as yourself."[44] We are to avoid no law and man's law. God's law is the rule for all of life.

In conclusion, the good is the end in itself, man's chief end, the highest value, sought for its own sake, the *summum bonum*. The beatific vision is said to be the immediate vision/experience of God, apart from creation, accessible to all in heaven. As we understand the good and the beatific vision, we will understand the good is not the beatific vision or heaven as the immediate fulfillment of human happiness.

---

37. *1 Corinthians 15:25.*
38. *SCQ. 103.*
39. *Joshua 1:7.*
40. *Psalm 19:7.*
41. *Deuteronomy 6:5.*
42. *Romans 2:15.*
43. *Matthew 28:20.*
44. *Matthew 22:37.*

3

THE GOOD AS THE
SOURCE OF UNITY

Paper delivered at the Sixth Annual Aquinas
Leadership International Congress

May 3, 2019

INTRODUCTION:
Common Ground, Contextual Background, and Relevance

AT THE OUTSET OF THIS PAPER, I MAKE some assumptions about
Common Ground, contextual background, and relevance. Some
of these assumptions, I hope, are shared by all now, and the rest will
be shared by all later.

Common Ground is the set of conditions necessary for thought and
discourse.[1] Common Ground consists in *reason*, *integrity*, and *Rational
Presuppositionalism* (which is critical thinking applied to basic beliefs),
which lead to the *Principle of Clarity* (vs. mysticism) as the needed response to the antinomy of skepticism and fideism.

The Historic Christian Faith is summed up in the creeds of the
Church councils of Historic Christianity: Jerusalem (A.D. 51), The
Apostles' Creed (*ca.* 180), Nicaea (325), Carthage (397), Chalcedon
(451), Orange (529), and Westminster (1648). Insight is historically
cumulative; what does not build on insight is tradition, not Historic

---

1. Gangadean, "Paper No. 2: Common Ground: The Necessary Condition for Thought and
Discourse," in *The Logos Papers*; Gangadean, Papers No. 50–53: Common Ground (Parts
I–IV) in *The Logos Papers*.

Christianity. The Historic Christian Faith is agreement that arises out of much discussion and is the relevant example of how we are to reach unity today.

Unity is necessary to function to achieve one's goal. Without unity, we are divided, individually and corporately: united, we flourish; divided, we perish. This is true always, in every age, from the beginning of mankind's history to the present. Longstanding divisions reveal deficiencies in our understanding of basic things. Divisions in the Church led to apostasy and loss of headship in the culture, which in turn led to the decay of the culture of Western Civilization, now nearing collapse.

We cannot simply return to the past (Protestant or Catholic) by mere re-assertion. As with past Church councils, we must respond to the challenges from the past. We must go deeper in understanding and lay foundation on the rock of clarity, not on the sand of uncertainty, without proof about basic things.

Challenges from the Modern world (to name a few) continue in varying admixtures of deism, mechanism, and naturalism: from Descartes, Newton, Hume, Kant, Hegel, Feuerbach, Marx, Darwin, Nietzsche, Russell, Freud, Heidegger, Foucault, and Rorty. Protestant responses of Paley, Schleiermacher, Kierkegaard, and Barth came short of clear general revelation. So too, did Catholic responses from de Chardin, Maritain, Gilson, and Copleston.

Western Christianity was built upon Augustine and Aquinas, who in turn built upon the Greek dualism of Plato and Aristotle. These Greek dualists never got to creation *ex nihilo,* affirmed in the Apostles' Creed (written against Greek dualism). Christianity, burdened by its Greek assumptions, and in reaction to Hebrew literalistic legalism, could not, therefore, affirm that creation is revelation, full and clear, as it is affirmed in the worldview of creation–fall–redemption, or affirm that man's work from the beginning was dominion for the knowledge of God,[2] or that Christ, in the place of Adam, by his rule now, will complete mankind's work to fill the earth with the knowledge of God.[3]

There is a set of arguments (the ontological, cosmological, and teleological—for both natural and moral design) which, when sufficiently revised and taken in sequence, shows the clarity of general revelation

2. *Genesis 1:26.*
3. *Isaiah 11:9.*

(that only some—God the Creator—is eternal, hence creation *ex nihilo* vs. all is eternal in some form or other).[4]

The challenge of skepticism, arising from naïve realism and naïve idealism, and the response of fideism leading to mysticism, is a recurrent problem in the West as well as in the East, in both ancient and modern times. Kant's error regarding causality as merely mind-imposed led to the split of the noumenal (unknowable) world from the phenomenal (the known but not real) world. But, in response, the noumenal must be the cause of the phenomenal, or we are left with an idealistic world based everywhere on uncaused events, which makes all of life unintelligible.

Greek naturalism, beginning with Thales, led to the split between Parmenides (change is unreal) and Heraclitus (only change/flux is real). Protagoras' solution that man is the measure of all things (one's own mind is the creative force) sank that world into skepticism, in response to which arose various gnostic forms of mystical ecstasies.

The split arose also in India and spilled over into the rest of Asia. In Hinduism, the world of change is *maya* (a shared illusion) or *avidya* (ignorance). Only *moksha/samadhi* (enlightenment, beyond thought) brings the realization that the self (*atman*) is the ultimate reality (*Brahman*). Buddhism, in response to the denial of change, affirmed that all is *dukkha* (impermanent, lacking self-existence—*swabhava*), *shunya* (empty), and dependently co-arising (*pratityasamutpada*)—approachable, if at all, only by the non-cognitive mystical experience of nirvana.

If it can be known with certainty that man is finite, temporal, and changeable in mind/soul and body, that he is neither animal nor God but the image of God, then we can have knowledge of the world and of God, and that the good for man as a rational being is the knowledge of God.

If human nature is rational, requiring cognitive meaning, then the good must be rational knowledge of God, not a non-cognitive, mystical experience, in either the East or the West. Nor can the good be a sensual paradise, or an Edenic paradise (without pain or physical death), or a literal city with mansions and streets of gold, all of which is vanity,

---

4. Gangadean, *Philosophical Foundation*, 71-161; Gangadean, *History of Philosophy*, 47-58; Gangadean, *The Westminster Catechisms*. See LCQ. 2; Gangadean, "Paper No. 3: The Principle of Clarity, Rational Presuppositionalism, and Proof," and "Paper No. 93: The Logic of Apologetics: The Goal, the Method, the Content," in *The Logos Papers*.

an opiate for the masses, utterly unable to satisfy man's deepest longing for an ever-increasing fullness of meaning in the knowledge of God.

THE GOOD IS THE END IN ITSELF

The good is the end in itself, the highest value (the *summum bonum*), chosen for its own sake and not for the sake of anything else. As the end in itself, it is the end of all ends of human activity and the source of unity, individually and corporately. As the highest value, the *summum bonum*, it is eternal life, the strongest motivation for one and all. As the end in itself, the highest value, it is existentially most basic and necessarily held by all, more or less consciously and consistently.

The end in itself is not the means to the end. The virtues, whether moral (as in faith, hope, and love or wisdom, courage, and temperance), or natural, or instrumental, are not the good, but the means to the good. The end in itself is not the effect of possessing that end. Happiness, pleasure, and relationship, as in friendship, is the effect of possessing what (we believe) is the good. The effect is lasting only if it is the good. Ethics is, therefore, teleological (aimed at the good), not deontological (aimed at virtue) or consequential (aimed at happiness). Most ethical differences originate at this level.

THE GOOD IS ONE

The good is one. If it were dual or plural, there would be no rational way to settle ethical disputes (as in Manicheanism and polytheism). Ultimate justification in ethics rests on metaphysics, knowledge of which rests on epistemology.

The good for a being is based on the nature of that being. This is held as an axiom. Common Ground assumes things have natures—there are identities and differences, and these are knowable. The nature or essence of a thing (or class of things) is the set of properties that all members have, that they always have, and that only members have.

A natural individual being is a unity of diversity in an ordered set of relationships of the diversity. A human has several layers of diversity. The good for a being, based on the nature of that being, is one for that being, based on the unity of that being. The good for a class of beings (all men) is one and the same since all members of the class have the same nature. The diversity in human nature gives rise to the varying virtues by which the good is achieved.

Real diversity in any being is always in unity as an ordered set of relationships. In the ordered set, the less basic does not set aside the more basic. Diverse levels or aspects of being do not conflict with but build upon what is more basic in the ordered set. We are first human before we are male or female, and can be fully so only if we affirm what is first. The good as the source of unity must integrate all diversity to serve the one end, the end in itself.

THE GOOD IS CLEAR

The good (for man) is based on human nature, which is immediately accessible (ordinarily) to every human being. Every source of knowledge, the philosophical (from clear general revelation—cGR), the theological (from special revelation/Scripture—SR), and the historical (from Historic Christianity—HC), agrees in its understanding the good.

From cGR: the good for man as a rational being is the use of reason to the fullest; reason is used to understand the nature of things; the nature of things created reveals the nature of God; therefore, the good for man as a rational being is the knowledge of God. From SR: the good for man as the image of God is the knowledge of God—eternal life is knowing God;[5] man is to know God through the work of dominion over the creation which reveals God, which revelation is full and clear; the outcome of the work of dominion is the earth shall be full of the knowledge of God as the waters cover the sea.[6] From HC: Man's chief end is to glorify God and to enjoy him forever;[7] we are to glorify him in all that by which he makes himself known;[8] God makes himself known by all his works of creation and providence.[9]

On a more existential note, circumstantial sufferings are trials of faith for the knowledge of God. Nothing separates believers from God's

---

5. *John 17:3.*

6. *Isaiah 11:9.*

7. *SCQ. 1.*

8. *SCQ. 101.*

9. *WCF 4.1, 5.1.*

love which seeks man's good; Job, and all who seek God, are brought to see God more fully.[10]

The means to the good are also clear: the moral law, summed up in the Decalogue, is written in the human heart (that is, structured into man's nature/being). Both Moses and Paul affirm this.[11]

ESSENTIAL CHARACTERISTICS OF THE GOOD

Before addressing the good, there are necessary conditions for rational justification in ethics or morality in general: a metaphysical absolute, which is God the Creator (vs. all is one or all is eternal), personal immortality, human freedom, clarity of general revelation, and rationality in man.

There are (at least) ten necessary characteristics of the good. The good itself must be continuing, inexhaustible, comprehensive, inalienable, corporate, cumulative, communal, fulfilling, ultimate, and transformative.

If there is no continuity from this life to the next, there is no unity of purpose; we are merely passing through or waiting in a vestibule. If there is continuity to and in the next life, forever, the good must be inexhaustible. Only the knowledge of God revealed in and understood through his Word/works is continuing and inexhaustible. Only understanding is comprehensive/complete/full/connected to all of life, and only understanding is inalienable.

Knowledge that is inexhaustible and comprehensive is achieved through dominion, by all men, throughout history, and in every land. Only the good as knowledge can be corporate, cumulative, and communal (increasing by being shared). Knowledge is fulfilling, and only the knowledge of God is lastingly satisfying; only knowledge of the logos, the eternal Word of God that creates and sustains all things, connects man to what is ultimate;[12] and only knowledge of the Truth has the power to transform and to make us free.[13] The knowledge of God, based on human nature, must be rational, cognitive, and meaningful,

---

10. *Job 42:5-6.*

11. *Deuteronomy 30:11-14; Romans 2:14-15.*

12. *John 1:1-18.*

13. *John 8:32.*

not mystical, without cognitive meaning, or apart from or against human nature.

THE GOOD AND HOPE

There is every reason to hope that the good will be achieved in history and enjoyed forever. From the nature of man: man needs the good; it is a matter of life and death. From the nature of the good: as cognitive/rational, the knowledge of God is only through the work of dominion, by all men and for all men. From the nature of God: infinite goodness, revealed in creation–fall–redemption, guarantees that the good will be achieved (good will overcome evil, belief will overcome unbelief).

There is a conflict between good and evil, penetrating to every degree of understanding and misunderstanding of good and evil itself, in each person, in every culture, through all of world history. Good retains integrity and meaning; evil by nature is self-contradictory and self-destructive. Only what retains meaning can last. All civilizations that lose meaning have perished.

The cultural mandate requires it: true hope in work (from the Garden to the City of God—the City with foundations), is opposed to no hope (of the City of Man—dominion apart from the knowledge of God), and to false hope (the knowledge of God without the work of dominion). The moral law mandate requires it: The law is teleological, aimed at the good. The law is near to each one of us (not a foreign thing); it is in our mouths and in our hearts that we should obey it. The mission mandate requires it: the Church is to make disciples of all nations, baptizing them and teaching them to obey all that Christ has commanded.

It is not the case that we have tried this vision and found it wanting, but rather the Church's foundation has been tried for a long time now and has been found wanting. It is now high time to awaken from our sleep, to work while it is day, and to lay foundation more deeply and fully by understanding the good and putting it into practice.

_____

4

REASON AND THE
WITNESS OF THE CHURCH

Public lecture delivered at Grand Canyon University[1]

March 5, 2019

INTRODUCTION

MY TOPIC IS REASON AND THE WITNESS of the Church. We should ask how we bring together reason and the Church. Recollect Tertullian asked, "What has Jerusalem to do with Athens?" What does faith have to do with reason? How do you bring these concepts together? Many people seem to separate the two, but we will see that they have everything to do with one another. The topic is puzzling, and we want to set the general tenor for the discussion. I am going to define reason from three sources: from general revelation, from Scripture, and from Historic Christianity. Historic Christianity is what has been summed up in the creeds and confessions/councils of the Church over the centuries. I will then explain what I mean by "witness"—what this witness is that is being called for. What is a witness of the Church? What do you mean by witness? Where does Scripture require us to make a witness? Again, I will look at three sources. And then, we will make several applications.

We will first examine reason from general revelation—what anyone, anywhere, at any time can and should know about reason. In any stage of history, in any phase of life, we can and should see what is clear

_____

1. Edited by The Logos Foundation Editorial Board.

about reason. We will begin with Common Ground. In its most basic sense, Common Ground is the set of conditions necessary for thought and discourse. There are many ways in which we can speak about common ground. We can speak about common ground psychologically or practically. Perhaps we are both from Flagstaff. Or we both went skiing at Telluride. We may connect in that way. Or we can speak of common ground as something we work toward. This is Common Ground in the most basic sense. It is a set of conditions necessary for thought and discourse. If we are going to think at all, if we are going to speak at all with one another, we need to identify the conditions necessary for thought and discourse.

The first part of Common Ground is *reason*, objectively speaking. Second, *integrity* is a concern for consistency, subjectively speaking. That is, you are committed to reason and applying reason personally. Third is *Rational Presuppositionalism*, which is to apply reason to your presuppositions. Presupposition is our most basic belief. So, Rational Presuppositionalism is critical thinking applied to basic beliefs, which are held more or less consciously and consistently. We have all heard of critical thinking. So, it should not be strange to apply critical thinking, or reason, to our most basic beliefs. That is, to our most basic beliefs conceivable. Reason, integrity, and Rational Presuppositionalism (which is the methodological approach) all lead to the fourth part of Common Ground, which is the *Principle of Clarity*, necessary for inexcusability. "Inexcusability" is a term we will return to a few times. If you believe in Jesus Christ and him crucified, crucified for sin, for your sin, our sin, and the sins of the world—that he is the Lamb of God who takes away the sin of the world—then we must deal with the question of inexcusability. Why do we need Christ? And him crucified? So, the Principle of Clarity is necessary for inexcusability. The Principle of Clarity simply says that some things are clear. The basic things are clear. The basic things about God and man and good and evil are clear to reason. We will see why we say they are "clear to reason." These are the four conditions for Common Ground. Here, we will just be focusing on reason. I want to see by the time we get through whether you are with me. If I had money, I would pay you for thoughtful questions. You say, "I knew there was a catch—thoughtful questions." What is a thoughtful question? A thoughtful question is one that builds on Common Ground. Otherwise, you are going to be raising questions about

Common Ground itself. So, as we go forward from here, we are expecting that whatever questions you have, you raise it from here. Let us go over the first part of Common Ground.

"REASON" FROM THREE SOURCES

From General Revelation

It is self-evident that we think. We form concepts, judgments, and arguments, the forms of all thought. When I say self-evident, you should keep in mind and contrast it with the well-known statement, "We hold these truths to be self-evident." I would say that statement is not self-evident. One would have to take steps to show that all men are created equal and that there is a God who creates. And also, when I speak about self-evident, you may want to contrast it with Descartes' *cogito ergo sum*, "I think, therefore I am." No, that has been tried and found wanting. The reason it was found wanting is that Modern philosophy, which was built on Descartes' foundationalism, ended in skepticism because it did not actually have a foundation. I am using "self-evident" in a sense that is stronger than Descartes. I am setting myself up to be knocked off easily, and I invite you to do that. It is self-evident that we think. To say "I think" is not to say "therefore I am."

It is self-evident we think in that we have concepts, judgments, and arguments, the forms of all thought. Thoughts begin with concepts, and they end with argument. There is nothing simpler than a concept and nothing more complex than an argument. An entire book could be a sustained argument with many premises and a conclusion. A concept is expressed by a word or term, which could be a group of words. "Table" is a word. "On the table," is a group of words together having meaning. "Red," "human," "mortal," "rational," and "hard," are words we use, and all of them express concepts. Forming a concept is the first act of thought. Concepts are expressed by a word or term, which assumes rationality. The law of identity is: *a* is *a*; *a* is not *non-a*. Book is not non-book. Book is not table. Terms are conventional. They are not natural; they are agreed upon by human beings. Terms can be used in a number of ways, as body language and sign language could be. But words particularly are conventional; they are agreed upon by human society. Words can be used in many ways. I want to specify that the rational use is not the non-cognitive use of words. Non-cognitive has to do with the practical and the psychological. You could give commands; you could express feelings, but that is not what we are talking about. Of all of the different uses of terms, the cognitive use is most basic. We cannot bypass and get around the cognitive use of terms. This is to say, we cannot bypass and get around reason. So, we begin with the claim that it is self-evident that we think, and what we mean by thinking, and I invite you to see if you can challenge that.

Secondly, **it is self-evident that there are laws of thought.** The laws of thought are, the law of identity: *a* is *a*; the law of non-contradiction: not both *a* and *non-a*, at the same time and in the same respect; and the law of excluded middle: either *a* or *non-a*. The laws of thought are properly called the laws of reason, which is reason in itself. Reason in itself is the most basic sense of the term "reason." There is legitimacy in always going back to appeal to the most basic when speaking about anything. So, I started with the most basic sense of Common Ground—reason. And then, the most basic sense of reason. The most basic sense of reason has priority and primacy. Many persons will use the term "reason," but not in its most basic sense—reason in itself as the laws of thought. If someone says "reason is fallen," they are not speaking about reason itself. They may be speaking about the human use of reason. Human beings are fallen, and that may affect their use of reason, but reason itself is not fallen. We do not need to be concerned about that objection and shy away from the use of reason in our witness. We will see that we are called very much, very strongly, to use reason in our witness. So, it is self-evident that there are laws of thought, and these are properly called the laws of reason, or reason in itself. Notice the words "properly called." That is, it is legitimate, makes good sense, and I do not think it can easily be contested.

Reason, as the laws of thought, is a test for meaning. If a law of thought is violated, then there is no cognitive meaning, no distinction between *a* and *non-a*, no distinction between being and non-being, true or false, good or evil. And if there is no cognitive meaning, then truth in any form is not possible. Meaning is more basic than truth. We often talk about truth, but we must recognize that truth applies to statements and judgments, not to concepts and arguments. Arguments are valid or invalid, sound or not. Concepts are well-formed or not well-formed. And statements or judgments are true or false. Judgments are the combination of concepts. "Socrates is mortal" or "all men are mortal" are judgments. Combine two concepts, and you have a statement that is true or false. So, before you can get to a judgment, you have to get a concept that is meaningful, where you distinguish *a* from *non-a*. If a law of thought is violated, there is no meaning, which is more basic than truth. There is no possibility of truth without meaning.

The strongest form of objection against any position is to show that what is being said is not logically possible—not simply that the position is false, but that it is not logically possible. We need to see that the clarity of God's existence is of that level and kind. You may say, "What are you saying? You are really setting the bar high, are you not?" Yes, I am, because it is God. And God's Word says it is clear. I will point to where it says it is clear and talk about the meaning of that—how clarity is the whole basis of the gospel. Clarity is the whole basis of the need for Christ. It is the whole basis of inexcusability. If it were not clear, you would not be inexcusable. So, when Paul begins to speak about the gospel, saying, "I am not ashamed of the gospel,"[2] he begins with clarity and inexcusability,[3] and the universality that no one seeks and no one understands what is clear about God.[4] From there, we may understand many other things, such as the universality of the curse in connection with not seeing what is clear.

So, reason is a test for meaning, and meaning is more basic than truth. Reason is not only the laws of thought, but reason is the laws of being. **Reason is ontological.** I am going to go step-by-step and come out in a place where you may ask, "How did you get there?" So, watch me closely. I will raise the meaning and significance of reason step-by-step. Reason applies to being as well as thought. There are no square-circles. There is no *a* that is *non-a*, at the same time and in the same respect, by the laws of reason. There is no being from non-being. Some play with the idea, but they really are merely flirting. They are not able to seriously say being came from non-being. In connection with that, there are no uncaused events. Including, against Kant, trying to make a distinction between the noumenal world (as it is in itself) and the phenomenal world (as we experience it), and saying that

---

2. *Romans 1:16-17.*

3. *Romans 1:18-20.*

4. *Romans 3:10-12.*

causality applies to the phenomenal realm but not to the noumenal. We will say that is not possible either. Reason applies to all being, to the highest being, to God's being. Which is to say, God is not both *a* and *non-a*, at the same time and in the same respect. God is not both eternal and not eternal, at the same time and in the same respect. Since God's being is eternal, reason in itself is eternal. See how I got there? Do you feel you want to back away? Do you feel this is too strong?

Reason is natural. It is the same in all men, in all human beings, as the light of nature. This light is that by which we see with the mind. That is, it refers to understanding, not to seeing with the eyes. Both the book of nature, that is, general revelation, and the book of Scripture, special revelation, are clear to reason and can be understood by all who seek. Seeking is a critical piece. What is involved in seeking? The Scriptures say, "He that comes to God must believe that he is and that he rewards those that diligently seek him."[5] But, Scripture also says, no one seeks, no one understands, no one is righteous, no not one.[6] What is it to seek and to see what is clear? Remember, the larger context is the witness of the Church, the witness of the believers in the Church, and what it is to which we are witness. Reason is the same in all, and all can understand. Reason is necessary to understand general revelation, which is the basis of the inexcusability of all men failing to know and acknowledge what is clear. In addition, reason is also used to understand special revelation. Reason is necessary for understanding both general and special revelation. It is more basic than, and is used to understand, both. Am I delivering what I promised? Whether you agree with it or not, we are giving a definition of reason.

Reason is man's essence as a rational animal. Would you agree that you have a body? You say, "I definitely agree with that." Do you agree that you have a mind? "Of course, I have a mind." Is the mind the same as your brain? That should be clear, right? Do you think with your brain or your mind? Do you think with the left side of your brain or the right side of your mind? Is the mind physical? Can the mind have a right side if it is not physical? We need a little pressure for clarification. Reason is man's essence as a rational animal. What we mean by essence is that reason distinguishes man from animals. We can

---

5. *Hebrews 11:6.*

6. *Romans 3:10-12.*

communicate with animals using many conventional signs, but this is not cognitive communication. Reason is man's essence as a rational animal. Man's essence is fundamental to all other aspects of his being. It is fundamental to his feelings and actions. Reason in man cannot be denied (because it is essential, fundamental) without sinking into meaninglessness—the loss of all meaning. Which is to say, reason cannot be denied without going against your very being, your essence. And if that is the case, then the good for man, based on human nature, as a rational being, must be rational, not mystical. You might say, "What is he talking about, and why is he talking about this?" A great portion of the Christian community is operating on a Greek model and thinking about a mystical vision of God in heaven, called the beatific vision, which has no cognitive content. And that is the good for most people. But, if man is rational and the good is based on human nature, then the good has to be rational; it is not mystical. Therefore, you might be able to see something about the state of the witness of the Church and why we are where we are.

Reason in man is transcendental. Reason stands above, and makes thought possible. It is authoritative; it cannot be questioned but makes questioning possible. You cannot use reason to question reason. You cannot use the laws of thought to question the laws of thought. If you are going to think at all, you have to use the laws of thought. We see that reason, as the laws of thought, is self-attesting. And only reason is self-attesting. The senses are not self-attesting. Intuition is not self-attesting. Nor is tradition or science. Only reason, as the laws of thought, is transcendental, self-attesting, and authoritative. The Scripture is not self-attesting. Reason is self-attesting. You can question Scripture, and you are called to do that in a number of places in Scripture itself. We are to know why we accept the Bible as Scripture but not the Quran as Scripture. Part of our witness is to be able to show this. We may be tempted to engage in friendship evangelism. You might end up with a nice club that way, but a club is not the same as a church. Furthermore, we do not want to separate love from the good. We often separate the two, but we should not.

From Special Revelation

Reason is the first form of the Word of God that comes to man.
John 1:1 says, "In the beginning was the Word [the logos], and the
Word was with God, and the Word was God." The word "logos" has
to do with account, reason, and explanation. That is the primary sense
of the term. In the beginning was the Word. John 1:4 continues, "In
Him [in the logos] was life, and the life was the light of men." The life
of the logos—the eternal Word of God, by whom God makes himself
known—comes into man as light, by which we see and understand.
This passage is the basis of saying reason is the first form of the Word
of God that comes to man. Scripture is the Word of God written.
Though, we cannot identify the Word of God simply with the written
Word of God. Why? There are other forms of the Word.[7] John 1:1 tell
us the Word of God is eternal. In the beginning was the Word. Scripture itself is using the term Word—Word of God—not just for the
written Word, but as eternal. It is the eternal Word of God. In addition, the Word comes to man in several ways, the first of which is that
the Word is in all men, made in the image of God, as the self-attesting light of reason. The Word of God in its fullness is truth. Truth in
its fullness makes God fully known. John 1:14-18 says, the only be-
gotten Son, who is the eternal Word of God, now incarnate, has made
God fully known. God the Word makes God known. So, from Scripture—John 1—we see the life of the logos is in all men as light. Reason
is the light—we see by the light—it is the light by which we understand. By reason, we grasp concepts, judgments, and arguments. Thus,
if we understand reason, we can then go on to see what reason has to
do with the witness of the Church. At this point, hopefully, your mind
should be stretched.

    Romans 1:20 is another relevant passage that says, "For the invisi-
ble things of him [God] from the creation of the world are clearly seen,
being understood by the things that are made, even his eternal power
and Godhead [or divine nature]; so that they are without excuse." Notice how Paul puts that together. The word "reason" is not used, but is
assumed. He cannot be speaking of seeing with the eye because the *invisible* things of God are clearly seen. Therefore, by good and necessary
consequences, they are not seen by the eye. Paul goes on to say, "being

---

7. Gangadean, "Paper No. 30: The Word of God: The Logos Is Truth," in *The Logos Papers*.

understood by . . ." The word "understood" implies reason. Knowing God is not an immediate intuition, as some have said. It is not the *sensus divinitatis*, a position that claims that everyone deep down knows God by some immediate intuition. Rather, the eternal power and divine nature are understood by reason.[8]

Romans 1:20 specifically singles out the eternal power and, secondly, the divine nature. Thus, if we are going to be witnesses to God, according to the gospel, as Paul introduces in verse 16 when he says, "For I am not ashamed of the gospel of Christ, for it is the power of God unto salvation to everyone that believes; to the Jew first, and also to the Greek," we need to begin our witness where he does. In introducing the gospel, he shows the need for the gospel by showing that all men are in sin—they fail to seek and understand what is clear. Romans 1:20 connects reason with understanding, and sin as the failure to understand what is clear to reason.

From Historic Christianity

The third source of the definition of reason is Historic Christianity. The opening lines of The Westminster Confession of Faith say, "Although the light of nature, and the works of creation and providence do so far manifest the goodness, wisdom, and power of God, as to leave men inexcusable; yet are they not sufficient to give that knowledge of God, and of his will, which is necessary unto salvation."[9] Again, the Confession does not literally use the word "reason," but it does use the words "light of nature." "Although the light of nature," although *reason*, and the works of creation and providence, *general revelation*, do so far manifest the goodness, wisdom, and power of God as to leave men inexcusable, it is not sufficient for what is needed for salvation. You need to go beyond general revelation. You need special revelation to get to the means of salvation. So, the opening words of the Westminster Confession of Faith, written in 1648 at Westminster Abbey, over about a five-year period, in the context of much discussion, affirms reason.

---

8. For a more detailed exposition of this point, see Part V, point 4 in: Gangadean, "Paper No. 120: Contra Voluntarism: The Will Is Not Independent of the Intellect," in *The Logos Papers*, 638-640.

9. *WCF 1.1.*

I emphasize the fact that the Confession was written in the context of much discussion because in John 16:13, Jesus says he is going to send the Holy Spirit, and when the Holy Spirit comes, "He will guide you into all truth." In John 17:17, we see the connection between truth and logos: "Your word is truth." Your logos is truth. Through the Holy Spirit, the logos is going to guide the Church into all truth—not each and every believer separately, but the body of believers together over time. The Westminster Confession is the high-water mark of Historic Christianity. There has been no major council since 1648. This is the work of the Holy Spirit, leading the Church into all truth.

Acts 15:7 is a reference to the first council, where the elders and apostles, the pastors and teachers, got together for much discussion. The context of the first council is that the gospel came to the Jews first, and they came into the Church with a mixture of understanding and misunderstanding, which lead them to believe, "Unless you are circumcised . . . you cannot be saved."[10] A dispute started over this claim and they came together to discuss it. And what happened? Acts 15:7 says that after there was much disputing or discussion, then the assembly was addressed. What was going on there? Here we see the work of reason, in the process of discussion, helping us to understand the truth of God. So, Historic Christianity is built upon the Holy Spirit leading us into all truth, and the logos is truth. After general revelation and Scripture, and the Word of God incarnate, then the Holy Spirit comes and does his work. Much discussion reflects the process by which we grow in understanding. The Holy Spirit leads the Church into all truth, through much discussion, by which the Church comes to understand.

This first major council of the Church was against a kind of literalism that distorted the truth of circumcision. The Jews did not see, as Nicodemus did not see, that you must be born again. And they failed to see that circumcision signified that you must be born again; you must circumcise your heart and not your flesh, which is new birth. And circumcision signifies the same thing as baptism. There are many ways in which the Church then, and the Church now, misread the Scripture with a false literalism rather than reading with contextualism, causing major divisions that affect the Church.

---

10. *Acts 15:1.*

With Acts 15 as the context, we should see how other councils follow. The second major council of the Church is the Apostles' Creed, which states:

I believe in God, the Father almighty, creator of heaven and earth.

I believe in Jesus Christ, his only Son, our Lord,
    who was conceived by the Holy Spirit
    and born of the virgin Mary.
    He suffered under Pontius Pilate,
    was crucified, died, and was buried;
    he descended to hell.
    The third day he rose again from the dead.
    He ascended to heaven
    and is seated at the right hand of God the Father almighty.
    From there he will come to judge the living and the dead.

I believe in the Holy Spirit,
    the holy catholic church,
    the communion of saints,
    the forgiveness of sins,
    the resurrection of the body,
    and the life everlasting. Amen.[11]

The creed emphasizes the physical creation, bodily existence, and the resurrection of the body. The Apostles' Creed was especially written against worldly Greek ideas influencing the Church. It is opposed to Greek influence from Plato and Aristotle and, with them, Greek dualism, which does not affirm that God created matter. Dualism claims some lesser being created matter and that matter is evil, and because matter is evil, one needs to be separated from the physical body to attain the good. The monastic movement, along with the beatific vision, was influenced by Greek ideas.

Continuing with other councils, Nicaea clarifies the Trinity; Carthage addresses the canon of the Scriptures; Chalcedon shows how Christ is fully God and fully man; and Orange shows the sovereignty of God's grace. And then, several of the creeds during the time of the

---

11. See: crcna.org/welcome/beliefs/creeds/apostles-creed

Reformation come to fullest expression in the Westminster Standards. Through these councils and creeds, God is leading the Church into all truth. From 1517, the beginning of the Reformation, to 1648, when the Westminster Confession is completed, is 130 years of intense discussion that brought about the Westminster Standards. This process is an example of how the Holy Spirit leads the Church into all truth. This does not mean that the councils are infallible or do not have errors, but errors can and have been corrected, and we are not to neglect that. To summarize: there are three sources of understanding "reason": general revelation, Scripture, and Historic Christianity, as it comes to expression through the councils, creeds, and in the Westminster Standards. So, does reason have anything to do with faith? Christianity?

"WITNESS" FROM THREE SOURCES

From the Moral Law

Let us now look at three sources of understanding "witness." The first and most basic sense of witness is from the moral law. The Ten Commandments, given in written form in Scripture, and the moral law written on the heart of all men, are the same in content. The ninth commandment is, "You shall not bear false witness against your neighbor."[12] This sense of witness is in the context of a court of law where one is called to testify and not bear false witness. This is a minimal sense of witness. One goes to court to seek corrective justice. What we need prior to corrective justice is preventative justice to prevent injustice from occurring. Truth is necessary for justice.

We are called to bear witness to the truth, the whole truth, and nothing but the truth, under questioning. Knowing and speaking the whole truth begins in Genesis 1:26 in recognizing that man is made in the image of God, from the beginning in Eden, and he is to name the creatures. In the temptation, the serpent says, "You shall be as God, knowing good and evil."[13] Adam putting himself in the place of God to determine good and evil, makes him the first existential atheist. As if you could define your own essence, rather than discover it. You are

---

12. *Exodus 20:16.*

13. *Genesis 3:5.*

going to determine good and evil? No, good and evil are based in human nature, which is already determined by God. You are not creator; you cannot determine your nature. This is part of knowing and speaking the truth, which is necessary for justice. When Adam failed to know and speak the truth about human nature, how much injustice came into the world? First, his relationship with his wife started to deteriorate. He took his eyes off the good and put them on her. And she said if you can do that, I can do that too. Girls can do anything that boys can do, only better. They take it, then take it one step further. That is what a suitable helper does; she develops.

From the Lord Jesus

The second main concern about witness is from the Lord, who says, "You shall be witnesses unto me in Jerusalem, and in Judea, and in Samaria, and unto the uttermost parts of the earth."[14] You are not to go tramping through the Amazon, come to some tribe, and expect to tell them the good news. You are going to have to deal with what they believe and with their gods. Jim Elliot, in the book by his wife Elisabeth Elliot, *Through Gates of Splendor*,[15] tried to go out and witness, but did not get where he needed to be. In the movie, *The Mission*,[16] the Indians cut the heavy paraphernalia off the main character's back. He was carrying a load of guilt, and the Indians raise questions about his king, saying, I am king here, and what about my word? The natives are capable of reasoning. So, if you are going to go into all the earth and be witnesses, you do not waltz in as if you have a free pass. Again, in the movie, *Silence*,[17] missionaries went to Japan and could not show what they needed to, and they are made to step on an image of Christ and renounce their faith. Jesus says, "You shall be witnesses unto me . . . unto the uttermost parts of the earth." This witness calls for knowing the truth, including knowing and showing how it is clear that they need to give up the worship of the sun to worship the Son—the Son of God. Witness, then, is for the truth, the whole truth, and

---

14. *Acts 1:8.*

15. Elisabeth Elliot, *Through Gates of Splendor* (Wheaton: Tyndale House, 1988).

16. Joffé, Roland, dir. *The Mission* (United Kingdom: Goldcrest Films, 1986).

17. Scorsese, Martin, dir. *Silence* (United States: Paramount Pictures, 2016).

nothing but the truth. This kind of witness leads to full justice as well as witnesses unto Christ in all the ends of the earth. We are to teach. In Matthew 28:19-20, Jesus says we are "to make disciples of all nations, teaching them to observe all that I have commanded you." In teaching and making disciples, we have to work through all the objections that human beings have in whatever field in which we teach, whether it be economics, politics, education, etc.

From the Nature of a Witness

The third consideration comes from the very nature of a witness. A witness is one who sees. In a court of law, when called to be a witness, a lawyer may ask were you in a position where you could see? Was there good lighting there? Do you have good eyesight? You are going to be cross-examined. You will have to describe what you saw, what you saw for yourself, and you cannot rely on what someone else told you secondhand. Secondhand testimony is not acceptable for a witness. When cross-examined, you can defend what you witnessed because you *know*. In witnessing to the truth of God, if you are a faithful witness, you must have indisputable proof of what is clear that can withstand cross-examination.

In my days of unbelief and atheism, when someone came to me and said "God loves you and has a wonderful plan for your life," I asked, "How do you know that God exists?" And, I persisted with that question and could not get an answer. I once persisted in asking the question of others on a forum for six months. When I asked the question "How do you know?" the forum went silent. I have asked that question of pastors and teachers in the Church, and they continually skirt the question. How do you know that God exists? There is a failure of witness. So, the question is, from Romans 1:20, do you see what is clear to reason about God? Do you see how it is that there must be something eternal and that only some—God—is eternal? Can you show that matter exists and matter is not eternal? And that the soul exists and that the soul is not eternal? And, therefore, only some is eternal.[18]

---

18. Gangadean, *Philosophical Foundation*, 71-161; Gangadean, *History of Philosophy*, 47-58; Gangadean, *The Westminster Catechisms*. See LCQ. 2; Gangadean, "Paper No. 3: The Principle of Clarity, Rational Presuppositionalism, and Proof" and "Paper No. 93: The Logic of Apologetics: The Goal, the Method, the Content," in *The Logos Papers*.

Should human beings all over the earth throughout history see what is clear about what is eternal? Should the abused, uneducated kid in 1800 B.C. see this? Should Abraham see this, and not worship his father's idols? Nor worship the sun? Can you see how the sun is not eternal? Is it clear to reason? Psalm 19 says the spacious heavens declare the glory of God, particularly the sun. "There is no speech nor language where their voice is not heard." You should be able to show how the sun is not eternal. Even before that, can you show that there must be something eternal? And even before that, can you show that it must be clear? Can you show the Principle of Clarity, that some things are clear to reason? This is what reason can give you. But remember, we are starting from the condition of sin where no one seeks, and no one understands the basic things that are clear about God. And this condition is what we need to repent of to fully enter into the life that God has for us. Otherwise, we will remain spiritual infants. Hebrews 5:12 warns, "For though by this time you ought to be teachers, you need someone to teach you again the first principles of the oracles of God; and you have come to need milk and not solid food." A faithful witness is one who sees and can withstand cross-examination.

APPLICATIONS

In conclusion, I will discuss a few applications. One application of reason, clarity, and inexcusability, is that a witness can show there must be something eternal and that only God is eternal, from Romans 1:20. The second application is that the good is man's chief end, and is eternal life, which is knowing God. Is the good based on human nature? Is the good for a being based on the nature of the being? Is that true almost by axiom? Is that almost a self-evident truth? Good for a horse is based on the nature of a horse. Good for a rabbit is based on the nature of a rabbit. And good for a man is based on the nature of a goat. No, based on the nature of a man. And can we know what the nature of man is? We can and should. And can we know what the good is? We can and should.

Someone might raise the question: are we privileging reason? Postmodernism speaks a lot about this. I ask, are we privileging thought? Thought is the necessary condition for everything. And reason is a necessary condition for thought. How about: are you privileging a group of people who may have gone further along in the use of reason because of the influence of the gospel and the logos? Are we privileging those people or are we saying what we esteem is reason and clarity? And all of us should privilege that. What if we say, reason is not something to be privileged, but it is that which makes privileging of anything else possible? There is much talk of groups of people being privileged. Can we be clear about what reason is in the most basic sense of reason? Can we know the relationship between reason and the Word of God? I am going to hold on to that to the very end. Should we guard the Word of God against reason, or should we guard the Word against the failure to use reason fully?

I want to focus attention on this last point a bit more. Can the Church come to unity on the several senses of the Word of God? Can we even agree on what the Word of God is? Now why is that important? The Lord prays that the Church might be one, as the Son and Father are one, that the world might believe.[19] This is most relevant for our witness. If the witness of the Church is to go out, then the Church needs to come to unity. Particularly, we need unity on the very starting point, the Word of God. Now, I referenced that need when I quoted John 1:1-18. I want to point out the verses and associations about the Word of God in John's Prologue and ask, can the Church come to unity on the several senses of the Word of God?

First, the Word of God is eternal. "In the beginning was the Word, and the Word was with God, and the Word was God."[20] Ask yourself if you agree with this. Secondly, the Word is in all men as reason. "In him was life, and the life was the light of men."[21] Thirdly, the Word is in creation. "He was in the world, and the world was made by him, and the world knew Him not."[22] This third sense of the Word of God is general revelation—creation and providence. Fourth, the Word of God is in special revelation/Scripture. "He came unto his own, and his own received him not." The Word came through the prophets—God came to the Hebrews and spoke—and they did not receive him. They often killed the prophets. And fifth, the Word came incarnate and

---

19. *John 17:21-23.*
20. *John 1:1.*
21. *John 1:4.*
22. *John 1:10.*

was rejected by crucifixion. The Word was rejected. First, the Word of God as reason was resisted—that is why Scripture says, "The light shines in the darkness, and the darkness has not overcome it"[23] or cannot withstand it. Then, in the creation, "the world knew him not." Then, in the Scripture, "his own did not receive him." And finally, he came incarnate, full of grace and truth. In grace, he forgives us for our rejection of the Word of God in the previous forms, and he comes in truth to make God known, which is eternal life. The sixth sense of the Word of God is in the Holy Spirit leading us into all truth in Church history.[24] And the seventh sense is that all those who are born again are born of the Spirit by the Word.[25] The Word and the Spirit bring us from death—spiritual death—to spiritual life. Scripture says, "unless one is born again, he cannot see the kingdom of God."[26] And further, the Holy Spirit sanctifies the believer by the truth—his Word is truth.[27] So, the Word is in each believer, who is truly a believer, by rebirth. We know that the life of God is in man as light. From the condition of spiritual death, we need to be restored to that light that was in Adam at the beginning. And we need to be sanctified through the truth. John 8:31 says, "If you continue in my word, then you are my disciples indeed; and you shall know the truth, and the truth shall make you free."

So, the answer to the question: "What does reason have to do with witness?" Everything—once we understand what is meant by reason and witness.

---

23. *John 1:5.*

24. *John 16:13.*

25. *1 Peter 1:23; John 3:3, 5.*

26. *John 3:3.*

27. *John 17:17.*

5

COMMON GROUND

For Public Discourse

Published in The Journal of Public Philosophy[1]

Issue 1, Summer 2019

INTRODUCTION

PUBLIC DISCOURSE HAS COLLAPSED IN THE recent culture wars. It is a predictable stage in the unfolding culture of every civilization that allows some freedom of thought. Freedom of thought apart from the laws of thought spins out of control. "Things fall apart; the center cannot hold; Mere anarchy is loosed upon the world . . ."[2] Can we have freedom without anarchy? Can there be rule by consent? We can and must have freedom and consent if we are to have any civilization, that is to say, a full common life, that is to say, human life, life that is beyond the birds and bees and beasts. Common life requires common ground. And common ground is to be found in human nature itself, understood more consciously and consistently.

Common Ground, in its most basic sense, is the set of conditions that make thought and discourse possible. The set unfolds naturally from the most basic, logically and objectively, to the existentially and subjectively basic; from the method of knowledge to the content of knowledge, all beginning, as it should, at the most basic level of our being. Common Ground consists of reason as the laws of thought,

---

1. See: publicphilosophypress.com/ppp-catalog
2. William Butler Yeats, "The Second Coming"
   See: poetryfoundation.org/poems/43290/the-second-coming

which make thought and discourse (the sharing of thought for consent) possible. This is not a mere professed, but actual commitment to the use of reason, a concern for consistency in thought and action, which is integrity. Applied consistently, reason is used critically to first test one's own basic belief for meaning. Reason, testing basic beliefs, is Rational Presuppositionalism. Reason, integrity, and Rational Presuppositionalism lead to the Principle of Clarity: some things are clear; the basic things are clear; the basic things in metaphysics (about God and man) and in ethics (about good and evil) are clear to reason (epistemology). Common Ground must begin with and build upon what is self-evident in epistemology.

REASON

It is self-evident that we think: we form concepts, judgments, and arguments, the forms of all thought—from the most basic concepts, expressed by a word or a term, to judgment—relating two concepts, to argument—the most complex thought, drawing a conclusion from premises. Thinking is cognitive, requiring judgments that are true or false and concepts that distinguish things, *a* and *non-a*. It is also self-evident that there are laws of thought: identity—*a* is *a*; non-contradiction—not both *a* and *non-a*, at the same time and in the same respect; and excluded middle—either *a* or *non-a*. These laws of thought are properly called the laws of reason, or reason in itself, to distinguish it from other, less basic senses of the term "reason."

From these two self-evident truths—that we think, and there are laws of thought—several other thoughts follow. Reason, as the laws of thought, is the test for meaning. Reason, as the laws of thought, makes thought possible. What violates a law of reason cannot be thought. *A* is *non-a* (fish is non-fish) cannot be thought. The words in the utterance become meaningless, emptied of meaning when joined together. Since truth requires meaning, loss of meaning brings the loss of truth. Reason is authoritative because it is transcendental—the laws of thought make thought possible. It, therefore, cannot be questioned without becoming self-referentially absurd. Only reason, as the laws of thought, is self-attesting. One can be free to think (to form concepts etc.) only by observing the laws of thought, that is, the laws of reason.

By nature, we think, even as we breathe; it cannot be prevented. It is common to all human beings as humans, regardless of other differences (age, gender, race, culture). We have bodies also, as animals, and sense experience. But a sense (bodily) impression, which is particular, is not a concept, which is universal. This distinguishes reason from the senses, thinking from perceiving, mind from body, man from animal. Because reason is natural, in our nature, it is universal, the same in all who think, and therefore reason is common ground.

Reason does not apply only to thought, but also to being. There are no square-circles, no *a* that is *non-a*. What is logically impossible is ontologically impossible; it cannot exist in any possible world. So, there are no uncaused events, no being from non-being. Reason applies to all being, to the highest being, to God's being (God is not both eternal and not-eternal, at the same time and in the same respect). Reason is eternal and uncreated. Miracles may override a created law of nature, but cannot override reason. Reason gives certainty, not just about relations among ideas, but in metaphysics also, about the world, about what is or can be eternal.

Reason in man is fundamental to desire (what we view as a good) and to action (what we choose to do in pursuit of the good). Since no experience (ordinary or extraordinary) is meaningful without interpretation, reason is fundamental (to the meaning of experience and to the meaning of truth statements). The psychological and the practical presuppose cognitive/rational meaning. Meaning is the deepest need and the highest good for man as a rational being and, therefore, the source of man's greatest happiness. Its absence is the source of man's deepest misery.

No area of life is exempt from thought, and no thought is exempt from meaning and, therefore, from reason. There is no religious exemption from reason. Faith is to reason as truth is to meaning. The deeper the understanding of what is not visible, the deeper is one's faith. Reason, therefore, is the beginning of Common Ground for all human beings, in all of life.

INTEGRITY

Integrity is a concern for consistency, both logical and existential. Without consistency, thought and dialogue become absurd/futile. Moral

evil is an act contrary to one's nature as a human being. It is to neglect, avoid, resist, and deny reason regarding what is clear. Suffering
calls us to stop and think. As humans, under the condition of natural and moral evil, we are more or less conscious and consistent. And
all agree we should be more conscious and consistent—we all should
have integrity.

With integrity, we would seek and understand basic things that are
clear to reason. We would come to agreement and grow in that agreement about what is clear. Either nothing (or not much) is clear, or
we generally lack integrity in not seeking and not understanding. But
no one, psychologically, can easily admit to a lack of integrity. Concern for truth is so inward and compelling that a special kind of self-
blinding (hypocrisy) is necessary to avoid what is clear. Hypocrisy can
be maintained only by a continual hardening of oneself by self-justification in order to excuse oneself from a sense of guilt in not seeking
and understanding.

Recognizing the propensity to hypocrisy requires the humility to be
open to correction through self-examination. Dialogue recognizes historically cumulated insight in others. Fear of human suffering should
spur self-examination. Challenges of different views call for thoughtful dialogue. We should seek out authority based on insight in order
to be challenged.

In light of reason and clarity at the basic level, integrity through
self-examination is necessary and sufficient for knowledge. What is
clear, and all that is clear, beginning with the self-evident and building on that, is easily knowable, with integrity. Integrity is necessary
as common ground. Without integrity, we cannot get off the ground.

RATIONAL PRESUPPOSITIONALISM

Critical thinking applies reason as the test for meeting, first at the basic
level and first in one's own basic beliefs (presuppositions). Reason used
to test presuppositions for meaning is called Rational Presupposition
(RP). RP is simply critical thinking applied more consciously and consistently. RP differs from other epistemologies by being alert to uncritically held assumptions and by attempting to be more conscious and
consistent in critical thinking at the foundational level.

There are two sets of basic beliefs in the three areas of basic be-liefs. 1) How do I know? (epistemology): either some things are clear or nothing is clear. 2) What is real/eternal? (metaphysics): either all is eternal (in some form or other) or only some is eternal. 3) What ought I to do? (ethics): either the good (the end in itself) is clear (because it is based on human nature, which is rational) or the good is not clear (because there is no rational human nature). In these three basic ques-tions, ethics (the good) is based in metaphysics (human nature), the understanding of which is grounded in epistemology. We must begin with epistemology.

RP presupposes integrity, and integrity presupposes what is self-evi-dent: that we think and that there are laws of thought—reason in itself. But no one is fully conscious and consistent in their presuppositions, given the factors of personality, background, and mood. Each person and every group of persons have an admixture of both sets of basic be-liefs held more or less consciously and consistently, with one set being more basic (at any time, from time to time, and over time). History is the outworking of the conflict of basic beliefs in each person and in every group of persons. Being contradictory, only one set can be true; only one set retains meaning. RP both intensifies and resolves con-flicts and brings things to a head—by making clear what is meaningful.

RP is to be contrasted with other epistemologies. Tradition is the default position of most human beings and is transmitted by testimo-ny (teaching of the elders). Scripture is passed on by testimony, but RP asks why any scripture, what makes this scripture, and why this scripture rather than another? When reasons are given without critical thinking, they are not rationally relevant. They are pseudo-arguments, not arguments; they appeal to the psychological and the practical, not the rational.

After tradition, common sense may be appealed to (a form of hoary tradition) as well as appeal to numbers also. Common sense is a form of naïve realism, which takes appearance for reality, a quasi-pragmatism that shifts the burden of proof to the opposing party. A less sophisticat-ed form is Thomas Reid's Scottish Common Sense philosophy. A more sophisticated form is Plantinga's Reformed Epistemology which focus-es on warrant, which may be lost, not on rational justification testing basic beliefs for meaning, which cannot so easily be lost. In common sense, taking appearance for reality, the earth may still be flat, and the sun still rise in the east.

Intuition as a source of knowledge assumes the sign is or is always accompanied by the reality. But "Beauty is truth, truth beauty—that is all ye know on earth, and all ye need to know,"[3] held true by the Romantics, may be true only in the world of art ("Ode on a Grecian Urn"). The urn (which speaks of death or timeless art) should remind us this is not a morally ideal world where sign and reality are insepa-rable. Pleasure may not be, and often is not, goodness.

Empiricism, which holds that all knowledge is based on sense expe-rience, ends in Humean skepticism or in science based on uncritical-ly held naturalism. But empiricism and its consequential metaphysical naturalism is not self-evident or evident to the senses, and cannot be merely imperiously or dogmatically assumed.

The alternative of rationalism has an equally sorry history—where reason is used as a source of truth (Descartes' *cogito* or Jefferson's *Dec-laration*) rather than a test for meaning; or used constructively (Plato or Hegel) and not first critically; or used critically, but insufficiently at the basic level (Kant or Nietzsche or Nagarjuna). RP seeks to learn from epistemological history and not repeat deadly errors from the past.

Thinking by nature is presuppositional: we think of the less basic in light of the more basic. In concepts, we think of the finite and tempo-ral in light of the infinite and eternal, which are most basic concepts. In judgments that are true or false, we think of truth in light of mean-ing and meaning in light of reason, which, as the laws of thought, is most basic. In argument, we think of conclusion in light of premis-es. In each case, if we agree on the more basic, we can and will agree on the less basic.

There is diversity and unity in all of life, if and only if the order of things is observed. In philosophy: epistemology, then metaphysics, and ethics; in theology: creation, then fall, and redemption; in human per-sonality: thought, then feeling, and will; aspects recognized in truth, beauty, and goodness; in knowledge, holiness, and righteousness; in modern Western civilization in rationalism, romanticism, and real-ism; in Indian thought in jnana, bhakti, and karma yoga; and in many

---

3. John Keats, "Ode on a Grecian Urn"
   See: poetryfoundation.org/poems/44477/ode-on-a-grecian-urn

other ways. If we observe RP, if we agree on the logically more basic in public discourse, we can and will agree on the logically less basic. In a step-by-step process, we can move from foundation to fullness. But in actual human situations, we must first address the existentially more basic (the subjective, the ethical, what is good and evil) in order that we can get back to the logically (objectively) more basic.

THE PRINCIPLE OF CLARITY

These three prior factors of Common Ground lead to the fourth and final, which is the Principle of Clarity (PC). PC states that some things are clear; the basics things are clear; the basic things (in metaphysics, about God and man) and in ethics (about good and evil) are clear to reason (epistemology). PC is opposed to skepticism (ancient, modern, and postmodern) and to fideism (theistic and non-theistic)—that is belief without proof based on understanding.

Some things are clear. If nothing were clear, then no logical distinction (between being and non-being, true and false, good and evil) would be clear. No distinction would be meaningful. Thought and discourse would be impossible insofar as we have integrity. Without integrity, we are left in logical and existential absurdity. Therefore, insofar as we think and talk, some things must be clear.

The basic things are clear. Given RP, if basic things were not clear, then nothing would be clear. But some things are clear from above. Therefore, basic things are clear. And the basic things are about metaphysics (God and man), ethics (about good and evil), and epistemology (meaning tested by reason—the laws of thought).

PC, at this point, says only that, in principle, basic things are clear to reason. It does not settle disputes between the two sets of presuppositions. PC says only that the disputes can and should be settled if we are, with integrity, to think and talk at all. But in saying this, PC overcomes in principle both skepticism and fideism. And that, given the history of mankind, is a giant leap for mankind. Thinking is not short-circuited, and discourse can begin.

Based on Common Ground, the steps ahead for RP can be identified. One, must there be something eternal? Two, if so, is all or only some eternal? Three, if only some is eternal (God, the Creator), is what is created by special creation? Four, if so, how can the problem of evil be answered in philosophy of religion? Five, only then can the necessity for a special revelation be addressed. Six, if so, which special revelation is consistent with clear general revelation (from one to five above)? Seven, is special revelation continuing or complete? Eight, can RP overcome fideism and settle disputes among theists? And finally, nine, given the problem of evil, can RP settle remaining disputes from skepticism? Can the work of settling disputes be completed based on Common Ground? The answer of RP, based on Common Ground, is yes.[4]

Without Common Ground for internal and external disputes, we will strain at gnats and swallow camels. This kind of public discourse leaves a bad taste in the mouth and intellectual indigestion within. With Common Ground, public discourse is honey, and it is money.

---

4. Gangadean, *Theological Foundation: A Critical Analysis of Christian Belief.*

———

6

CHRISTIAN HOPE

Faith, Hope, and Love

Eulogy given for Dr. Rodney Tussing

August 31, 2019

I HAVE KNOWN ROD TUSSING, MY BROTHER, for fifty years, as mentor, as colleague, and as friend. I have known him from the hour of his birth in Christ, to the hour of his departure to be with Christ. I have been his church elder for his first ten years, and his pastor for the past few years. He was to assist me as pastor to carry on the work of Westminster Fellowship. It is a privilege, therefore, with some sadness, to speak the Word of God, that was on his heart, to you his family and friends.

Hear what the Word of God says concerning life and death, as all men live before God, and as we live in Jesus Christ:

> But I would not have you to be ignorant, brothers, concerning them which are asleep, that ye sorrow not, even as others which have no hope.
> For if we believe that Jesus died and rose again, even so them also which sleep in Jesus will God bring with him.
> For this we say unto you by the word of the Lord, that we which are alive and remain unto the coming of the Lord shall not go before them which are asleep.
> For the Lord himself shall descend from heaven with a shout, with the voice of the archangel, and with the trump of God: and the dead in Christ shall rise first:

Then we which are alive and remain shall be caught up together with them in the clouds, to meet the Lord in the air: and so shall we ever be with the Lord.
Wherefore comfort one another with these words.[1]

Resurrection and Reward are foundational doctrines of the Christian faith.[2] Foundation consists of first principles which are necessary for maturity, fruitfulness, unity, and fullness in God.

Jesus said to Martha, and to all who grieve the departure of loved ones, "I am the resurrection and the life; he that believes in me, though he were dead, yet shall he live: And whosoever lives and believes in me shall never die. Do you believe this?"[3]

There are *two* kinds of resurrections, physical and spiritual, for the body and for the soul. But there is only one physical resurrection of the dead, which is general, for all persons, both of the just and the unjust.[4] Spiritual resurrection comes when a person is regenerated or born again. Physical resurrection comes at the end of history. "For he must reign, until he has put all enemies under his feet. The last enemy that shall be destroyed is death."[5] After this resurrection, comes the rapture of those who are alive and remain. So shall we ever be with the Lord. We sorrow not, therefore, even as others who have no hope. Wherefore, Paul says, comfort one another with these words.

Christians have hope in every way. We hope we shall see the departed once again, as whole persons, in the unity of our body and soul. God, who made man in his own image, has made it clear to all who would seek, that we are a unity of body and soul. Many, who walk by sight, lack faith. But true faith is not blind; it is grounded in understanding. Rod's faith was awakened by understanding proofs for the existence of God given in a philosophy class. It is clear to one who seeks that death is not the end of our existence; that the mind is not the brain; that the thinker is not the thought; that our self is *most* real; that our soul is most precious, and not to be sold through unbelief. Faith leads

---

1. *1 Thessalonians 4:13-18.*
2. *Hebrews 6:1-2.*
3. *John 11:25-26.*
4. *John 5:28-29.*
5. *1 Corinthians 15:25-26.*

to hope and hope to love, by which we serve God and not ourselves. "For what shall it profit a man if he gains the whole world and loses his own soul?"[6] As we have faith that God imposed death on man as a call back from sin, so we have hope that God will remove death when sin is removed by God's work of redemption.

Christians have hope that our labor in the Lord is not in vain. Rod's faith called him to be a witness to the truth. He eventually engaged with current unbelief in his doctoral dissertation. He grew in faith and came to understand God's Word, through the apostle Paul, that the basic things about God and man and good and evil are clear to reason.[7] Ten years ago, he began teaching college classes in religion and philosophy. He has built up the faith of others, through his writing[8] and by witness to the truth of the Historic Christian Faith. He labored in all the relations of life to advance the kingdom of God on earth, knowing it is Christ who works, through his people, to advance his kingdom. Rod labored in the hope of the Sabbath, that Christ, in the place of Adam, will complete the work of dominion (originally given to all in Adam, but now, through all in Christ)—that the earth shall be full of the knowledge of the Lord, as the waters cover the sea.[9]

Christians have hope in the wisdom and goodness of God's providence. We have hope that we will complete *our* part of the work God has given to *us*. At times we may be perplexed, and think otherwise. God's ways are above our ways and past finding out, until our sin is removed. Job came to see God through suffering, and repented. His witness of faith remains to this day, to men and angels. If a picture is worth a thousand words, then a life well lived is worth a thousand sermons. If we cannot hear the witness of unspoken words, then we will not hear though one *preaches* a thousand sermons. For our sake, Jesus suffered hunger in the wilderness and agony on the cross. While, for us, to depart and be with the Lord is better by far, for the sake of the body of Christ, we remain, to build up *their* faith. We preach the gospel by our lives; we use words if necessary. Those who die in faith, seal

---

6. *Mark 8:36.*

7. *Romans 1:20; 2:14-15.*

8. Rodney W. Tussing, *Religion and Science: Deconstructing a Modern Paradigm* (Phoenix: Public Philosophy Press, 2019).

9. *Isaiah 11:9.*

their witness to us the living. When our witness is finished, we say—with Jesus, and with Paul—"It is finished!"

Christians have hope in the redemptive love of God. Suffering cannot separate us from the love of God. "Deep calls unto deep. All your waves and billows are gone over me."[10] But many waters cannot quench love. In all these things, we are more than conquerors through him that loved us. In the face of the final suffering, Rod kept the faith. "Though he slay me, yet will I trust in him" is the response of faith. He went through to the victor's crown, the crown of a martyr, a faithful witness under intense suffering.

Suffering, under redemption, is *never* wasted. It does not deny, but *in* God, it increases our dignity. All things work together for good to those who love God. Nothing can separate us from the love of God that is in Christ Jesus. "Our light affliction, which is but for a moment, works for us a far more exceeding and eternal weight of glory."[11] By suffering—of the cross—we die to self, so that our capacity to see God is enlarged. We thereby obtain a better resurrection.

In the intermediate state, between our departure and the consummation of history, we wait, we watch, and we wish, with all in Christ who have gone before. We wait for the completion of the work, for the resurrection of our bodies, and for our inheritance in the kingdom of God, *together*. We watch those who are now running the race set before them, and silently (to them) we cheer them on, if only they had ears to hear. And, we wish. We wish that our work will bear lasting fruit. The departed have not yet received what was promised. God has provided something better for us, that they without us will not be made complete.[12] "Wherefore, seeing we also are compassed about with so great a cloud of witnesses, let us lay aside every weight, and run with patience the race set before us, looking unto Jesus, the author and finisher of our faith."[13] Therefore, comfort and exhort one another with these words.

---

10. *Psalm 42:7.*

11. *2 Corinthians 4:17.*

12. *Hebrews 11:39-40.*

13. *Hebrews 12:1-2.*

7

UNITY OF THE FAITH
Common Understanding of Foundation

Public lecture delivered at Grand Canyon University[1]

September 24, 2018

INTRODUCTION

THE TOPIC OF OUR DISCUSSION IS "Unity of the Faith: Common Understanding of Foundation." There are many reasons for thinking this topic may not be relevant. That is, the Church and whatever is going on in the Church, is not relevant to what is going on in the culture. I will respond to that general concern. If we get that far, with agreement, we can look at the substance of settling disputes and securing agreement. I am going to say, boldly, "It's really not that hard." And this is intended to be provocative, but I will stand by this statement, "It's really not that hard." If we agree on the more basic, we should be able to agree on the less basic. So, the first part of our discussion is relevance. The second part is the substance of how we can achieve agreement and settle disputes. Lastly, we will consider practical and psychological motivational factors to actually get us moving and get us off the ground towards securing agreement and settling disputes.

I will present an extended argument, and what I present will be by premise, premise, and conclusion, which then becomes the premise for more conclusions. As we go through each point, you may want to indicate whether you agree or disagree. I welcome strong engagement

---

1. Edited by The Logos Foundation Editorial Board.

and strong opinions, especially if it is not just how you feel, but what you think about what I am saying. I welcome you to push back, and hopefully, we will get some real engagement so we can make real progress in our understanding/faith.

THE CHURCH:
God's Ordained Institution for Redemption

To begin, what is the Church? The Church is God's ordained institution for redemption. We have to contrast the Church with the family, the state, and subsidiaries of these institutions. The Church is not simply a suggestion, it is ordained by God for the purpose of redemption.

Creation–Fall–Redemption

Redemption is to be understood in the context of two other basic ideas, that is, creation and the Fall. Redemption assumes the order of creation: that man is created in the image of God, he is to have dominion over the creation, he is given a helpmeet, and through an age-long process of multiplying and filling the earth, he is to accomplish the work of dominion. We might speak about dominion today in terms of the humanities and culture, which includes human nature and the moral law, and developing all the powers latent in ourselves; and the sciences and technology, which includes naming the creation in all of its parts and developing all the powers latent in the creation. We still have quite a ways to go in this work. God said, "Let us make man in our image, and let him have dominion."[2] It is not often that we hear discussion about man made in the image of God for the work of dominion, but dominion is a central part of the order of creation that was crowned by the Sabbath day, which signifies that the work God gave to man will be completed, even as God completed his work of creating. So, in the beginning, from the order of creation, we have some basic things. In the Fall, man turned away from the work of dominion. He fell into the condition of sin and death, in connection with the warning from God, "In the day that you eat you will surely die."[3]

---

2. *Genesis 1:26-28.*

3. *Genesis 2:17.*

The result of sin is spiritual death, not physical death. We will see that physical death is imposed later as part of redemption.

The Doctrine of Clarity and Inexcusability

Redemption assumes the order of creation and man's fall away into sin and death. Sin assumes the objective clarity of general revelation. To get into the idea of clarity, ask yourself: assuming the historic position of final judgment, of heaven and hell, or life and death (which are the primary terms), what happens to those who have never heard of Jesus Christ? What happens to them when they die? I am sure that we have heard that question, or that it has crossed our mind. The context that we are raising about the clarity of general revelation is that there is an objectively clear revelation of God's eternal power and divine nature, revealed in the way he has created the world. In Romans 1:20, as he begins to present the gospel, Paul says, "What may be known of God . . . his invisible qualities—his eternal power and divine nature—have been clearly seen, being understood by the things that are made, so that they are without excuse." No person of ordinary development, of average intelligence, apart from education, and even if they didn't have the "best parents in the world," has any reason to think that they are excused from knowing what is clear about God. This is the doctrine of clarity and inexcusability. Sin assumes clarity, and if we define sin as less than failure to know what is clear, we will end up with all kinds of problems, such as we see now in the Church and in the culture.

We should elaborate on clarity a little further. Psalm 19 says, "The heavens declare the glory of God." The firmament shows his handiwork from day to day, especially the sun, and the heat of the sun. "There is nothing hidden from its heat." This psalm speaks about the eternal power of God. That the sun, which is perhaps the most lasting thing that we know, is clearly—upon a little reflection, insofar as we reflect at all—not eternal. Nor are the stars or the galaxies composed of stars. None of them is eternal. The sun and stars are temporal, they came into being, they were created by the eternal and infinite power of God. This is an example of how it is clear that God has created the world and that no man is excusable for failing to know.

In the movie, *Silence*,[4] which takes place in Japan, a Japanese monk said, "We worship the sun," and a Christian priest replied, "Well, we worship the Son." I thought the priest had an opportunity to speak to the Japanese and prevent World War II, by showing how it is clear that the sun is not eternal and is not to be worshipped—not in Japan, not in China, not in India, not among the Incas, or in Egypt, or anywhere in the earth. It is clear that God, and only God, is eternal. Nor can we allow the dualists to say that matter and souls are eternal. It should be clear to all of us that the soul exists—the mind is not the brain—and that the soul is not eternal, contrary to what reincarnationists might think.

It is clear that only some, only God, is eternal, and God is the Creator.[5] Many other things follow, including the nature of God the Creator, and the goodness of God in the way he created the world originally. Some ask the question, "Why is there evil, why is there physical death?" Physical death was not part of creation originally. The original creation was all very good. Furthermore, death will be removed in the end, at the consummation of redemption. Scripture says, "The last enemy to be destroyed is death."[6] All of this is part of the doctrine of clarity and inexcusability.[7]

These things are in Scripture, and what I am doing is taking things that are familiar to us—clear to us—and I am making connections between these things, and by making connections, deepening the understanding of things that we already believe. That is essentially what I am speaking about here. Through this process, we can come to a deeper level of understanding and unity, and overcome the divisions that are in the Church.

So, some things are objectively clear. Yet, Scripture says in our fallen condition, no one seeks and no one understands God,[8] and that we are without excuse for this. Sin is universal in the strong sense that

---

4. Scorsese, Martin, dir. *Silence* (United States: Paramount Pictures, 2016).

5. Gangadean, *Philosophical Foundation*, 71-161; Gangadean, *History of Philosophy*, 47-58.

6. *1 Corinthians 15:26.*

7. Gangadean, "Paper No. 35: The Clarity of General Revelation," "Paper No. 41: What Is Clear About God: The Clarity of General Revelation," and "Paper No. 112: Why General Revelation Is Basic in the Christian Worldview," in *The Logos Papers*; Gangadean, *The Westminster Catechisms*. See LCQ. 2 and Appendix 4.

8. *Romans 3:10-12.*

"not even one" seeks or understands who God is. Paul speaks of this sin before he preaches the gospel, to show the need for the gospel, the need for redemption from sin and death. He also speaks about how we progress, without our focus on God, deeper into moral corruption: first sexual impurity, then sexual perversion, and then into the condition of being senseless, faithless, heartless, and ruthless.[9] It is not surprising that this pattern has occurred again and again in the history of mankind. We have seen the collapse of many civilizations. Of the twenty-plus civilizations counted by Arnold Toynbee,[10] he says that only four remain, and it does not look good for those that remain.

What is objectively clear, insofar as we are concerned for consistency, which is integrity, becomes subjectively clear. If we are concerned with following the implications of what I am saying and hold consistently to those implications, then we can come to understand what is clear. So, clarity increases subjectively with integrity.

Pillar and Ground of the Truth

The Church—the "ecclesia"—which is ordained by God, consists of those who have been called out of the state of sin and death—spiritual death. By spiritual death I mean a lack of understanding of the meaning of things, or meaninglessness, or the state of having less and less meaning—and with that boredom, lack of satisfaction, and with boredom, excess to the point of perversion, and guilt. That is spiritual death, connected inherently with not seeking and not understanding what is clear about God. So, the Church consists of those who have been called out by God from the state of sin and death—called out by way of God's gracious redemption. In that context, we can say that the Church is the pillar and ground of the truth.[11] This statement may seem bold, perhaps arrogant, but it is understood in the context that the Church is the body of Christ, as is clearly and commonly acknowledged among Christians.[12] The Church is the body of Christ, and Christ is the Word of God, the logos incarnate. "In the beginning was

---

9. *Romans 1:21-31.*

10. Arnold Toynbee and David Churchill Sommervell, *A Study of History* (New York: Oxford University Press, 1987).

11. *1 Timothy 3:15.*

12. *1 Corinthians 12:27.*

the Word, and the Word was with God, and the Word was God . . . and the Word was made flesh and dwelt among us."[13] Christ indwells the Church, his body. Because the Church is the body of Christ, who is the Word of God—truth incarnate—the Church is, therefore, the pillar and ground of the truth.

Salt and Light

Matthew says that the Church is the salt of the earth and the light of the world.[14] By bringing the law of God to the world, making disciples of all nations, teaching them to observe everything Christ has commanded,[15] the Church is salt to the earth in that it preserves the culture. And, the Church is the light of the world, bringing the light that is needed in place of fundamental falsehood/darkness. If this is the case, the relation between the Church and the world is that the Church preserves the world. If the Church fails, the world also fails. Is the Church failing?

Division, Apostasy, Decay, and Collapse

There are divisions in the Church and those divisions are due to manifold apostasy. Apostasy means departing from the faith. There have been many forms and degrees of apostasy throughout the Church. Someone said recently that there are over 40,000 divisions within the Church. And even if we do not count those—what we might call minor divisions—there are major divisions that have persisted for a long time between Eastern Orthodoxy and the historic Roman Catholic position. Then there are divisions between the Catholics and Protestants. And then within Catholic circles, there are Dominicans, Jesuits, Carmelites, Benedictines, and Franciscans—they have many different orders, different flavors, and tensions. Within Protestantism, there are the Presbyterians, Baptists, Methodists, Lutherans, and the Assemblies of God. The Church is divided greatly. Each of these groups has some distinctive doctrine that they hold to. Yet, when seen in relation

---

13. *John 1:1, 14.*

14. *Matthew 5:13-16.*

15. *Matthew 28:18-20.*

to Historic Christianity, these distinct doctrines are seen as a departure from the Historic Christian Faith. And that is apostasy, a departure from the faith.

As a result of apostasy, the culture is in decay. You may not agree, but consider the state of the family and modern divorce. What is a family, what is marriage, what gender are you? Must we allow transgender people in the girl's bathroom or in the Girl Scouts? These questions have recently been in the news. There are many concerns in the culture right now that are very different from what has been practiced widely and historically as "traditional values." We see opposition in the media, entertainment, and the news. We see it in the universities in the postmodern perspective and the question as to whether truth is possible. We see it in the economy, in the growth of national debt, and how public monies are being spent, or not being spent. We see it in politics and the circus-like atmosphere in Washington D.C. these days. People are saying, "I've never seen anything like this in all my days." There has always been some division, but has there been anything like what there is now? There is decay in the culture and it is nearing a state of collapse. How close are we to collapse? We can speculate, but seeing what has happened in other cultures throughout history, it would not be surprising if we go in the direction that many others have gone over the centuries, over millennia. If the Church fails, the culture fails.

The Church is now the tail of the culture where it was once the head. In most of the Ivy League schools—Harvard, Yale, and Princeton—the idea of a Christian perspective even getting a hearing is no longer there. Rather, naturalist, humanist, and secular views to the extreme dominate. And what is going on in higher education passes into the law schools, and then passes from the law schools into the culture. The Church was once the head of the culture, and now it is the tail—it is in captivity. This is not only true in the United States and Europe, but worldwide, because what has happened in the West has been transported to the East. We hear of some places where there is vitality in the Church, but the overall condition is a reflection of the West.

IS THERE HOPE FOR UNITY?

Having painted that picture, I want to ask, is there hope that we can overcome the divisions? To be more particular, is there hope that we can overcome the division between historic Protestantism and historic Catholicism? Is it relevant? Do we need to? Is it possible for us to get to the good without overcoming our divisions? Particularly, if we understand the good as: if you die, and you are in Christ (and some may say even implicitly in Christ), you go to heaven, and in heaven you receive the fullness of the blessing? If that is true, do we need to concern ourselves with these divisions? Why not say, "In the essentials unity, in the non-essentials charity, acceptance, tolerance, and everything else"? That is a kind of motto that is going around. Some think that we do not need to settle these divisions. This is probably said because there is not a connection in our minds between sin and death in the Church and death in the culture—we do not make this connection. We need a deeper understanding of sin that leads to death, and in that context, we see the motivation of the fear of the Lord that is the beginning of wisdom. The fear of the Lord is the fear of the meaninglessness of spiritual death—is not the end, but the beginning of wisdom.

Three Kinds of Unity

When we speak about the unity of the faith, we want to distinguish three different kinds of unity. Ephesians speaks about these kinds of unity in verses 4:3, 4:13, and 4:16. There is *the unity of the Spirit* that we are to preserve; it already exists: there is one Lord, one faith, one baptism, one God and Father over all.[16] The unity of the Spirit is to be *preserved* by walking in humility, meekness, and love. Later in the chapter, Paul speaks about *the unity of the faith*—the work of the apostles and prophets and evangelists and pastor-teachers. That work is being continued now, ordinarily, in the Church through the pastors and teachers, through the councils that they have, and through the process of much discussion. Through their work, we are to *attain* to the unity of the faith where we have a common understanding of basic things. If we have the unity of the faith, we can have a *functional unity* where we are *operating* as members in the body of Christ, with each part doing its particular work.

I am particularly addressing the *unity of the faith*—having to do with *understanding*—and I think that overcoming divisions can be

---

16. *Ephesians 4:4-6.*

done, should be done, and will be done. I believe the divisions among us will be dealt with in due time, by the sovereign, gracious, rule of God in the lives of his people. The greatness of the promise in Christ is matched with the greatness of the power of God, who raised Christ from the dead and seated him at his own right hand. And we are seated with Christ in the heavenlies.[17]

As we understand this reality, build on the basics, and get the foundation in place, we can begin to overcome these disunities. We cannot merely go back to the standard points of difference. If we go back only that far, we will get locked into the same problems. We have to go back deeper to the assumptions. If we get to the assumptions, and get to what is more basic, and if we can agree on what is more basic, then we will agree—not merely can agree—we *will* agree on what is less basic. There is a process to get back to the more basic, and we will see how basic we can get, and I think we will agree, "Yeah, that is pretty basic; we cannot get more basic than that." Reason is the laws of thought. *a* is *a*. I do not think anyone would disagree with this. Something cannot be both *a* and *non-a*, at the same time and in the same respect. And, something is either *a* or *non-a*. The contrast is not black or white, but rather black or non-black; that particular shade of grey and not that particular shade of grey. We do not need to play fast and loose with the laws of thought and consider, "Well, here is an exception." No, that has been thought of and addressed.[18]

SOURCES OF UNITY

The Good/The Goal

Let us start more existentially and then go to the logical starting point. The *existential* starting point is the good, or the goal. The good is the end in itself. It is sought for its own sake. It is the highest value—the *summum bonum*—and it is what everything is for. Love is not the good. Happiness is not the good. Virtue is not the good. The good is other than these. Virtue is a means to the good, and love is the greatest of the virtues—it binds them all together in perfect unity. Happiness is

---

17. *Ephesians 2:6.*
18. Gangadean, *Philosophical Foundation*, 293-309.

the effect of possessing what is the good. The good is not another person, as in romantic love, or even God. The good is what is achieved by human choice and action.

We are going to look at the three basic sources of revelation and answer the question: "What is the good?" Revelation in nature—or general revelation, revelation in Scripture, and then revelation in the history of the Church—through the Church councils seeking to more deeply understand the faith. All three of these are in agreement concerning what is the good. First, I present this by way of an argument from general revelation. See if you agree with each of these points as they are brought up. The good for a being is according to the nature of a being. The good for a horse is according to the nature of a horse, the good for a rabbit is according to the nature of a rabbit, and the good for a human is according to the nature of a human. What distinguishes human beings from animals? Rationality—which is the capacity for rational thought. We could entertain objections, but that has been the understanding historically. Thus, what is good for man is according to his rational nature, since reason distinguishes him from the animals. The good for man as a rational being is the use of reason to the fullest. And reason is used to grasp the nature of things. Every time we use a word, we are expressing a concept, which grasps the essence of a thing, or the nature of a thing. So, "apple," "atom," "man," "matter"—and we could go on to name all the particulars of man and all the parts of the material world. In naming, we are grasping the nature of a thing. All things are to be named in the process of our work of dominion. As we understand the creation, we come to understand what it reveals. What is created reveals the nature of the Creator. Therefore, from all of these premises, the good for man—from general revelation—is the knowledge of God.

What do the Scriptures say? From special revelation, man is made in the image of God, to know God, through the work of dominion.[19] John 17:3 says that eternal life *is* knowing God. So, Scripture affirms the good as the knowledge of God.

And what about Historic Christianity, especially as summed up in the latest of the creeds, the Westminster Confession of Faith? From Historic Christianity, which may be familiar to us, "Man's chief end

---

19. *Genesis 1:26-28.*

is to glorify God and to enjoy him forever."[20] These are the opening words of the Shorter Catechism. In addition, in considering the first petition of the Lord's Prayer, which is "Hallowed be thy name," we are taught that man's chief end is to glorify God, "in all that by which he makes himself known."[21] How does God make himself known? In all of his works of creation and providence. God created to reveal his glory, and rules to reveal his glory.[22] So, if we put these together—Glorifying God, in all that by which he makes himself known, in all of his works of creation and providence—we come out in the same place: the good is the knowledge of God, in great fullness. If we just say the first part (the good is the knowledge of God), without connecting it up with the others, then we do not get as deep and as full a picture of the good.

I am characteristically going after fullness in order to get to unity. I think when we reflect on the good, we will come to agreement, and say, "Yes, the good is the knowledge of God, and it is the knowledge of God through the work of dominion." If we agree on the good, we will have the *cornerstone* in place, from which we can build together and come to unity and fullness. The good is the source of unity in *all*, in each person—each and every person, and *among all* persons and in all the relations of life. If we have the good in place from these three sources, strongly reaffirmed, we can go on and hope that the good will be achieved.

What I am presenting is an interesting contrast with the view that you die and go to heaven and receive the fullness of the blessing. For a long time in the history of the Church, this view has been referred to as the beatific vision.[23] The good as the knowledge of God, and the earth being filled with the knowledge of the glory of God, is in contrast to popular views of heaven, as well as the beatific vision that has been common in the Church for both Protestants and Catholics. If we get the good in place, we can go further.

---

20. *SCQ. 1.*

21. *SCQ. 101.*

22. *WCF 4.1, 5.1.*

23. Gangadean, "Paper No. 106: The Good and Heaven: The Good Is Not the Beatific Vision," in *The Logos Papers*; In this work, see the essay: "The Good and the Beatific Vision"

The Moral Law

The second source of unity is the moral law. The moral law is summed up in the Ten Commandments. And the moral law is the means to the good. The first commandment says do not put yourself in the place of God, as Adam did, to determine good and evil, other than what God has given, going contrary to our nature. The last commandment is about covetousness, and the discontent that comes with it. It is unsettling that we have various kinds of natural evil to contend with. If we have the good in place, we would not be discontent. Paul, the apostle, says, "I have learned in whatever situation I am to be content."[24] So, all the Commandments, each and every one, are focused on the good and achieving the good.

The Commandments are central to the faith and central to the believer. First of all, the moral law is clear. "The moral law" is a general revelation term; "The Ten Commandments" is a special revelation term. Paul, in Romans 2, says the law is written in the hearts of all men.[25] And interestingly, Moses, who brought the law of God, by special revelation, explicitly says in Deuteronomy 30:11-14, you do not have to go up to heaven to bring it down, you do not have to go across the sea to get it, it is very near you, in your mouth and in your heart that you may obey it. Moses, who brought the Ten Commandments by way of special revelation, is saying that this law is near to you, even though it is given by special revelation—he received it from heaven— otherwise, we may have to go across the sea to get it. He says no, is it very near you, it is in your mouth and your heart. The law of God is written in the hearts of all men, believer and unbeliever. The law is universal, perpetual, total, spiritual, reaching to every level. Its consequence, if we obey it, is a matter of life, spiritual life—abundance, fullness, richness, the riches of Christ. And if we disobey it, the consequence is death, spiritual death. Because the law is present in all of our lives, and clear and easily knowable, it is a source of unity.

We are going step-by-step. Is there moral law that is structured into our very being? And, can we show it? Can we show there is such a thing as morality? We can start with the reality of choice. All people make choices. That is common, that is general revelation. Some things are

---

24. *Philippians 4:11-13.*
25. *Romans 2:14-15.*

chosen as means and some as ends, and some are chosen as the end in itself, the good. We get the concepts of the good and the means to the good. We can raise the question: how do we know that the good is according to the nature of a being? The nature of a being is created by God, and thus, the good for a being is determined by God. With this understanding of the good, we are not to put ourselves in the place of God as Adam did in the Garden to determine good and evil for himself.

When we determine the good to be the knowledge of God in heaven apart from creation and providence, we are violating the first commandment. When we determine the good is happiness, as if that were a self-evident truth—life, liberty, and the pursuit of happiness—we violate the first commandment. No, Mr. Jefferson, the good is not happiness. Neither is it self-evident that all men are created equal. And it is not self-evident that God exists. You jumped the gun; you went to a kind of intuitive knowledge—common sense intuition—from Thomas Reid and the Scottish Enlightenment. Common Sense realism has been tried and found wanting. Yet, we do need to start with the self-evident. And we need to start with the epistemological first principles, the metaphysical first principles, and the moral first principles. We did not get to them then, and now we are in trouble and need to rebuild. The Church is to be salt and light. The Westminster Shorter Catechism says, "Man's chief end is to glorify God," which was in place in 1648, as against 1776. What happened? How did the Church lose that focus?

The moral law is both central and basic. It is central in Israel's worship. The tablet of the law was under the mercy seat in the holiest of all—in the holy of holies. The mercy seat was the place of God's throne, where he ruled among his people, according to that law. Aaron's rod that budded was also in the most holy place, along with the pot of manna. Yet the moral law continued in effect as the perfect rule of righteousness. So, it is central and basic, and it is the source of unity objectively, and should also be subjectively.

Common Ground

A third source of unity, which is the *logical* starting point, is Common Ground. Common Ground is the most basic source of unity, as the requisite for all thought and discourse. If you are thinking, and conversing with another, there is a prerequisite. The prerequisite is Common Ground. If we have Common Ground in place, and agree on the most basic, then we can agree on other things that come after. We can and will agree. For example, if we agree that there is a distinction between being and non-being, and that you cannot get being from non-being by its very nature, and if we can agree that there are no square-circles, and there are no uncaused events,[26] then we can answer Kant when he sets aside the law as merely something imposed by the mind on the data of intuition. We can overcome those who might try to say, "And then something happened," whether it is in modern quantum physics, or whether it is in the ancient world through Epicurus with the atomic swerve (versions of uncaused events). We can say, no, you cannot get out of the problem of entropy with regard to the material universe by appeal to an uncaused event.[27] There are no uncaused events, just as there are no square-circles. If we can agree on these things, we can agree that there must be something eternal, and we can agree that matter exists and matter is not eternal, the soul exists and the soul is not eternal—that only some is eternal—and we can get to the eternal power and divine nature.[28]

So, if we can agree on the more basic, we can agree on the less basic, and we cannot get any more basic than reason as the laws of thought. The laws of thought include the law of identity: *a* is *a*; the law of non-contradiction: not both *a* and *non-a*, at the same time and in the same respect; and the law of excluded middle: either *a* or *non-a*. These laws apply to being as well as thought. Remember, there are no square-circles. And we do not know that by experience—by going and checking the cupboards, or the dark side of the moon, or in a quasar or any such thing—we know it by reason alone, that it cannot be. And we know the certainty of that. That certainty is the clarity of general revelation. And if we agree on the more basic, we can and will agree on the less basic.

So, Common Ground begins with *reason* as the laws of thought, which apply to being also. We notice that Nietzsche attempted to deny

26. Gangadean, *Philosophical Foundation*, 63-68.

27. Gangadean, *Philosophical Foundation*, 73-80.

28. Gangadean, *Philosophical Foundation*, 61-161; Gangadean, *History of Philosophy*, 47-58.

the connection between reason and being.[29] That was his killer shot, and in doing so he opened the gates toward skepticism and nihilism. We need to confront that Nietzschean claim, squarely, to see if he really is saying reason does not apply to being, and to see whether he wants to be consistent with that claim.

The second point of Common Ground is an application, a concern for consistency. We are not to have ideas that are contradictory, and we are not to say one thing and do another. *Integrity* is both logical consistency and existential consistency. It was existential consistency that got me out of Sartre and Camus, to see that their positions were not livable, which opened the way for the Word of God to come into my heart. "It is He who has made us, and not we ourselves."[30] I am not my self-creator. And I could not create in the way Sartre or Camus may have intended or suggested—not with integrity. I would have to give up integrity, and I was not willing to do that, which made the difference between life and death for me back in December of 1961. The second feature of Common Ground is integrity, which is a concern for consistency, both logical and existential.

The third feature of Common Ground is *Rational Presuppositionalism*, which is critical thinking applied fully. Reason, as the laws of thought, is most basic. It is more basic than meaning in that reason is the test for meaning, and nothing is more basic. Rational Presuppositionalism is reason applied as a test for meaning to your most basic beliefs: How do I know? What is real? What ought I to do? How we answer those questions are our presuppositions. Rational Presuppositionalism is the most consistent form of critical thinking, and it becomes clear at that point, at that basic level. And if we agree on what is more basic, we will agree on what is less basic. And these three together; reason, integrity, and Rational Presuppositionalism, lead to the Principle of Clarity.

The *Principle of Clarity*, the fourth feature of Common Ground, can be introduced by saying first, some things are clear. Secondly, the basic things are clear. Because, if the basic things are not clear, then nothing is clear. And thirdly, the basic things, which are about God

29. For a critique of Nietzsche's denial of reason as applied to being, see: Kelly Fitzsimmons Burton, *Retrieving Knowledge: A Socratic Response to Skepticism* (Phoenix: Public Philosophy Press, 2018).

30. *Psalm 100:3*; See at the beginning of this work, "The Testimony of Surrendra Gangadean"

and man and good and evil, are clear to reason. So, on that third point, we have God and man (metaphysics), good and evil (ethics), clear to reason (epistemology). The Principle of Clarity pulls these three together.[31] So, that means if we were to start talking, I would ask you, "Are we agreed on the Principle of Clarity?" Do you think that some things are clear, and if not, then we will focus on that to see if we can get agreement before moving on. If we agree on the more basic, we can and will agree on the less basic.

Scripture

Scripture is the fourth source of unity. We will look at two aspects of Scripture—the biblical foundation given in narrative form (in Genesis 1–3) and in theological form (in the Seven Pillars of the faith). The opening section of the Scripture, in Genesis 1–3, clearly teaches the biblical worldview of the creation, the Fall, and redemption, which is the basis of understanding the rest of the Scripture. We need to go into the narrative of creation–fall–redemption to see the particulars of what is being said. The curse, in the form of physical death, comes into the world in Genesis 3. It comes in the context of redemption, when God gives the promise—the seed of the woman will crush the head of the serpent.[32] The curse is given, and it is given not as punishment, but as a call back, from not only sin, but from self-deception and self-justification. Adam repents after being given the curse and the promise. If we read Scripture step-by-step and pay attention to the particulars— if we look at it, and notice it—and see if we agree on creation–fall–redemption, then we can agree on the rest of Scripture very easily.

The things that are stated in Genesis 1–3 are stated in other places in Scripture as the foundation. And the foundation can be summarized in Seven Pillars.[33] As a place to focus, consider what the Scripture says,

---

31. Gangadean, *Philosophical Foundation*, 3-5, 287-292; Gangadean, *The Westminster Confession*. See Question 4; Gangadean, "Paper No. 53: Common Ground (Part IV): The Principle of Clarity," in *The Logos Papers*.

32. *Genesis 3:15*; Gangadean, *Philosophical Foundation*, 156-161; Gangadean, "Paper No. 147: The Biblical Worldview (Part VII): The Fall: Death and Theodicy," in *The Logos Papers*; In this work, see the essay: "The Problem of Evil: An Ironic Solution"

33. Gangadean, "Paper No. 36: The Pillar and Ground of the Truth: Rebuilding the Church's Foundation" and "Paper No. 37: The Seven Pillars: A Brief Summary," in *The Logos Papers*. Also see: Gangadean, *Theological Foundation: A Critical Analysis of Christian Belief*.

"Wisdom has built her house, she has hewn out her seven pillars."[34] The Seven Pillars may be summed up: 1) clarity and inexcusability, 2) sin and death, 3) curse and promise, 4) repentance and faith, 5) justification and sanctification, 6) baptism and calling, and 7) resurrection and reward. These are stated in Hebrews[35] and Romans,[36] put together with some of the implications filled in. So, if we can agree on the first principles—what is called the milk of the Word, not meat—we can agree on other things. And if we do not agree here, we should push back to see if we can agree.

The Historic Christian Faith

The last source of unity is the Historic Christian Faith, which is grounded in the promise of Jesus to his disciples—the Holy Spirit will come, and he will lead/guide you into all truth.[37] This promise is not for each and every person, but for the Church as a whole.[38] The work of the Holy Spirit enables us to understand the Scriptures in response to challenges, coming together in councils, and after much discussion, coming to agreement, then putting the agreement into writing and sending it out to the whole Church for the unity of the faith. The first such instance of this process is seen in Acts 15 when there was a dispute about

---

34. *Proverbs 9:1.*

35. *Hebrews 5:11-6:2.*

36. The Book of Romans is a systematic statement of the Christian faith. All men have clear general revelation of the nature and existence of God and the law of God and so are without excuse for unbelief and sin (1–2). Since no one is righteous, a person is accepted by God on the basis of the righteousness of God, which comes through faith in Jesus Christ. Abraham, too, was accepted by faith (3–4). This reconciliation by grace through Christ's atoning death has benefits far greater than the effects of Adam's sin. It not only forgives sin but also frees from the power of sin. It extends to the whole of creation and triumphs over every opposition (5–8). This grace comes into a person by God's sovereign choice and though Israel does not now believe, God will bring both the Gentiles and Israel to believe (9–11). In view of God's mercy, men are to devote themselves to God and to do his will in all things. The will of God in many applications of the law is urged upon those who believe (12–16).

37. *John 16:13.*

38. Gangadean, *The Westminster Confession.* See Questions 39-61; Gangadean, *The Westminster Catechisms.* See LCQ. 30-90; Gangadean, "Paper No. 148: The Biblical Worldview (Part VIII): Redemption: The First and Second Calls to Repentance," "Paper No. 149: The Biblical Worldview (Part IX): Redemption: The Third Call to Repentance," and "Paper No. 150: The Biblical Worldview (Part X): Redemption: Justification and Sanctification," in *The Logos Papers.*

whether one had to be circumcised to be saved. There was much discussion, they came to agreement, and they sent their agreement out
to the Churches.[39]

The second major expression of this process is the Apostles' Creed,
which is set over and against Greek dualism and the otherworldliness
of Plato, and by implication, in some ways against Aristotle. The Greek
dualist challenge had to be answered, that is why the emphasis is on
physical and bodily existence: God is the creator of heaven and earth;
Jesus is born of the virgin Mary; he suffered under Pontius Pilate; was
crucified, dead, and buried; he rose again on the third day; he ascend-
ed into heaven and sits at the right hand of God, from whence he will
come to judge the quick and the dead. And, "I believe in the resurrection of the dead." The resurrection of the dead was foolishness to
Greeks and their dualistic ontology. But the Church worked through
Greek assumptions. It is not that the God of the Old Testament is the
God of matter and the God of the New Testament is the good and
loving God. There is no such distinction.

The Church is not to have an otherworldly view that developed under
the influence of Greek thought. We are not to be mere this-worldly,
nor are we to be mere otherworldly, but our focus is to be the earth
filled with the knowledge of God as the waters cover the sea. Today,
we are still working through this Greek influence. We are still having
to work through the notion that we "die, go to heaven, and get the
fullness of the blessing,"[40] rather than engaging in the work of dominion to fill the earth with the knowledge of God. I was recently by the
sea for a week, and while walking and entering into a meditation, the
thought came back, "as the waters cover the sea." As I walked along
the sea, a number of times "as the waters cover the sea." And I asked,
"Will it come about, Lord?" Will it come about that the earth will be
filled with the knowledge of God as the waters cover the sea? Isaiah
11:9 says that this will be the result of the Messiah's rule. And, the lion
will lay down with the lamb, and the bear with the calf, and the child
shall put his hand in the den of the adder, and they shall not hurt or

---

39. Gangadean, "Paper No. 16: The Historic Christian Faith: The Holy Spirit Guides the
Church into All Truth," in *The Logos Papers*.

40. Gangadean, "Paper No. 106: The Good and Heaven: The Good Is Not the Beatific Vision," and "Paper No. 113: Historic Christianity: Contrasted to Popular Christianity," in
The Logos Papers.

destroy on all my holy mountain.[41] Can this really come about? That is what we are talking about in terms of the unity of the Church. That is why the unity of the Church is necessary. I believe it can come about if we get what is more basic in place.

There are seven major creeds of the Church, and the creeds are cumulative, starting with Jerusalem in A.D. 51, going up to the Westminster Assembly in 1648. These include the Council of Jerusalem, the Apostles' Creed, Nicea, Carthage, Chalcedon, Orange, and all of the Reformation creeds summed up in the Westminster Confession of Faith in 1648.[42] The cumulative insight of the creeds and confession is the work of the Holy Spirit leading the Church into all truth. This truth is Historic Christianity, it is the holy catholic and apostolic faith, and to depart from Historic Christianity is to divide the body of Christ. We need to come back, examine, and affirm whether there is such a thing as Historic Christianity, whether it comes to us in the creeds, through the councils, after much discussion, and whether we need to give heed to that reality before we depart or disregard it.

THE NECESSITY FOR DISCIPLESHIP:
To Understand and Obey the Truth

So, these are the five sources of unity: the good, the moral law, Common Ground, foundation from Scripture, and the Historic Christian Faith. Can you conceive of a program where the Church, by giving heed to these things, comes into unity? It can happen. Church discipline is necessary for discipleship. Jesus said, "Go and make disciples."[43] Through discipleship, through Church discipline, we come to understand and to obey the truth. He goes on, "Teaching them to observe all that I have commanded." He does not say, teach them *what* to observe, but teach them *to* observe, to put the Word into practice. The Word of God, or the logos, is truth in its fullness.[44] And the logos

---

41. *Isaiah 11:6-9.*

42. Gangadean, *The Westminster Catechisms*, xvii-xxvii; Gangadean, "Paper No. 16: The Historic Christian Faith: The Holy Spirit Guides the Church into All Truth," in *The Logos Papers*.

43. *Matthew 28:18-20.*

44. *John 8:31-32; 17:17.*

is the eternal Word of God. From John 1:1, "In the beginning was the Word [the logos], and the [logos] was with God, and the [logos] was God." The logos is not merely a principle, but he is a person. He is the second person of the Trinity. He is the Son of God, who makes God fully known. God makes himself known through His Word. And that Word of God comes to us in a number of ways: It comes to us first as *reason*. John 1:4: "In him [the Logos] was life, and the life was the light of men." Reason in itself, about which I have been speaking, is the first form of the Word of God that comes to us, and it is in all men. Reason is not neutral with respect to truth and meaning. It is the first form of the Word of God in all. And then the logos is present in the creation as *general revelation*. He was in the world, and though the world was made by him, the world knew him not.[45] Then the logos comes to us in *Scripture* in the history of redemption through the prophets.[46] And the Word, which was rejected as reason, as general revelation, and as Scripture, comes once again, *incarnate*, to be crucified for our sins, and comes full of grace and truth—to forgive and to bring us to the knowledge of God.[47] This one is Christ, the anointed one, who is anointed by the Spirit, and who sends the Spirit to lead the Church into all truth.[48] And that very Spirit works in the heart of each believer, to regenerate them, that they may be born again by the Word of truth.[49] And by being regenerated, the same Spirit works in the life of each believer to sanctify them, to make them holy, to be devoted to God and the good with their whole heart.[50] It is in this sense that the Word of God makes God fully known objectively and subjectively, through history. And we have that Word with us, and the Spirit with us, which can work to bring about this end. Church oversight and discipleship will bring this about, as the Church seeks to nurture its members in the truth.

---

45. *John 1:3, 10.*

46. *John 1:11.*

47. *John 1:14.*

48. *John 16:13.*

49. *1 Peter 1:23; John 3:3, 5.*

50. *John 17:17.*

MOTIVATION:
Fear and Love

On the motivational level, the fear of the Lord is the beginning of wisdom.[51] Fear is the beginning, not the end. Fear begins when we see the connection between sin—the *root* sin of not seeking and not understanding what is clear about God—and death. *Spiritual* death as meaninglessness, boredom, and guilt, is inherent in root sin. This is where the fear of the Lord begins. If we do not see the connection between sin and death, we will not learn the fear of the Lord, and we will not be motivated to seek. While wisdom begins with fear, it does not end there. It is by the love of God, love of the good, seeking the good with our whole heart, that we come into the fullness of the knowledge of God, by grace. Not just individually, but increasingly through history, corporately. The motivational factors that are to bring us to seek the good as the knowledge of God are the fear of the Lord and the love of God.

THE NECESSITY FOR UNITY

In closing, I want to say why the unity of the faith is necessary. The unity of the Church is necessary to disciple all nations. We are called to go and make disciples of all nations. Yet, we are divided, we are not being heard, and we are counterproductive to each other. We have to come into unity, as Jesus prayed, that we might be one, that the world might believe.[52] Unity of the faith is necessary to disciple all nations. We are to complete the work of dominion given to mankind in the Garden, being carried out now through discipling the nations. We are to subdue all things to Christ.[53] He is to reign until all his enemies are put under his feet, the last enemy to be destroyed is death—physical death—which occurs with his coming.[54] In the process of reigning with Christ, we are to take every thought captive to the obedience of Jesus Christ. Given the doctrine of clarity, we are to demolish arguments and every pretension that is raised up against the knowledge

---

51. *Proverbs 9:10; 1:7.*

52. *John 17:21.*

53. *1 Corinthians 15:28; Ephesians 1:22-23.*

54. *1 Corinthians 15:25-26.*

of God.[55] This is part of the spiritual war. Unity of the faith is necessary for this work to be completed, and then for Christ to return. This work is not being done apart from the Church, but in and through the Church. When Christ returns, then believers together will inherit the kingdom of God.[56] We will inherit the City of God—the City with foundations—that is pictured in the Book of Revelation, into which all the kings of the earth bring their glory, because even in unbelief, God rules, and causes men to uncover his glory.[57] And then we will experience the fullness of joy in enjoying the fullness of God.

RECOVERY

If this seems like a lot, let me focus it as clearly and simply as I can. Recovery. We need recovery. Recovery begins with preaching the gospel *in its fullness*. What is the gospel in its fullness? In the words of Scripture, "Repent, for the kingdom of heaven is at hand."[58] Now we are giving greater depth to that verse. Repent of what? Sin. Of what sin? Root sin. We are to repent of not seeking and understanding what is clear about God. Repent, for the kingdom of heaven—which is directed toward the glory of God, the good—is at hand. In that very word of the gospel, we have both sin (evil) and the good, the kingdom of God. This is not an individualistic otherworldly sense of heaven, but the kingdom is coming on the earth now, through the Church.

---

55. *2 Corinthians 10:4-5.*

56. *Revelation 21–22.*

57. *Revelation 21:24*; Gangadean, *The Book of Revelation: What Must Soon Take Place—Doxological Postmillennialism* (Phoenix: Logos Papers Press, 2023).

58. *Matthew 3:2.*

8

MY LAST LECTURE
Focus on Foundation

Lecture presented at Logos Theological Seminary

April 2018

M Y LAST LECTURE REFLECTS MY YEARS OF teaching in philosophy, religion, and the humanities in the academy, in theology
at Logos Theological Seminary, and pastoral teaching in the church.
It calls for a focus on foundation.

THE NECESSITY FOR FOUNDATION

In general, foundation is necessary for maturity, fruitfulness, unity,
and fullness. Without foundation, there is division and apostasy in the
Church, and decay and collapse in the culture. In Scripture, foundation is called for as first principles,[1] for endurance against tempests,[2] for
lasting fruit,[3] for unity of the faith and fullness,[4] for a lasting culture
in the City of God.[5] Current divisions in the Church and decay in the
culture show a longstanding lack of foundation and the need to get to
bedrock. Foundation must get to the certainty of clarity, the cornerstone, from which arises inexcusability. It must overcome skepticism

---

1. *Hebrews 6.*
2. *Matthew 7.*
3. *1 Corinthians 2.*
4. *Ephesians 4.*
5. *Hebrews 11:10; Revelation 21.*

and fideism by faith.[6] Failure to achieve comprehensiveness to attain to fullness of life is not new; it has been recurrent throughout history in the collapse of civilizations. A mere return to the past is insufficient for bedrock.

THE CORNERSTONE:
Understanding good and evil (and life and death, and heaven and hell); without the cornerstone, the foundation cannot be laid and the worldview cannot be built.

The good is the highest value, the end in itself, chosen for its own sake and not for the sake of something else; it is neither virtue (means to the good) nor happiness (the effect of the good). The good is clear: the good for a being is according to the nature of that being; the good for man as a rational being is the use of reason to the fullest to understand the nature of things. The nature of things created reveal the nature of God. It is *not* a non-cognitive state of a beatific vision. The good is one: it is the source of unity in each person and the source of unity among all persons. The good must have several characteristics: continuing, inexhaustible, comprehensive, inalienable, corporate, cumulative, communal, fulfilling, ultimate, and transformative. The good is the first *moral* concept, depending on one's epistemology and metaphysics. It is the most basic *existential* concept that moves a person to or from critical self-examination.

Moral evil is an act contrary to one's nature as a rational being; all have sinned, all come short of the glory of God. It is to neglect, avoid, resist, and deny reason regarding basic things that are clear to reason. Clarity makes unbelief inexcusable. Moral evil of not seeking and not understanding is *root* sin and is the source of all *fruit* sin.

Natural evil (toil and strife, and old age, sickness, and death) is due to autonomy in moral evil; it is a lasting and final call back to stop and think, to restrain, recall from, and to remove moral evil. The inherent consequence of moral evil is meaninglessness, boredom, and guilt; it is *not* a state that is merely future or imposed.

---

6. *Romans 1:20; Hebrews 11:1.*

COMMON GROUND AND THE WORD OF GOD

Common Ground is the set of conditions necessary for thought and discourse. It consists of reason (as the laws of thought), integrity (as a concern for consistency), critical thinking (applying reason critically as the test of meaning to basic beliefs/presuppositions) and the Principle of Clarity, that the basic things (about God and man and good and evil) are clear to reason (vs. skepticism and fideism).

The *Logos* is the eternal Word of God, Truth in its fullness, who makes God known.[7] The Logos, by which all things were made, is in all men as light/reason,[8] in creation as general revelation,[9] in history, through the prophets,[10] in person, incarnate in Jesus Christ, full of grace and truth.[11] He sends the Spirit of truth to lead the Church into all truth,[12] to bring unbelievers into the truth by regeneration,[13] and to sanctify the believer through knowing the truth.[14]

It is self-evident that we think and it is self-evident that there are laws of thought. Reason as the laws of thought (identity, non-contradiction, and excluded middle) is the most basic form of the Word of God to all men. Only the Word of God as reason is and can be self-attesting, and therefore authoritative. What is self-attesting does not need justification *and cannot be* questioned because, as the laws of thought, it makes questioning possible. By reason we understand the clarity of general and special revelation. Reason as the beginning of Common Ground and of the Logos in man is not neutral ground. Any act of thought (including unbelief) assumes reason and the darkness of unbelief cannot withstand the light of reason.[15] One must stop thinking and talking to avoid the use of reason, and no one can stop the spontaneity of thought. The use of reason leads to belief in God, and consequently, in Scripture. And, belief in God assumes reason is ontological, for

---

7. *John 1:1-18.*

8. *John 1:4.*

9. *John 1:10.*

10. *John 1:11.*

11. *John 1:14.*

12. *John 16:13.*

13. *John 3:3.*

14. *John 17:17.*

15. *John 1:5.*

neither God's being *nor any being* can be contradictory (both eternal and not eternal at the same time and in the same respect).

THE CLARITY OF GENERAL REVELATION:
It is clear to reason that God the Creator and Ruler exists.[16]

The concept of God: God is not only a higher being (one among many) but the highest being (above all else). He is not only eternal (uncreated) but *the only eternal* (the Creator of all). It is clear to reason that there must be something eternal (being cannot come from non-being), and that only God is eternal. Matter exists (vs. idealism) and matter is not eternal (self-maintaining). The soul exists (the mind is not the brain), and the soul is not eternal (having all knowledge in infinite time).

It is clear that creation is revelation, necessarily, intentionally, and exclusively. Man is created a body/soul unity, a rational animal, created in the image of God, not in the image of (or from) non-rational animals, to rule over the creation, to know and make known the glory of God. Original creation was very good, without natural evil (toil and strife, and old age, sickness, and death). The good for man, grounded in human nature, is the knowledge of God.

It is clear to reason that man is fallen, that God rules over man by an act of *special* providence, that *by covenant* the act of one affects all. Since God's eternal power and divine nature are clear, unbelief is without excuse. No one knows and acknowledges what is clear about God; no one seeks and understands—all have sinned and come short of the glory of God and all are in self-deception and self-justification about seeking and understanding.

It is clear that natural evil, which is not original, is now *imposed on all* (by God, through covenant) to restrain, recall from, and remove moral evil, that a call back is not punishment but mercy, that mercy requires special (redemptive) revelation to show how God can be both just and merciful to man in sin and death. Since moral evil is permitted in order to deepen the revelation, it must be removed gradually if the revelation is both to be deepened and be seen. In the conflict between

16. Gangadean, *Philosophical Foundation*, 71-161; Gangadean, *History of Philosophy*, 47-58; Gangadean, *The Westminster Catechisms*. See LCQ. 2; Gangadean, "Paper No. 3: The Principle of Clarity, Rational Presuppositionalism, and Proof" and "Paper No. 93: The Logic of Apologetics: The Goal, the Method, the Content," in *The Logos Papers*.

good and evil, belief will gradually overcome unbelief, through another in place of the first covenant head.

The clarity of general revelation regarding God and man and good and evil is necessary metaphysical foundation for the unity of mankind scattered in every form of unbelief.

MORAL LAW:
It is clear from general revelation that there is a moral law which is clear, comprehensive, and critical.[17]

1) Good and evil are grounded in human nature. God, as Creator of human nature therefore determines good and evil for man. Man is not, and cannot be, the author of his being (vs. all forms of *autonomy*).

2) Misconceptions of God arise from likening the infinite (Creator) to the finite (creature), rather than thinking of the finite/less basic in light of the infinite/more basic (vs. all forms of *idolatry*).

3) Lack of integrity (concern for consistency, both logical and existential) empties words of meaning. *Hypocrisy* is without excuse and leads to mental stupor.

4) Man's work of dominion is based on God's work of creation. As creation is revelation, dominion brings knowledge of revelation. As creation is completed, dominion will be completed (vs. false and no hope).

5) Authority is rational and is based on insight, which is historically cumulative. Authority based on insight must be honored; authority without insight must be changed where possible.

6) Human dignity is based on man's capacity to understand. Human society is a society of rational beings. Participation in human society is based on the exercise of one's capacity to understand.

7) Lack of love in marriage is due to lack of love of the good. Ordinary adultery is rooted in spiritual adultery.

8) Value arises from the exercise of talent in pursuit of the good. Talent, given in one's being, is from God, the author of our being. Only

---

17. Gangadean, *Philosophical Foundation*, 171-284; Gangadean, *History of Philosophy*, 61-69; Gangadean, *The Westminster Catechisms*. See LCQ. 91-148.

God therefore owns value absolutely; man is steward of the talent given to him.

9) Truth is necessary and sufficient for justice. One must know and speak the full truth to attain full justice.

10) The good is inalienable. Natural evil is a call back from moral evil. All things work together for good to those who seek the good.

The moral law, given in human nature, is universal, perpetual, total, and spiritual; it is teleological (aimed at the good), and defines what love is. It is therefore foundational and the source of unity in all and for all.

BIBLICAL FOUNDATION (NARRATIVE FORM):
Creation–Fall–Redemption (Genesis 1–3)[18]

Scripture

Clear general revelation through the problem of evil requires special revelation/scripture. Only what is consistent with clear general revelation (4–5 above) can be special revelation. Only Biblical revelation (Genesis 1–3 and what builds on it) affirms creation–fall–redemption (CFR), as it is understandable from clear general revelation. Therefore, only Biblical revelation, and no other text, can qualify as special revelation from God.

Creation

God's purpose in creation is revelation: necessarily, intentionally, and exclusively. This revelation is full and clear. Man's purpose, as created in the image of God, is for dominion. The good for man, man's chief end, eternal life, is the knowledge of God through dominion. The Sabbath signifies the hope that man's work of dominion will be completed, that the earth will be filled with the knowledge of God as the waters cover the sea.

---

18. Gangadean, "Paper No. 14: The Biblical Worldview: Creation–Fall–Redemption (Expanded Version)," in *The Logos Papers*; Gangadean, Papers No. 141–150 on The Biblical Worldview (Parts I–X), in *The Logos Papers*.

Fall

God relates to man by covenant; by representation, the act of one affects all; the visible covenant of marriage established in the Garden of Eden reveals the invisible covenant of creation. In probation, man's understanding of good and evil is tested—knowing what is the good and the ground of the good is tested by the claim: "you shall be as gods knowing good and evil." Had Adam been seeking God he would have understood that only God as Creator can determine good and evil. Adam's sin revealed that left to oneself no one seeks God and no one understands what is clear about God. All have sinned and come short of the glory of God. God permits the Fall of man to deepen the revelation of his glory, especially his justice and mercy.

Redemption

Man is called back from sin and death, first through conscience (shame regarding nakedness), which is avoided by self-deception (the covering of leaves). Man is then called to self-examination by the question "where are you?" which is resisted by self-justification, blaming the woman and God. Man's final and enduring call back is through the curse (toil and strife, and old age, sickness, and death) and the promise—"I will put enmity between you and the woman" (through a spiritual war, which is age-long and agonizing, good will overcome evil). Through the seed of the woman, Christ to come in the place of Adam, will undo what Adam did (as the Lamb of God signified by the coats of skin) and do what Adam failed to do (make God known by crushing the lies of the devil (the head of the serpent)). Adam believes the promise, repents, and obeys (he wears the coats of skin—he is *justified* in being covered through the death of another), and he calls his wife's name Eve, the mother of all living—he will be fruitful for the work of dominion. Adam is to be *sanctified* by knowing the truth through suffering; he is driven from the Garden to live under the curse.

CFR is a complete summary of the biblical worldview.

CFR is affirmed in Genesis 1–3, the foundation of all of Redemptive Revelation. All of Scripture must be understood in light of CFR. If we do not understand CFR, we cannot understand Scripture. CFR gives unity to all of Scripture and to all who affirm Scripture.

BIBLICAL FOUNDATION (THEOLOGICAL FORM): The Seven Pillars[19]

Foundation has many layers; the City of God[20] has 12. Theological Foundation is summed up in Hebrews[21] in its assumptions and implications, and in the proclamation of the gospel—repent, for the kingdom of heaven is at hand. *Repentance* assumes *sin and death*, which assumes *clarity and inexcusability. Faith* towards God assumes the *promise* of redemption, given with the *curse* as God's continuing call to repentance. Repentance and faith is accompanied by *justification and sanctification*.

A repentant sinner is received by the Church through *baptism* (signifying regeneration and identification with the work of each person of the Triune God). The Church prepares its members for their particular work (*calling*) in the kingdom of God, based on God's work. Commitment to work in the kingdom is renewed in corporate worship each Lord's Day and in the sacrament of the Lord's Supper *until he comes*. Christ returns when all things are subdued to him, consummated by the *resurrection* of the dead, followed by the Last Judgment and *reward*, each according to one's work.

1. Clarity and Inexcusability

Basic things about God and man and good and evil are clear to reason so that unbelief is without excuse. If there is no clear general revelation, there is no possibility of meaning or morality, no sin and death, and no need for Christ as redeemer. All who fail to acknowledge clarity and inexcusability, in some degree, fail to repent of (root) sin and (spiritual) death, and persist in self-deception and self-justification. The Church disciples its members to deepen their faith in understanding the first principles of the faith, and not to remain spiritual infants, unable to teach others.

---

19. Gangadean, "Paper No. 36: The Pillar and Ground of the Truth: Rebuilding the Church's Foundation" and "Paper No. 37: The Seven Pillars: A Brief Summary," in *The Logos Papers*.

20. *Revelation 21.*

21. *Hebrews 6:1-2.*

2. Sin and Death

Sin is an act contrary to one's nature as a rational being. In sin, man neglects, avoids, resists, and denies reason regarding what is clear about God. Root sin is universal: no one seeks God and no one understands; all have sinned and come short of the glory of God.

The wages of sin (spiritual suicide) is spiritual death: meaninglessness, boredom, and guilt, ever increasing in this life and the next. Root sin is *not* fruit sin, and spiritual death is *not* a literal lake of fire.

3. Curse and Promise

The curse consists of toil and strife, and old age, sickness, and death, and is imposed by God on all as his continuing and final call back to stop and think, to restrain, recall from, and remove moral evil. As sin increases culturally, the curse increases corporately to war, famine, and plague.

The promise, given with the curse, is that through a spiritual war (between belief and unbelief), which is age-long and agonizing, good will overcome evil.[22] Christ, the seed of the woman, in place of Adam, will undo what Adam did (as the Lamb of God he will take away the sin of the world), and will do what Adam failed to do (rule through the work of dominion to make God known).

4. Repentance and Faith

Man is called by the gospel to repent of (root) sin and to seek first the kingdom of God by which God is glorified and through which man enjoys eternal life—the knowledge of God now and ever increasing forever.

Repentance in principle must grow in practice: faith grows as man through discipleship becomes more conscious and consistent in understanding and in obedience, putting away all sin, root and fruit.

5. Justification and Sanctification

Upon repentance and faith in Christ's atoning sacrifice on the cross, a person receives forgiveness of sin and is justified solely on the basis of Christ's righteousness imputed to him and is received by faith. This

---

22. *Genesis 3:15.*

imputation of Christ's righteousness to those in him is real, even as Adam's sin is imputed to all in him, and as our sin is imputed to Christ. Imputation of Christ's righteousness for justification is once for all and is not by any works or to be confused with sanctification, by which a believer continues to be cleansed from sin throughout his life.

Sanctification comes through knowing the Truth, the fullness of the Word of God.[23] Knowing the Truth comes through trials of faith by which we are disciplined through suffering under the curse in this life. Sanctification is completed at and through death and does not continue in the next life through any kind of purgatory.

6. Baptism and Calling

Upon a credible repentance and faith, the Church receives a repentant sinner by baptism in the name of the Father, Son, and Holy Spirit. Baptism signifies regeneration, and union with God, even as circumcision under the Old Testament, and is similarly applied, in principle.

In light of the work of the Triune God, each man is called to a particular work in the kingdom of God, recognized, at times, by the laying on of hands. Commitment to discipleship in following Christ is renewed in corporate worship on the Lord's Day and in the Lord's Supper, done in remembrance of him *until he comes*.

7. Resurrection and Reward

Christ returns when all has been subdued to him. The last enemy, physical death, is removed by the resurrection of all, followed by the rapture of believers who remain alive at the time.[24]

In the Last Judgment, believers, separated from unbelievers, inherit, in Christ, the kingdom of God, the City of God with foundations, built throughout history, according to plan, from the beginning.[25] Christ is ruling now through the Church in a spiritual war through history to make God known; there is no future millennium in which he will come to rule from any place. The reward of believers is the kingdom of

---

23. *John 8:32, 17:17.*

24. *1 Corinthians 15:51; John 5:28-29; 1 Thessalonians 4:15-17.*

25. *Matthew 25:31-34.*

God now being advanced on earth, not a beatific vision of God apart from the earth being filled with the knowledge of God.

THE HISTORIC CHRISTIAN FAITH[26]

Christ sends the Holy Spirit to lead the Church into all Truth.[27] In response to challenges, the pastor-teachers, building on the work of the apostles and prophets, after much discussion come to agreement, expressed in creeds and confessions delivered to the Church for the unity of the faith.[28] This is the holy, catholic and apostolic faith, the basis of the magisterium—the teaching authority of the Church, departure from which divides the body of Christ.

The Council of Jerusalem (A.D. 51) addressed the question of sacrament and salvation: must I be circumcised (or be baptized) to be saved? Since any sacrament is a sign and not the reality of grace, the Church's answer is no. The First Council rejected the underlying principle of literalism which confuses sign and reality and both polarizing antinomies of this error: the sign is *not* the reality, nor is it always accompanied by the reality.

The Apostles' Creed (*ca.* 180) rejected Greek dualism which denigrated the reality and value of bodily existence in the incarnation, crucifixion, and resurrection of Christ. Creation is very good and is revelation and the knowledge of God through dominion is man's original and lasting calling. It therefore implicitly rejects celibacy as a regular calling for the priesthood, monasticism as a higher service, and direct, mystical contemplation as the good.

The Council of Nicea (325) affirmed the unity of diversity in the Trinity: One God in three Persons, Father, Son and Holy Spirit; the ultimate reality of personhood; diversity and relationships of persons who are equal in power and glory, and ordered without subordination. The Word of God (the *Logos*) is the co-eternal Son of God, who makes God known.

---

26. Gangadean, "Paper No. 16: The Historic Christian Faith: The Holy Spirit Guides the Church into All Truth," in *The Logos Papers*; Gangadean, *The Westminster Confession*. See Questions 1-3.

27. *John 16:12-13.*

28. *Ephesians 4; Acts 15.*

The Council of Carthage (397) confirmed the canon of the New Testament to be all and only the writings commonly received. The Old Testament canon, affirmed by the Hebrew priesthood to whom it was entrusted, consists of all and only the writings commonly received, and excludes all inter-testamental writings. The canon of Scripture is the Word of God *written* and is authoritative over all other special revelations of spirits and traditions of men. Scripture itself affirms the authority of the Word of God in its manifold forms in John's prologue, and throughout Scripture, understood by good and necessary consequences.

The Council of Chalcedon (451) affirmed the unity of two natures (the Godhead and manhood) united in one person, Jesus Christ, without conversion, composition or confusion. The infinite (God) includes the finite (man) without contradiction or paradox. The finite cannot include the infinite. The mysteries of the faith are neither from reason, nor against reason, but in accord with reason, and requires care not to be misrepresented.

The Council of Orange (529) affirmed the Fall of man against all degrees of Pelagianism. Only sovereign grace can restore man from sin and death. Man is always free (to seek and to understand), but left to himself, no one seeks and no one understands.

The Westminster Confession of Faith (1648) (and its Catechisms) builds upon earlier confessions of the Reformation in response to the Church of Rome. Salvation is by faith alone, by grace alone, through Christ alone, based on Scripture alone, for the glory of God alone. Westminster affirms the earlier creeds prior to the Reformation and represents the current high-water mark of the Historic Christian Faith.

FROM THE REFORMATION TO THE PRESENT:
Challenges from the past continue.

Divisions in Christendom

Divisions among Christians persist since the Reformation, and have increased. A false magisterium in Rome has been opposed by no magisterium in current Protestantism. The true magisterium in the Historic Christian Faith, the work of the Holy Spirit leading the Church into all Truth and which is the holy catholic and apostolic faith, is the source of unity for all who believe.

The Enlightenment

The Enlightenment, whose motto was "Dare to Reason," failed to see what was clear to reason, that there must be something eternal, and only some (God) is eternal. The Enlightenment split into the antinomy of rationalism (Descartes, Spinoza, Leibniz) and empiricism (Locke, Berkeley, Hume). The synthesis proposed by Kant failed and resulted in varying degrees of idealism (Hegel, Schopenhauer, Bradley).

Secularism

Secularism affirmed the reality perceived through the senses alone. In the name of naturalistic science, it pronounced against the invisible realities grasped by reason alone: essences, the soul/mind, personal immortality, and God (Marx, Darwin, Nietzsche, Freud).

Postmodernism

Post-Kantian modernism in existentialism (Kierkegaard/Barth, Heidegger, Sartre) and Positivism's verification theory (Russell, Ayer) or Ordinary Language (Wittgenstein, Moore) gave way to Postmodern pragmatic skepticism (Dewey, Rorty) and its eventual nihilism (Derrida, Foucault, and cultural Marxism).

The spiritual war (between belief and unbelief) that is age-long and agonizing is currently being expressed in the many dimensions of the culture war today. Response still requires the fullness of redemption through Christ.

RESPONSE OF THE WORD OF GOD (THE LOGOS):
Redemption from the sin of unbelief and the death of meaninglessness is by Christ through the Church.

The Church is the body of Christ, the Word of God incarnate, who rules to make God known.

The Church is the pillar and ground of the Truth. It is the salt of the earth and the light of the world, without which the culture decays and collapses. The first principles of the foundation must be in place for the Church to be the pillar and ground of the Truth.

The Church is for worship and discipleship. We are to worship God in spirit and in Truth. Only the Psalms for singing in corporate worship preserve pure and entire the biblical worldview of creation–fall–redemption.

The Church is to make disciples of all nations, teaching them to observe all things that Christ has commanded. Only the Church which holds to the Historic Christian Faith has the authority of cumulative insight to make disciples.

The Church is to be sanctified by the Truth that it may be one that the world might believe. The Holy Spirit is sent to lead the Church into all Truth in the Historic Christian Faith, the basis of the unity of the faith.

The Church is to preach the gospel in the fullness of Truth: repent of (root) sin of not seeking and not understanding what is clear, and seek first the kingdom of God in all relations of life by which God is glorified.

The Church has and must affirm the promise that through a spiritual war (between belief and unbelief) which is age-long and agonizing, good will overcome evil.

The Church, by the Word of God (the *Logos*, Truth in its Fullness) is to demolish arguments and every pretension raised up against the knowledge of God and take every thought captive to Jesus Christ.

The Church, under Christ, through the work of dominion, is to fill the earth with the knowledge of God as the waters cover the sea.

The Church, under Christ, builds the City of God with foundations, and inherits that kingdom, into which all nations flow, and which lasts forever.

9

ON THE NECESSITY FOR THE
UNITY OF THE FAITH

Public lecture delivered at Arizona Christian University,
Unity of the Faith Conference[1]

April 18, 2015

I AM GOING TO ADDRESS THREE QUESTIONS: what is the unity of the faith? Is it necessary and urgent? And, what proposals for unity are there?

WHAT IS THE UNITY OF THE FAITH?

The unity of the faith is about the *basic* beliefs of the Christian faith—what is foundational—about God and man and good and evil. The unity of the faith is not about making converts. It is not about what is fundamental for initial conversion, for being saved, or for entering into the kingdom of God. It is about what is foundational, which is necessary for maturity in Christ.[2] Foundation is for fullness, and what is maximal includes what is minimal. Unity of the faith is not to be equated with the unity of the Spirit in professing one Lord, one faith, one baptism, *which already exists* among believers and is to be preserved in the bond of peace.[3] Unity of the faith is about the fullness of Christ *to be attained*, as mentioned in Ephesians 4:13. It is not about

---

1. Edited by The Logos Foundation Editorial Board.

2. *Hebrews 6:1.*

3. *Ephesians 4:3-6.*

ecclesiastical unity, that is church government, which comes naturally if there is unity of the faith. It is not about what is less basic, the
outward before the inward, whether in piety, in law, or sacrament. If
we agree on what is more basic, we can and will agree on what is less
basic. That is a theme I will emphasize—always getting the more basic
in place—and then we can address what is less basic. Unity of the faith
is about *basic* beliefs that are clear from general revelation (philosophical foundation),[4] from Scripture (theological foundation),[5] and from
Church history (historical foundation).[6]

The unity called for is the unity that is in the Trinity. As Jesus prays
in his high priestly prayer, "that they all may be one, as you, Father, are
in me, and I in you; that they also may be one *in us*, that the world may
believe that you sent me."[7] This is the most comprehensive and deepest
unity possible. All diversity originates in God who is one. This includes
male and female, rich and poor, bond and free, barbarian, Scythian,
and all the nations. All of this is in God and God is one. The unity
called for is the unity in Christ himself. The response of Paul to the divisions in the Corinthian church is to ask, "Is Christ divided?" Christ,
in his office as prophet, priest, and king, is not divided. But note, the
division between prophetic, priestly, and kingly may penetrate within any church, even those that profess the same thing. We are not to
say, "I am of Paul, or I am of Apollos, or I am of Cephas."[8] The unity
of the faith is unity in the Truth, capital T. Truth is attained by the
work of the Holy Spirit, through the work of the pastors and teachers
in Church history.[9] This is where the historical foundation comes in.
Unity of the faith requires unity in the good, which is the philosophical idea corresponding to "eternal life" in Scripture, and to the words
in Historic Christianity, "man's chief end."[10] Unity of the faith is a
unity in the meaning and purpose of life, in man's chief end, which is

---

4. Gangadean, *Philosophical Foundation: A Critical Analysis of Basic Beliefs,* Second Edition;
Gangadean, *History of Philosophy: A Critical Analysis of Unresolved Disputes.*

5. Gangadean, *Theological Foundation: A Critical Analysis of Christian Belief.*

6. Gangadean, *The Westminster Confession of Faith: A Doxological Focus*; Gangadean, *The Westminster Shorter and Larger Catechisms: A Doxological Understanding.*

7. *John 17:21.* Emphasis added.

8. *1 Corinthians 1:12-13.*

9. *John 16:13; Acts 15; Ephesians 4:11-13.*

10. *SCQ. 1.*

to glorify God. Jesus prays for this at the beginning of his high priestly prayer, "Glorify your Son, that your Son also may glorify you."[11]

IS THE UNITY OF THE FAITH
NECESSARY AND URGENT?

We come to the crux of the matter. The necessity for unity depends on one's view of the good. There are two views. In one view it is not necessary, in the second view it is necessary. We will need to decide where we are in our thinking, taking into consideration the background from which we are coming. In the popular view of knowledge by direct experience, regardless of what has happened on earth, when you die, in heaven you receive the fullness of blessing by direct experience. And, it is regardless of the idea that creation and history are revelation, and that through the work of dominion, the revelation is exposed. This is one view. It is often correlated with other beliefs, such as the view that only by Christ's return and direct rule on earth can evil be removed. Rather, it is by his rule through the curse of toil and strife, and old age, sickness, and death, that moral evil is removed. Christ restrains evil, he calls us back from evil through regeneration, and he further sanctifies us through the Truth. In the popular view, unity of the faith is not necessary for attaining the good.

On the other hand, in the view that knowledge of God is by understanding God's self-revelation in creation and history, the fullness of blessing is received only by Christ ruling through the Church to complete the work of dominion given to man in the Garden of Eden. In this view, unity of the faith is necessary for the good. That is the crux of the matter, depending on your view of the good. If we do not have the good in common, we cannot go on to speak about unity of the faith being urgent, and there is no point in considering proposals.

Is the unity of the faith urgent? Consider this: without foundation (understanding basic things, beginning with the meaning and purpose of life), we do not thrive. We do not go on to maturity, fruitfulness, unity, and fullness.[12] We remain infants rather than become teachers, "For though by this time you ought to be teachers, you need someone

---

11. *John 17:1-4.*

12. *Ephesians 4:11-13; John 15:8, 16.*

to teach you again the first principles of the oracles of God; and you have come to need milk and not solid food."[13]

Without foundation we have meaninglessness. We not only do not thrive, we shrivel and fade, and we lose meaning. Meaninglessness is a state in which we continue to lose more and more meaning of every word that we speak and profess. And consequently, with the loss of meaning, boredom (with transgression to overcome boredom), and with that, guilt. We are in a state of spiritual death.

Without foundation the family breaks down. Not just families, but the very idea of family breaks down. Christ said, "I have come that they may have life, and have it to the full."[14] Have it to the full. He said, "Let anyone who is thirsty come to me and drink. Whoever believes in me, as Scripture has said, rivers of living water will flow from within them."[15] We will be like "a tree planted by the water that sends out its roots by the stream. It does not fear when heat comes; its leaves are always green. It has no worries in a year of drought and never fails to bear fruit."[16] "And in old age, when others fade, their boughs of fruit shall bend."[17] Life more abundantly. We need it, our children desire it, and without it they will try to find it in the world in cheap imitations—it is not there. The world is full of emptiness. Foundation is needed for the family—it is not only individual, but it is corporate.

By divisions and apostasy in the Church, the Church ceases to be pillar and ground of the Truth. It is taken captive and it does not take thoughts captive. We are to demolish every pretension that raises itself up against the knowledge of God[18] and yet we are in captivity. Foundation is for fullness, to prepare us to do this work. Currently, the Church is not salt and light. It is the tail of the culture, not the head. The universities that lead the way, Princeton and Harvard, are hotbeds of unbelief. The culture without God, in education, in economics, and in politics, decays and collapses. How far along are we? We may differ,

---

13. *Hebrews 5:12.*

14. *John 10:10.*

15. *John 7:37-38.*

16. *Jeremiah 17:8.*

17. Psalm 92B, *The Book of Psalms for Singing* (Pittsburgh, PA: Crown and Covenant, 1973).

18. *2 Corinthians 10:4-5.*

but the cup appears to be nearly full. Not being salt and light, we will be cast out and trampled underfoot. If this is so, then unity is urgent.

WHAT PROPOSALS ARE THERE FOR PROGRESS TOWARD UNITY?

My proposal begins with five areas of basic agreement and seeking to be more conscious and consistent. By taking a step-by-step approach to unity, we hope we can identify where differences arise and address those differences. So, I am going to speak of five areas.

The Knowledge of God: Man's Chief End, the Good, Eternal Life

The first source of agreement, something I believe that all Christians affirm, is that "Man's chief end is to glorify God and to enjoy him forever." I am going to try and show this step-by-step and reach towards fullness. We will also do this for the other areas. Let us see how much we can agree with as we go step-by-step.

Man's chief end, also referred to as "the good" in philosophy, and "eternal life" in Scripture, is the knowledge of God. According to Westminster Shorter Catechism, Question 1, "Man's chief end is to glorify God and to enjoy him forever."[19] This is part of the ABC's—the milk. And the Catechism goes further—we are to glorify God "in all that by which he makes himself known." This is how Question 101 of the Shorter Catechism is answered, connected to the first petition of the Lord's Prayer, "Hallowed be thy name." How does God make himself known? He makes himself known by all his works of creation and providence.[20] This is comprehensive. Through everything that comes to pass, we are to glorify God.

Jesus said, eternal life is knowing God.[21] Putting these thoughts together, relating them, and connecting the dots, we come to infer that the good is grounded in human nature and therefore, never changes. Human nature is established by God. So, the good, which is the

---

19. *SCQ. 1*; Gangadean, *The Westminster Catechisms.* See SCQ. 1 and Appendix 4; Gangadean, *The Westminster Confession.* See Question 25; Gangadean, *Philosophical Foundation*, 171-177, 208-211; Gangadean, *History of Philosophy*, 61-64.

20. *WCF, 4.1, 5.1.*

21. *John 17:3.*

knowledge of God, has been the goal from the beginning. God said, "Let us make man in our image . . . and let them have dominion . . ."[22] The goal then was the knowledge of God—it was knowledge of God through dominion. So, the good was given to man from the beginning and the good never changes. And the work of dominion now extends, after the Fall, over sin. "Sin shall not have dominion over you, for you are not under law but under grace."[23] We are to overcome and have dominion; we are to take thoughts captive. Dominion extends over sin and the program has always been, always, to move from the Garden of Eden to the City of God.[24] What is said in the first two chapters of Genesis, is completed in the last two chapters of the Book of Revelation. Fully and clearly there—Jesus is the Alpha and the Omega who will bring this about.

From the beginning, we are told that the work of dominion will be completed, as God completed his work and hallowed the Sabbath. The Sabbath signifies the completion of the work. Christ, through the Church, will rule to complete the work of dominion in place of Adam. He will do what Adam failed to do—he will rule through the Church. Christ is to rule through mankind, and mankind together must do this work of dominion. The result is that "the earth shall be full of the knowledge of the Lord as the waters cover the sea."[25] Through the rule of Christ the curse will be removed, consummated in nothing less than the resurrection of the dead. "For he must reign until he has put all his enemies under his feet. The last enemy to be destroyed is death."[26] This is the Christian mission; this is the fullness of life. By believing it, understanding it, and giving our lives to it, out of our innermost being will flow rivers of living water.[27] Remember the picture of the water flowing out from under the threshold of the temple in Ezekiel, and it became greater and greater until it could not be crossed.[28] It is the

---

22. *Genesis 1:26-28.*

23. *Romans 6:14.*

24. *Revelation 21–22.*

25. *Isaiah 11:9*; Gangadean, "Paper No. 104: Eschatology: The Earth Shall Be Full of the Knowledge of God" and "Paper No. 118: Eschatology: Based Upon the Doxological Focus," in *The Logos Papers.*

26. *1 Corinthians 15:25-26.*

27. *John 7:38.*

28. *Ezekiel 47:1-12.*

same river that appears in the last chapters of Revelation, the river of life and the tree of life on either side, bearing fruit in twelve seasons.[29] Fullness of life. So, this is the goal. How far did we get in agreeing?

Common Ground

The second source of agreement is Common Ground. It is a necessary condition for thought and discourse for all human beings—all thought, all discourse.[30] It begins with what is self-evident—that we are thinking beings, having been made in the image of God. We are thinking beings and reason in itself is the laws of thought, which is more self-evident than what Jefferson said and, therefore, more certain. *Reason*, as the laws of thought, is most basic. It is therefore the test for meaning and it is self-attesting and authoritative.

Next, we should be committed to reason as rational, thinking beings. We should have *integrity*, a concern for consistency, both logically and existentially. There are premises and conclusions, and premises are more basic than conclusions. We have assumptions, and we should be aware of our assumptions—critically aware of them. We should be aware of the assumptions of others, be able to address them, and test them for meaning using reason. There must be something eternal—we can know this with certainty. Only some is eternal—we can know this also with certainty. There are many basic things we can know with certainty and we should have those things in place.

A third feature of Common Ground is *Rational Presuppositionalism*, which says thinking is presuppositional. We think of the less basic in light of the more basic. If we agree on the more basic, we can agree on the less basic. Rational Presuppositionalism tests basic beliefs for meaning. This is what I have been involved with for 45 years in philosophy and teaching. I was aware this was not going on as I went through undergraduate and graduate school, and I said to myself, "If I ever teach philosophy, I will always consider assumptions and address those assumptions." By the grace of God and the opportunities given to me, I have been giving myself to this for 45 years with the added benefit

---

29. *Revelation 22:1-2.*

30. Gangadean, "Paper No. 2: Common Ground: The Necessary Condition for Thought and Discourse," in *The Logos Papers*; Gangadean, Papers No. 50–53: Common Ground (Parts I–IV) in *The Logos Papers*.

of Historic Christianity, as that came into focus, and the riches of the faith became so much more beneficial.

The fourth feature of Common Ground is the *Principle of Clarity*, which states: some things are clear; the basic things are clear; the basic things about God and man and good and evil are clear to reason.[31] The Principle of Clarity is opposed to skepticism, which dominates the thinking of the world, and fideism—believing in God without being concerned to prove the existence of God based on understanding the basic things. By faith we understand. Both skepticism and fideism fail to see that basic things are clear. As the apostle Paul said, what may be known of God is clear so that men are without excuse.[32] The lack of clarity ends eventually, sooner or later, in nihilism, the loss of all meaning. Understanding clarity, we can see why unbelief is inexcusable and why Paul says this. One has to neglect, avoid, resist, or deny reason to not see what is clear. Understanding the Principle of Clarity is necessary to understand sin and spiritual death. If there is no sin and death, there is no need for Christ and him crucified. This is where Paul begins: "For I determined not to know anything among you except Jesus Christ and him crucified."[33] If we cannot account for the crucifixion of Christ by going back to sin and death, we cannot begin our witness. If we do not get to clarity and inexcusability, we will not get to Christ crucified.

The Moral Law

The third source of agreement is the moral law. The moral law is clear, comprehensive, and critical, and the law is basic. It is given in special revelation from Mount Sanai, it is in the ark under the mercy seat, and Jesus says, "Go therefore and make disciples . . . teaching them to observe all that I have commanded."[34] The moral law is also given in human nature as is stated in both Romans 2:14-15 and Deuteronomy 30:11-14. Moses says:

---

31. Gangadean, *Philosophical Foundation*, 3-5, 287-292; Gangadean, *The Westminster Confession*. See Question 4; "Paper No. 53: Common Ground (Part IV): The Principle of Clarity," in *The Logos Papers*.

32. *Romans 1:20.*

33. *1 Corinthians 2:2.*

34. *Matthew 28:18-20.*

For this commandment which I command you today is not too mysterious for you, nor is it far off. It is not in heaven, that you should say, 'Who will ascend into heaven for us and bring it to us, that we may hear it and do it?' Nor is it beyond the sea, that you should say, 'Who will go over the sea for us and bring it to us, that we may hear it and do it?' But the word is very near you, in your mouth and in your heart, that you may do it.

This is the law that is in the heart of all men—this is what makes it *clear:* it is grounded in human nature. We should be able to derive the moral law—the Decalogue—from human nature.[35] The law, therefore, is universal for all men and it is perpetual for all times. The law is *comprehensive:* it is total for all choices, it is spiritual for all levels, and it is summed up in the commandment to love. Love is not higher than the moral law, but is expressed in obeying God's law. The moral law is *critical:* its consequences are a matter of life and death. Spiritual life (the knowledge of God in the kingdom of God) or spiritual death (both personal and cultural). In the first four moral laws is revealed the real meaning of autonomy, idolatry, hypocrisy, and hope in connection with the Sabbath.

The moral law as given in human nature is neither arbitrary—merely posited by divine command (as in the divine command theory), nor is it strange to us (foreign to human nature) as if we are being imposed upon. Rather, it is in our nature. The moral law is teleological—it is aimed at the good. It is not deontological—aimed at virtue. We have to be careful about this—virtue is the means to the good. And the law is not consequential—aimed at happiness. Happiness is the effect of possessing what is the good.

The moral law, aimed at the good, is corporate, cumulative, and communal. This was so from the beginning: "Be fruitful and multiply and fill the earth and subdue it, and have dominion over [it]."[36] This work is *corporate:* it is going to take all of mankind to complete. It is throughout history, so it is *cumulative* and it is *communal*—it involves active cooperation and sharing. The moral law is for oneself as well as for others. It is personal as well as cultural. We achieve the good

---

35. Gangadean, *Philosophical Foundation*, 171-284; Gangadean, *History of Philosophy*, 61-69; Gangadean, *The Westminster Catechisms*. See LCQ. 91-148.

36. *Genesis 1:26-28.*

through the kingdom of God, which is the City of God. The moral law is over all institutions of culture; no institution is total—over any other. I mention this because when we talk about the law we tend to fall into theocracy. I am not talking about theocracy. Sanctions differ according to the form and function of each institution. We can and should be able to distinguish each institution—the family from the Church, the state, business, education, etc. Civil law only applies to crime, which is but one distinct aspect of moral evil, so we do not criminalize sin. We understand the difference between crime and sin and apply the civil law appropriately, so we do not fall into a theocracy, which is a common objection when talking about the law of God.

Foundation in Scripture: Creation–Fall–Redemption

The fourth source of agreement is the foundation in Scripture. And that foundation is creation–fall–redemption. Foundation consists of elementary truths of the faith. It is milk, not meat.[37] It is the ABC's. It is necessary for a lasting culture in the City of God. Abraham was looking for a city with foundations.[38] What we find at the end of history is a city with foundations in Revelation 21:14 and 19-20. Foundation is necessary, as we said earlier, for maturity, fruitfulness, unity, and fullness. It is possible not to have the foundation in place. Hebrews 5:12 speaks about this. And so, it has to be laid again. Or, it is possible to hear about the foundation but not build upon it, as Jesus said, not building on the rock but on sand.[39] And Paul says, let every man take heed how he builds on it— gold, silver, precious stones or wood, hay, stubble—every man's work shall be made manifest.[40] Jesus said we should have fruit, much fruit, fruit that will last.[41] It is by having the foundation in place that we can go on to maturity and fruitfulness.

Foundation from Scripture is found in Genesis 1–3. Creation–fall–redemption.[42] We do not have to wait until the New Testament to

37. *Hebrews 5:12-14.*

38. *Hebrews 11:10.*

39. *Matthew 7:24-27.*

40. *1 Corinthians 3:10-15.*

41. *John 15:8, 16.*

42. Gangadean, "Paper No. 14: The Biblical Worldview: Creation–Fall–Redemption (Expanded Version)," in *The Logos Papers*; Gangadean, Papers No. 141–150 on The Biblical

know this foundation. It is there from the beginning. The account of creation reveals God's purpose for creating man in the image of God. We see the good and the means to the good through the work of dominion, and the Sabbath hope that the good will be attained. The account of the Fall reveals the covenant of creation—there is a covenant that is corporate. We see clarity and inexcusability, temptation and sin, and spiritual death in meaninglessness. Adam was not thinking when the serpent said, "You shall be like God knowing good and evil." We are to understand that God knows good and evil by determining the nature of things by creation. Adam could not possibly do this. He was not seeking and was already lapsing into misunderstanding. And when confronted, he was in a state of self-deception—they used the coats of leaves to cover sin instead of face it—and then self-justification in blaming his wife and God, instead of accepting responsibility. That is the condition revealed in the Garden.

In the account of redemption, the curse comes with the promise—the seed of the woman will crush the head of the serpent, and, cursed is the ground because of you. The curse is imposed, not as punishment, but as a merciful call back to repentance. We also find the teaching of vicarious atonement in God providing the coats of skin (the animal was killed), and also, we see justification—we are covered through the death of another. And finally, they are expelled from the Garden to live under the curse so that we might, through suffering, come to seek God diligently and understand. The doctrines are there—justification and sanctification—from the beginning. So, Christ in the place of Adam will undo, as the Lamb of God, what Adam did. And he will do, as King, what Adam failed to do—that is, exercise dominion through his people.

Historic Christianity

The last source of agreement is Historic Christianity. Historic Christianity is the work of the Holy Spirit leading the Church into all Truth,[43] according to Jesus, in John 16:13. This work is through the pastor-teachers, in response to challenges, and it is after much discussion. As in

---

Worldview (Parts I–X), in *The Logos Papers.*

43. Gangadean, "Paper No. 16: The Historic Christian Faith: The Holy Spirit Guides the Church into All Truth," in *The Logos Papers.*

Acts chapters 15–16, they come to agreement, and this agreement is summed up in the creeds and delivered to the churches for the unity of the faith. The process is depicted in the first council in Jerusalem.[44] The Council of Jerusalem (A.D. 51) addressed the question of sacraments, specifically, the question, "Is circumcision necessary for salvation?" And the answer was, "We gave no such command." We have to draw the implications of this ruling for the history of the Church.

Next, the Apostles' Creed (*ca.* 180) addressed Greek gnosticism and otherworldliness, which minimized the value of creation as revelation, and all that went with that view—our failure to engage with the world, and withdrawal from the world in many ways. Then, Nicea (325) addressed the Trinity and the unity and diversity in God. The Council of Carthage (397) particularly spoke about the New Testament canon. The Old Testament was addressed by the Church in the Old Testament, based upon what the Jews included, and only what they included, as Scripture. The Council of Chalcedon (451) addressed Christ as both God and man. He is fully God and fully man, two whole natures joined together in one person, without conversion, without composition, without confusion. And the Council of Orange (529) addressed the question of Pelagius and semi-Pelagianism on the topic of free will. The Reformation built on the previous councils, continuing those— that is the holy, catholic, and apostolic faith. And the Westminster Confession (1648) built on the six earlier creeds of the Reformation.

The councils, creeds, and confessions are the work of the Holy Spirit leading the Church into all Truth. We can say the work of the Holy Spirit leading the Church into all Truth is continuing and will continue until the end of history. A base was laid in the first five centuries of the Church. It needs to be, but has not yet been, developed. There is much more to say, but in closing, thanks be to God for the measure of unity that we do have as his people. And may that unity increase.

---

44. Gangadean, "Paper No. 60: The Spiritual War (Part II): Church Councils and Settling Current Divisions in the Church," in *The Logos Papers*.

10

CHRISTIANITY, PHILOSOPHY, AND PUBLIC EDUCATION

*Reflections Upon Retirement:
For all those who would sit in the chair of Philosophy*

Paper Published for the Evangelical Philosophical Society[1]

April 2014

T HE IDEA OF A CHRISTIAN PHILOSOPHER in a secular university raises a set of related concerns. First, there are Church and State First Amendment issues (more generally, religion and public life). Second, the definitions of philosophy and religion and their relation to each other. Third, what special obligations are there for a Christian who is a philosopher in public education. (I assume there is no such thing as Christian philosophy or Christian math.) And fourth, is there any resolution to the dilemma inherent in the very notion of public education today.

There is an ever-increasing presumption of a wall of separation between religion and public life. In private life, one is free to be religious; in public life, one is to be free from religion. It is either not good form or unconstitutional (or both) to expose one's religion in public life. The public realm is either common ground or neutral ground and religion appears to be neither. But common ground and/or neutral ground

---

1. See: epsociety.org/articles/christianity-philosophy-and-public-education

appear equally elusive. Can philosophy offer help? Can the philosopher who is a Christian offer wisdom?

What are some minimum characteristics of philosophy that lead us to expect help from philosophy?[2] There is public philosophy and philosophy addressed primarily to fellow philosophers (that is, academic philosophy). Public philosophy deals with questions that are of interest to the public at large. These are the questions that moved us at first to love philosophy, the big questions, the basic, enduring questions, what may be called the classic tradition in philosophy. These are the questions of epistemology (how is knowledge possible?), metaphysics (what is real/eternal?), and ethics (what ought I to do?). And is it still philosophy if we have left our first love, if we do not seek answers to the big questions?

We had wanted (needed) knowledge if at all possible, and if it was not possible, then we faced despair.[3] (Could we, with integrity, be heroes of the Absurd?) We critiqued every answer for a sufficient reason, having outgrown mere authoritarianism. If nothing is clear, if knowledge is not possible, if we don't (can't) even know what knowledge is, have we become mere sophists (if we get paid for teaching) or nihilists (if we don't sell out)? And if knowledge *is* possible, must we be the gadfly (or midwife) to our fellow citizens who are complacent in mere opinion (fideism)? And what is our knowledge about if not about basic things, about what is eternal (God, *or not*) and about human nature (man) and about what we ought to do as *human* beings (about good and evil)? If philosophy is not about what is clear to reason about God and man and good and evil, what is it about?

Philosophy engages in critical thinking about basic things; therefore, philosophy is not neutral about basic things. Some views will not withstand scrutiny.[4] If philosophy concludes one way or another about what is eternal, is that a *religious* conclusion? If so, is critical thinking in public education therefore unconstitutional? Are we then to avoid critical thinking and merely list opinions? Would that still be philosophy? When Socrates exposed false claims to knowledge, those so exposed struck back. Questioning authority (by reason) was said

2. Gangadean, *Philosophical Foundation*, 6-10; Gangadean, *History of Philosophy*, 73-78.

3. Gangadean, *History of Philosophy*, 169-170.

4. Gangadean, *Philosophical Foundation*, xxiii-xxvi; Gangadean, *History of Philosophy*, xxi-xxvii.

to "corrupt the youth." Instead of countering Socrates' reasoning or else acknowledging the conclusions of reason, he was condemned by popular vote, based on widespread prejudice, and executed, not being willing to retract.

If we think out loud (do public philosophy and question illegitimate authority *du jour*) there will be push back. What shall we do? We can deny God (give up his call to think, that is, to be human) or do the expedient thing (leave Athens/the Academy/public life), or, we can seek to dispel popular prejudice (on what is religion and on the wall of separation) while there is still time.[5]

One such popular prejudice concerns the definition of religion. Religious Studies departments are still "working on it." Clergy are still "working on it." Philosophy can/should offer help. So, I make a modest proposal, without irony, because it is truly modest, not a clever innovation, but merely a reminder. Religion is the belief or set of beliefs we use to give meaning to our experience. Both theists and non-theists give meaning to their experience. All who hold any belief about what is eternal, implicitly or explicitly, hold a belief about the existence (or the non-existence) of God. All who hold beliefs about God, affirmative or negative, using these to interpret experience, are therefore equally religious. Consequently, we can readily admit that all are religious. And since basic beliefs affect all other beliefs, then all of life (public and private) is religious.

This does not mean there is no distinction between public and private life. A further distinction about religion is to be made. Some religions are revealed, based on special revelation (on a sacred text or tradition handed down by testimony), and some religions are natural, based on general revelation (what can be known about God and man and good and evil by all men, everywhere, at all times). All human beings have equal access to general revelation. Equal access to knowledge is a natural requirement for public life. Natural religion belongs in public life; revealed religion belongs in private life. The credibility of this application depends on understanding the boundaries of what is public and private, and the (objective) clarity and comprehensiveness of general revelation.

---

5. Gangadean, *History of Philosophy*, 3-9.

Public life in America began with the *Declaration of Independence*, which affirms basic beliefs in epistemology, metaphysics, and ethics. "We hold these truths to be self-evident *(epistemology)*, that all men are created equal *(metaphysics—about God and man)*, that they are endowed by their Creator with certain unalienable Rights *(ethics)* . . ." There is no revealed religion here, only general revelation. The *principle* of beginning with basic beliefs which are clear to all is right; the *claim* that these are the self-evident truths on which all can agree is dubious. The assumptions of Reid's Common Sense philosophy used in the Declaration encounter defeaters by which they lose their *prima facie* warrant. More work is needed, without which the Declaration sinks into a mere assertion of *fideism* and is therefore inadequate for public life, even though it is natural and not revealed religion. Social doctrine based on naturalism or spiritual monism is currently equally fideistic and equally inadequate for public life. We need, in place of fideism and skepticism, what is clear to reason, with proofs to show clarity.[6] This is a job for public philosophy. But given the long history of disputes, is there hope to show what is clear about basic things?[7]

It is not enough therefore to avoid revealed religion in public life by appeal to natural religion. It is necessary to avoid fideism in natural religion as well, beginning with any dogmatism in epistemology. Currently (in Postmodern Academic life) a dogmatic skepticism prevails, as much as dogmatism has prevailed in the past in revealed religion. We face dogmatism in the antinomy of skepticism and fideism. We are at an impasse unless public philosophy can show what is clear to reason as a basis for public life as well as for private life. Public philosophy must use critical thinking to attain knowledge for the benefit of both the individual and society. Discourse in public philosophy must not be hindered by the prejudice that it is establishing a (revealed) religion if it reaches a conclusion in natural religion, or that it is prohibiting anyone in the free private exercise of religion if it critiques any form of fideistic religion (revealed or natural).

Christian philosophers (as persons of wisdom) are committed in principle to special (redemptive) revelation found in the Scriptures of the Old and New Testaments, the written word of God. They understand

---

6. Gangadean, *Philosophical Foundation: A Critical Analysis of Basic Beliefs*, Second Edition.

7. Gangadean, *History of Philosophy: A Critical Analysis of Unresolved Disputes.*

good and evil in basic ways. They understand the difference and relation between general and special revelation (GR and SR): that if there is no clear GR, there can be no (need for) SR;[8] that understanding the claims of GR leads to understanding the necessity for and the existence of SR; that SR presupposes clear GR. They understand that the good for a being is according to the nature of that being, and that the good for man, the image of God, a thinking, sentient being, is the knowledge of God gained through self-knowledge, attained by the full exercise of one's powers.

Understanding good and evil motivates by fear and love the Christian philosophers' search for the *Logos*, the Word of God in its fullness, revealed in every aspect of life.[9] They are willing to prepare themselves through much discussion and historically cumulative insight to glorify God in all that by which he makes himself known, in all his works of creation and providence. They speak prophetically the law of God, deeply structured into human nature[10] to all of life, in Church and State and Family; in economics and law and psychology. Wherever we go, behold, he is there!

He is there in public education. Wisdom stands in the high places and cries out at the city gates to all, both wise and simple. The university is the life of the mind, enabled through dialogue. It is not the silence of the mind in mysticism or skepticism or fideism. Without the life of reason, the university loses its *raison d'être* and fragments into voices muttering from the dust. Without reason as common ground, public education splits into antinomies: if it is public, it must be religiously neutral; but if it is education, interpreting life through basic beliefs, it cannot be religiously neutral. The dilemma can be resolved by recognizing that common ground is not neutral ground. The critical use of reason is not and cannot be neutral with respect to meaning and truth.

Since reason as the laws of thought and the test for meaning is common to all (and to which all have equal access), and since the public square (including public education) must be accessible to all, we must abandon the chimera of religious neutrality for the universality of natural

---

8. *Romans 1:20.*

9. *John 1:1-18.*

10. *Romans 2:15.*

religion, accessible to all through reason as common ground. In place of the dilemma, we can say: If it is public, it must be rational; if it is not rational, it must be (kept) private. Through reason, legitimate authority is upheld. No one is killed/enslaved/oppressed/loses freedom as a rational being. Only those who use brute force rather than reason are restrained. Philosophy has a role to play in public life. The Christian who is a philosopher has a double obligation to lead the way.

All human beings are more or less conscious and consistent in holding their basic beliefs. Philosophy, through critical thinking, must lead the way in becoming more conscious and consistent. All the more so must Christian philosophers lead the way as persons of the Logos, the Word of God in its fullness. Nebuchadnezzar found Daniel ten times wiser than others because he was not taken captive by the worldview of the court astrologers.

All discourse requires common ground, all the more explicitly if it addresses longstanding disputes. If we cannot agree on anything (even that *a* is *a*), how can we begin to think or talk? Common ground is not arbitrary. Philosophy merely points out the necessary conditions which make discourse possible. Reason as the laws of thought makes thought (and therefore discourse) possible. As such, reason is the test for meaning which is necessary for truth (a meaningless utterance is neither true nor false). The laws of thought (identity, non-contradiction, and excluded middle) are most basic and authoritative (they cannot be questioned, but make questioning possible). Reason, objectively, and commitment to reason, subjectively (as a concern for consistency both logical and existential), are the beginnings of common ground.

Thinking by nature is presuppositional; we think of the less basic in light of the more basic: truth in light of meaning; conclusion in light of premises, etc. If we can agree on the more basic, we can agree (settle disputes) on what is less basic. Applied in principle, if any discourse is possible at all, we will hold to the Principle of Clarity as self-evident: that some things are clear; that the basic things are clear; that the basic things (about God and man and good and evil) are clear to reason. Reason, Integrity (concern for consistency), Rational Presuppositionalism (the less basic in light of the more basic), and the Principle of Clarity are elements of common ground, the basis of discourse and public life.

The task of the Christian philosopher then is to make dialogue possible by establishing common ground through which we can find meaning and settle disputes. And, failing that, we can point out that the lack of common ground in the most basic matters is the cause of the death of dialogue. Since dialogue is the source of public life, we must live or die together. Let us live together!

11

———

MODERNITY AND
MORAL LAW

Paper presented at the West Coast
American Academy of Religion Conference

Spring 2006

PART I

M ODERNITY MADE CLAIMS TO KNOW BY REASON. Current as-
sessment by Postmodernism is that the project of Modernity
has failed. This is seen not merely as the failure of particular persons
in the modern period to use reason fully, that is, to use reason critically at the basic level, but as a failure in the project itself. Reason itself
is now thought to be incapable of delivering knowledge, and so, incapable of our deliverance. No metanarrative, it is said, can assume intellectual hegemony. We have only individual narratives maintaining
their hold on us by their rhetorical power.

We have been down this road before. The early Greek philosophers,
seeking explanations beyond the stories about the gods, failed to achieve
an adequate account of reality by reason and so lapsed into sophistical
skepticism.[1] In those troubling times, power was to be achieved not by
rational explanation, but by rhetorical persuasion. Socrates and his disciple Plato sought to build a dam against the floodwaters of skepticism,
but cracks appeared in the dam when Aristotle departed from Plato's

---

1. Gangadean, *History of Philosophy*, 81-85; Gangadean, *Philosophical Foundation*, 71-73.

epistemology.[2] A more sophisticated skepticism then emerged in the Academy, as we find in the Universities today. No universal claim to knowledge can stand. We lapse again into a neo-tribal world of multiculturalism, guarded only by a hermeneutic of suspicion of reason.[3]

The Limits of Reason

Are we to settle back and live in this world as the real world, the final world, or is this multicultural world also a constructed world? Is it always and everywhere only a matter of interpretation? To acknowledge the ubiquity and inescapability of interpretation is to acknowledge the need for meaning seen in the constructive use of reason. Worldviews are constructed upon basic beliefs. What can be said in a worldview is constrained by reason. To acknowledge resistance to the universal claims of worldviews in their current forms is to acknowledge the critical use of reason. To acknowledge change and development within a worldview through the internal and external challenges to meaning is to acknowledge that history has not ended, that reason is still at work and still has work to do in history. Are there deeper levels in the critical use of reason yet to be attained or have we exhausted the use of reason in Modernity? I believe the common ground of reason in its critical and constructive uses is still intact and that current challenges are grounds for hope that a deeper use of reason can be attained. In this paper, I will offer comments on preliminaries needing clarification in the area of moral law and make suggestions of how moral law arises by rational analysis of the fundamental features of human nature.

Before doing so, a brief word about epistemological assumption is in order. In all dialogue, there is a constant need to become more aware of assumptions in operation, to recognize that thinking is presuppositional. Presuppositional thinking means simply that we think of what is less basic in light of what is more basic. We think of truth in light of meaning, experience in light of basic belief, conclusion in light of premises, finite and temporal in light of infinite and eternal, special revelation in light of general revelation, the constructive use of reason in light of the critical use of reason. Presuppositional thinking

---

2. Gangadean, *History of Philosophy*, 87-105.

3. Gangadean, *History of Philosophy*, 171-174, 185-187.

is an alternative to standard empiricism and rationalism, which often fail to recognize assumptions at work. It calls attention to the need for clarification of meaning in the use of basic terms like "truth," "meaning," and "reason." Presuppositional thinking maintains that agreement on what is more basic is necessary for agreement on what is less basic, and that proof and persuasion proceed in a step-by-step process.[4]

Delineating the Concept of The Good

Moral law, which is teleological, stands both in relation to and in contrast with natural law ethical theories which are deontological (virtue ethics), and to hedonic theories which are consequential. It is based upon the concept of the good as the end in itself, chosen for its own sake, the goal or telos. An account therefore is required for teleological ethics to distinguish it from alternatives which have dominated modern ethics and which reach back to ambiguities in earliest ethical theories. Further, it must be considered whether there is one good for all persons and whether the good and the ground of the good are knowable by all persons accounted morally responsible.[5]

There are two lines of thought which converge on the notion of the good. Ethics assumes the fundamental human reality of choice. Choice is made between things varying in value. A hierarchy of values assumes what is of highest value, which is the good, the *summum bonum*. Again, what is chosen is either chosen for its own sake or chosen for the sake of something else. What is chosen for its own sake is an end in itself. What is chosen for the sake of something else is a means to an end and derives its value from its relation to that end. The end in itself (assuming there is one chief end of man) is the good. What are means to the good are virtues. Virtues may be of different kinds—moral, natural, and instrumental. It can be seen by analysis that money is not an end in itself, but is an instrumental virtue. Love, which seeks the good for

---

4. Gangadean, *History of Philosophy*, 19-23; Gangadean, "Paper No. 2: Common Ground: The Necessary Condition for Thought and Discourse," "Paper No. 52: Common Ground (Part III): Rational Presuppositionalism," "Paper No. 95: Rational Presuppositional Apologetics: Prolegomenon," and "Paper No. 96: The Project of Rational Presuppositional Apologetics," in *The Logos Papers*.

5. Gangadean, *Philosophical Foundation*, 165-183.

the other, is a moral virtue. Talent, which is an ability to achieve some aspect of the good, and which is present from birth, is a natural virtue.

The good is of highest value. Believing that one possesses the good is the source of happiness. The good, therefore, is not happiness. Happiness itself is not what is of highest value, or anything that can be sought directly. Happiness depends on and is the effect of a belief regarding what the good is and of possessing what is believed to be the good. When belief about the good changes, happiness also changes. Happiness is not directly connected to virtue apart from the good.

The good is the central concept of ethics. It is the moral absolute. Other ethical concepts are relative, that is, they are to be understood in relation to the good. Virtue is the means to the good, and happiness is the effect of (possessing) the good. Pursuit of the virtues apart from the good, as if they were ends in themselves, is virtue ethics or deontology, not teleology. In deontology, duty is pursued for its own sake, not for the sake of happiness, and not as a means to the good. Kantian ethics is a classic form of deontology. Hedonism uncritically assumes happiness is the good, rather than the effect of possessing what is believed to be the good. It then sinks into an antinomy between individual happiness (ethical egoism) and group happiness (utilitarianism). Much of modern ethics is a contest between deontology and forms of hedonism, based on a failure to distinguish and to relate the good, virtue, and happiness.[6] It is necessary to resolve this question if we are to hope for progress in ethical discourse.

There Is One Good for All Persons

Assuming at this point that the good is distinct from virtue and happiness, many ethical questions would have been resolved, yet some remain. Is there one good for all human beings, and, is this good knowable? The first step in arguing that there is one good for all persons is based on the premise that "good for a being is based on the nature of that being." For example, the good for a horse is based on the nature of a horse; the good for a rabbit is based on the nature of a rabbit; and the good for a human being is based on the nature of a human being. There are assumptions here taken as common ground accepted by all.

---

6. Gangadean, *Philosophical Foundation*, 172-174.

It assumes that there are differences among classes of things and that there is some knowledge of these differences. It assumes there is such a thing as human nature, however it may be conceived, and that all human beings, rich and poor, male and female, Western and non-Western, share alike in this human nature. It further assumes that in the diversity within common human nature, there is a unity, that knowledge, feeling, and will are not in themselves formally or structurally opposed, and that by nature, each person is one (unified) being.

Since the good for a human being is based on human nature and human nature is one in each person, there is one good for each person. Again, since the good for a human being is based on human nature, and human nature is the same in all persons, the good is one and the same in all persons. While there may be agreement that the good is one, there are many views of this good since there are many views of human nature. Naturalists, theists, dualists, and pantheists view human nature differently because they begin with different views of reality. The view of the good, grounded in one's view of human nature, is thus grounded in one's view of what is real. The moral absolute is grounded in the metaphysical absolute. Knowledge of the good, mediated through knowledge of human nature, depends on knowledge of the real. So, the question is raised, "Can we know what is real?"

Modernity and Metaphysics: Is the Real Knowable?

On the topic of metaphysics, Postmodernism has turned away from the project of Modernism. From Descartes to Deism, from Locke to Hume, from Kant to Hegel and Marx, from Kierkegaard to Camus, one can agree that no agreement has been reached. Is it therefore time to give up the project? According to the method of Rational Presuppositionalism, if we agree on what is more basic, we can agree on what is less basic. Have we disagreed on what is more basic only after having made what is more basic explicit? I think not. Therefore, this is not the time to give up the quest, but to look more closely at assumptions.[7]

Descartes' *cogito* as a starting point is not shared by Vedantic Philosophy. His version of the ontological argument, from the concept of God to the existence of God, makes assumptions about concept

---

7. Gangadean, *History of Philosophy: A Critical Analysis of Unresolved Disputes.*

formation as well as the concept of what is the highest being. Thomas Jefferson's *Declaration* about self-evident truths are based on Thomas Reid's Common Sense Realism, which is insufficient as an enduring response to Hume's skepticism. Hume developed the empiricism of Locke to show it ends in utter skepticism—no self, no substance, no causality. Kant's attempt to make a place for science on the one hand and for faith and ethics on the other sought to limit causality to the phenomenal realm. The noumenal realm, without any causal connection whatsoever, internally and externally, became an unknowable, filled differently by Hegel and Marx and others. Kierkegaard's defense of the individual pit faith against universalizing reason. Camus chose the way of the absurd hero over sacrificing the intellect in a leap of faith. Attempts to go further in Analytic and Continental philosophy have not broken the impasse. There is a need to back up to what is more basic.

Only a very little can be done on the question of what is real in the space of this paper. The concept of being is basic, and the concept of eternal being, when talking about the real, is most basic.[8] There are three judgments based on the concept of eternal, by which worldviews can be classified and by which one's view of human nature and the good are determined: All is eternal, in some form or other (naturalism, dualism, pantheism), or only some is eternal (God the Creator), or none is eternal (radical process philosophy—Heraclitus, Buddhism). Only a first step will be attempted here: can it be known if there must be something eternal? The following argument is basic. Disagreement on a basic argument will only bring more basic things to light, things on which the possibility of thought itself rests. Is reason in itself the laws of thought? Can a statement be both true and not true, at the same time and in the same respect? Does reason apply to being as well as to thought? Can there exist something which is both *a* and *non-a*, at the same time and in the same respect? How does this apply to knowing if there must be something eternal, and secondly, to knowing if only some (that is, God) is eternal?

Argument to Show There Must Be Something Eternal:

The contradiction of (i) "some is eternal" is (ii) "none is eternal." Both cannot be true and both cannot be false, at the same time and in the

---

8. Gangadean, *History of Philosophy*, 25-44; Gangadean, *Philosophical Foundation*, 61-68.

same respect. If one is false, the other must be true. "None is eternal" implies a contradiction. If none is eternal, then (iii) all is temporal, which implies (iv) all had a beginning, which implies (v) all came into being, which implies (vi) all came into being from non-being. Since (vi) "being from non-being" is not possible, its original (ii) "none is eternal" is not possible. Therefore, its contradiction (i) "some is eternal" must be true. (vi) would not be implied from (v), if one allows for an infinite regress of creation *ex nihilo*. Historically, this has not been asserted, perhaps for good reason. Or, one may allow totally uncaused events—being from non-being, in which case there would be no meaningful ontological distinction between being and non-being, and no meaningful logical distinction between true and not-true. The possibility of meaningful distinctions regarding the metaphysical notion of "being" ends, and with it, the possibility of meaningful distinctions in thought ends. All possibility of meaning ends.

So far, I have argued for three basic points. 1) There is a distinction and a relation between the good, virtue, and happiness. 2) The good is based on human nature and there is one good for all human beings. 3) One's view of the good and of human nature is based on one's view of what is real/eternal, and we can know by reason that there must be something eternal. To argue from the concept of an eternal being to the existence of an eternal being is a modest, and hopefully, sound form of the ontological argument. To show some is eternal does not prove that God exists. One would have to show only some is eternal, that is, some is eternal and some is not eternal, understanding that what is eternal would bring into existence or create what is not eternal, hence, God the Creator.

Moral Law 1: The Good and God

If God is creator of human nature, then God is the determiner of good and evil for man since good (and evil) is based on human nature. To show only some is eternal, one would have to show that the material world exists, and that matter is not eternal; that the soul exists, and that the soul is not eternal. The attempt to show this is not part of this paper.[9] But if it were shown, the first moral law, requiring a recognition of human nature, would be established and would be stated simply as follows: God, as creator of human nature, is the determiner of good and evil for man. This law would be opposed to a number of things: it would be opposed to all forms of non-theism, to both skepticism and fideism, to all forms of ethics which historically has been based on human autonomy—that human beings apart from God determine good and evil, and it would be opposed to both heteronomy and positivism (divine command theory). The inherent consequence of an act according to or against one's rational nature, by observing or not observing what is clear about the good and God, would be the beginning of meaningful or meaningless existence.

Allowing for now that one could get this far, how much further could we get? Could we get to a moral law which is clear (because it is based on human nature), comprehensive (applying to all expressions of that nature in choice), and critical (since the consequence of acting according to or against human nature is a matter of (spiritual) life or death)? The second half of this paper will sketch how moral concepts are grounded in human nature and how moral judgments or moral laws are derived from the analysis of these moral concepts. In all, I will sketch nine additional moral laws based on the following moral concepts: thinking and presupposition, integrity and knowledge, work and hope, authority and insight, human dignity and rationality, sex and love, value and talent, truth and justice, and suffering and the good.

PART II

Moral Law 2: Thinking and Presupposition

By nature we think. And by nature, we think of basic concepts which apply to the nature of God. Thinking by nature is presuppositional: we think of the less basic in light of the more basic. We think of the finite and the infinite, and the temporal and the eternal. If we act according to the nature of thought, we should think of the less basic—the

---

9. Gangadean, *Philosophical Foundation*, 71-161; Gangadean, *History of Philosophy*, 47-58; Gangadean, *The Westminster Catechisms*. See LCQ. 2; Gangadean, "Paper No. 3: The Principle of Clarity, Rational Presuppositionalism, and Proof" and "Paper No. 93: The Logic of Apologetics: The Goal, the Method, the Content," in *The Logos Papers*.

finite and temporal—in light of the more basic—the infinite and eternal. We should think of finite man in light of the infinite God (man as the image of God), and not think of the infinite God in light of finite man (God as the image of man). Building upon the existence of God from moral law 1, this moral law is applied to divisions among theists in how the divine nature is conceived. Specifically, it applies to conceptions of the divine justice and goodness, which divide deists from theists and which divide the historic forms of theism—Judaism, Christianity, and Islam. It also applies to divisions within historic forms of Western Christianity. There are a few questions which are to be addressed here: Is infinite goodness compatible with natural evil in the original creation? Is redemptive revelation in theism necessary to understand how God can be both just and merciful at the same time? Are popular forms of understanding divine justice (as future and imposed vs. present and inherent) compatible with infinite justice?[10]

Moral Law 3: Integrity and Knowledge

There is a natural unity in our being and there is a natural concern for consistency to maintain the unity of our being. This concern for consistency in all we think and say and do is integrity. By nature, then, we should have integrity. Integrity is necessary and sufficient for knowledge. Self-examination and at least a beginning measure of discipline are necessary for integrity. Lack of integrity is hypocrisy, which finds ways to overlook one's own inconsistencies and makes correction in thought and life impossible.[11]

Moral Law 4: Work and Hope

By nature we must work. To bring into being and to sustain in being requires work. But work is not an end in itself. It is a means to the end in itself, which is the good. If the good is understood, work as a means to the good will be understood. Several formal characteristics of the good (for example, comprehensive, inexhaustible, fulfilling) show that achieving the good requires the cumulative work of mankind through history. Hope as certainty that the good will be achieved,

---

10. Gangadean, *Philosophical Foundation*, 195-197.

11. Gangadean, *Philosophical Foundation*, 199-205.

given the reality of moral and natural evil, requires understanding the nature of things. The existence of Infinite Goodness guarantees that the good will be achieved. True hope is opposed to all forms of false hope (that the good can be attained without work), and to no hope (that work cannot serve to achieve the good). We should work for the good with true hope.[12]

Moral Law 5: Authority and Insight

We are born ignorant and need to be taught the good and the means to the good. Authority in teaching is based on insight into the good and the means to the good. Authority, therefore, is rational, not personal, based on insight, not might, and insight is historically cumulative, from generation to generation. Authority, wherever it occurs, must be questioned to see if it has insight. Authority based on insight must be honored; authority without insight must be changed where possible. This applies first to principles of authority. The highest form of authority is self-attesting; it cannot be questioned because it makes questioning possible. Testimony (divine or human) and experience (inner or outer) are not self-attesting; their meaning is understood and analyzed by reason. Persons without insight should not be in positions of authority, and change is to be made where possible, whether in church, in state, in family, in education, or in business. Jurisdiction of an institution is limited to its area of competence. No institution is total, over all others in authority, but each institution is equally under the moral law according to its form and function.[13]

Moral Law 6: Human Dignity and Rationality

We are born human. Therefore, we are to be treated as humans, differently than animals. Human dignity consists in the capacity to understand. Human society is a society of rational beings. Freedom and responsibility in every aspect of social life depends on the degree of the exercise of this capacity. To affirm human dignity is to affirm the freedom and responsibility of human beings for the use of reason. It requires resolving differences rationally, at the basic level where they

---

12. Gangadean, *Philosophical Foundation*, 207-219.

13. Gangadean, *Philosophical Foundation*, 221-229.

arise, rather than by emotional manipulation or by the use of force. Intellectual, psychological, economic, ethnic, and gender differences are
real, but are built upon and do not override our common humanity.
Circumstances of fortune or misfortune cannot mitigate our humanity, but only reaffirm deeper levels of one's humanity. While denial of
one's own dignity, and consequently that of others, may separate one
from human society, human dignity is ineradicable and hence inalienable. We are human by nature and can never cease being human.[14]

Moral Law 7: Sex and Love

We are born of a sexual union of one man and one woman. Sex is a
sign and seal of love. Love seeks the good for and with others. The
physical union is not to be separated from the spiritual union. There
is a natural boundary as to what constitutes a physical union. Sex and
love together constitute a full union of persons. The sign of sex without the reality of love is emptied of significance. It dehumanizes persons and becomes a source of contempt. A full union of one man and
one woman is a monogamous and lasting relationship, which is marriage. Since the good is achieved by and for persons, love in marriage
is therefore the source of the origin of our being and the nurture of
our being for the good. As a social institution, designed to protect and
promote the common good, marriage is to protect and promote the
natural connection between the origin and the nurture of human beings. To ensure the connection between sex and love and marriage and
the good, there is a social order for entering into marriage, designed to
protect marriage and to promote the good.[15]

Moral Law 8: Value and Talent

As human beings, we naturally value things and reveal what we value
by our choices. No one values all things alike. Value is a function of
supply and demand. Demand is a function of our view of the good,
and supply is a function of talent. Talent is an ability to achieve some
aspect of the good. Talent is in each, grounded in the uniqueness of
our personality, originating from the origin of one's being at birth. It

---

14. Gangadean, *Philosophical Foundation*, 231-243.

15. Gangadean, *Philosophical Foundation*, 245-254.

is thus given to each, for all. It is known by interest and ability and developed by the cumulative nurture of others as well as by one's own efforts. It is developed fully only in the vision of the good, and when fully developed, it creates forms by which to express its function. One is therefore to develop one's talent, in pursuit of the good, to create what is of lasting value, in service to others. In the creativity of talent, there is not a practically finite supply. Social policies are to promote, not to hinder, development of talent. Stewardship of talent and the resulting increase of supply are opposed to absolute ownership of value by man, either by the individual or by society. As one has received from the commonwealth, one is to contribute to the commonwealth. Use of one's talent in pursuit of the good increases the richness of life for all.[16]

Moral Law 9: Truth and Justice

We are born equal. In justice, equals are to be treated equally, all things considered. Ontological justice is inherent in the nature of things. Social justice requires human action and is first distributive, then contractual, and finally retributive. Truth is necessary and sufficient for justice in a court of law. Full social justice must both correct and prevent injustice. Knowing and speaking the whole truth is necessary for full social justice. Some worldviews fail to recognize human equality and to provide equal opportunity. At the same time, some worldviews fail to encourage the use of opportunities which are available. To correct and prevent injustice, one must know and speak the relevant truth regarding worldview assumptions which permit or support injustice. In one's obligation to do justice, there is an obligation to know the truth about basic things which are clear. Ignorance is not excusable, and mere belief without knowledge nullifies one's testimony concerning the truth. Justice based on truth requires freedom of speech as a right to rational discourse and equality of access to the public forum. There is no right to privacy for decisions affecting public affairs, but there is a right, as well as an obligation, to privacy for what is private.[17]

---

16. Gangadean, *Philosophical Foundation*, 255-265.

17. Gangadean, *Philosophical Foundation*, 267-275.

Moral Law 10: Suffering and the Good

We are born changeable. We can change from true to false beliefs concerning the good. Suffering arises when we believe we cannot possess what we falsely consider to be the good. Given a misconceived notion of the real, we will fail to understand moral evil and its consequence, as well as natural evil in relation to moral evil. A false view of the good can bring about envy, or cynicism, or indifference, or resentment, or depression, or self-indulgence, or resignation, or any combination of these. Where natural evil is seen as a call back from moral evil, where suffering is seen as a call to stop and think deeply about basic things, suffering is not considered worthless. And where moral evil is seen to be made to serve the good, it can be said that all things work together for good.[18]

---

18. Gangadean, *Philosophical Foundation*, 277-283.

———

12

THE PROBLEM OF EVIL

An Ironic Solution

Paper presented at the C. S. Lewis Conference

2005

INTRODUCTION AND SUMMARY

O F ALL PROBLEMS, THE PROBLEM OF EVIL challenges us most pro-
foundly and most universally. If God is all good and all powerful, why is there evil? Do the intellectual leaders of our culture have
an answer? Does the Christian theist in the academy have an answer?
The answers given so far have been less than satisfactory, or insufficient. God cannot be Creator and be morally indifferent (Hume). Free
will may be necessary to explain evil, but free will is not sufficient to
explain it. There need not be moral (or natural) evil in order to pass
from innocence to virtue (Hick). To show that the reality of evil does
not contradict the power and goodness of God (Plantinga) still leaves
the question unanswered. There is a need to go further.[1]

There are two aspects to the problem of evil—natural evil and moral
evil. In this paper, I grant the assumption of the question regarding natural evil—natural evil is not necessary in creation. It was not present
originally in the creation. Before responding to the question of moral
evil, I offer a basic definition of good and evil, with explanation, illus-
tration, and application, giving attention to the assumptions of this
definition. I argue from this particular understanding of good and evil

---

1. Gangadean, *Philosophical Foundation*, 145-161.

that moral evil serves the good and that natural evil is imposed as a final call back from moral evil. If this definition is warranted, then the problem of evil must be reformulated, in a way that is ironic.

NATURAL EVIL IS NOT ORIGINAL; IT IS IMPOSED

Natural evil is not original. By natural evil is meant suffering that comes upon us apart from our own action. It consists of toil and strife, and old age, sickness, and death. These three become intensified in war, famine, and plague. They all become focused in physical death. In saying that natural evil is not original, we are saying that physical death is not original. God created the world without physical death. If God is all powerful, he could do so. If he is all good, he would do so. If he could and would, then he must have done so. And if he must have done so, then he did. While the original goodness of creation is taught in historic, biblical theism, this knowledge is accessible from general revelation. It is the intuition present in the common formulation of the problem of evil: If God is all good and all powerful, why is there evil? In the beginning, there was no evil. For any thoughtful person, natural evil requires an explanation.

Since natural evil is not inherent in our actions, it is not inherent in moral evil. There is no intrinsic connection between moral evil and physical death. As such, natural evil is something imposed upon man. If it were imposed as punishment for moral evil, without intrinsic connection to moral evil, it would be arbitrary. Thus, natural evil is not original nor inherent, but imposed; and it is imposed for a sufficient reason, but not as punishment. Since natural evil is imposed because of moral evil, the reason for its imposition will depend on our understanding of moral evil. We will come back to the reason for natural evil after thinking further about moral evil.

GOOD AND EVIL: Defined and Explained

Why is there moral evil? Given objections to past answers, there is need for a clearer understanding of good and evil. The problem of evil itself gives a point of entry into this understanding. The problem of evil is a problem for man as a rational being. The problem of evil is not practical, but intellectual. The concern is not to remove it, but to explain it, given certain other beliefs. The question is: "Why is there evil?"— not "How can it be removed?" Making sense of the world is primary over changing the world. Good and evil must be understood in the context of man as a rational being.

We should not be surprised, in thinking about the need to define more clearly our understanding of good and evil, that the first manifestation of evil is in our misunderstanding of good and evil itself. Evil reverses the order of things, and calls good evil and evil good. And it also should not come as a surprise that, in the long struggle between good and evil, progress can be made in understanding good and evil.

In general, it must be said that good for a being is based on, or is according to, the nature of that being. For example, good for a horse is according to the nature of a horse; good for a rabbit is according to the nature of a rabbit; and, good for man is according to the nature of man. Good for man as a rational being is the use of reason to the fullest. By reason, in its most basic sense, is meant the laws of thought (the law of identity, non-contradiction, and excluded middle.) Reason is used to understand the nature of things. Since the natures of things created reveal the nature of God, good for man is the knowledge of God. This view of good for man assumes that the existence and nature of God are clearly revealed in the things created.

Moral evil, on the other hand, is an act that is contrary to the nature of man. It is the failure to use reason to understand the nature of things, and therefore the failure to know God. This view of evil assumes that it is clear that God exists. (It also assumes that knowledge is sufficient for morality, that knowing the truth sets us free.) The failure to know God can be described as unbelief. If there were no clear general revelation regarding the existence and nature of God, there would be no inexcusability for unbelief and for the actions that flow from this unbelief. What is clear is objectively clear to reason, so that one must neglect, avoid, resist, or deny reason to avoid what is clear. What is clear is that something must be eternal and that only some (God) is eternal. All else is temporal, that is, created. From the idea of God as Creator arises understanding of other attributes of the divine nature.

There are inherent consequences of the failure to use reason to see what is clear. Since reason is the source of understanding meaning, the failure to use reason empties one's life of meaning. With meaninglessness comes boredom, and with meaninglessness and boredom comes guilt. These three are inseparable and together constitute the condition of spiritual death, which corresponds in degree to the failure to know what is clear about God. Lack of meaning can be seen when basic terms lack meaning for a person upon a little critical analysis. Here, words are used with little understanding of their meaning, for example, good and evil, life and death, heaven and hell, love and law. Failure to see what is clear is manifest when objections to what is clear cannot be answered.

St. Paul's exposition of the gospel in his letter to the Romans begins by explaining the reality of evil—sin and death—in light of clarity and inexcusability.[2] The eternal power and divine nature are clearly revealed so that men are without excuse for unbelief. The moral law too is written on the hearts of all men, increasing inexcusability. Paul cites the words of the psalmist to sum up the human condition without God: no one seeks God; no one understands; no one is righteous. This is the original sin, in which all follow. To the degree one fails to see what is clear, to that degree the root of evil remains in us. If one has truly come to see what is clear, one should be able to answer objections to what is clear. All come short of knowing God. We differ only in degree of understanding and misunderstanding and in which of the two (understanding or misunderstanding) is more basic.

THE PROBLEM ILLUSTRATED:
The Parable of the Prodigal Son

Jesus spoke to men in parables concerning good and evil. The problem of evil can be illustrated in the parable of the prodigal son spoken by him.

> There was a man who had two sons. The younger one said to his father, 'Father, give me my share of the estate.' So he divided his property between them.
> Not long after that, the younger son got together all he had, set off

---

2. In this work, see the essay: "Romans 1: The Biblical Doctrine of Clarity and Inexcusability"

for a distant country and there squandered his wealth in wild living. After he had spent everything, there was a severe famine in that whole country, and he began to be in need. So he went and hired himself out to a citizen of that country, who sent him to his fields to feed pigs. He longed to fill his stomach with the pods that the pigs were eating, but no one gave him anything.

When he came to his senses, he said, 'How many of my father's hired men have food to spare, and here I am starving to death. I will set out and go back to my father and say to him: Father, I have sinned against heaven and against you. I am no longer worthy to be called your son; make me like one of your hired men.' So he got up and went to his father.

But while he was still a long way off, his father saw him and was filled with compassion for him; he ran to his son, threw his arms around him and kissed him.

The son said to him, 'Father, I have sinned against heaven and against you. I am no longer worthy to be called your son.'

But the father said to his servants, 'Quick! Bring the best robe and put it on him. Put a ring on his finger and sandals on his feet. Bring the fattened calf and kill it. Let's have a feast and celebrate. This son of mine was dead and is alive again; he was lost and is found.' So they began to celebrate.[3] (Here, I omit the account of the older brother.)

The younger son was in unbelief regarding his father's teaching. His unbelief was without excuse. His evil (unbelief) served to obscure to him the revelation of his father's love; he saw it every day without understanding it, so he longed for something else. His evil (unbelief) also served to deepen the revelation of his father's love. He experienced the loss of everything in departing from his father, and he experienced forgiveness and restoration in his return to his father.

Application 1: Moral Evil Serves the Good

Some implications follow from this understanding of good and evil. If evil (unbelief) is removed abruptly, the revelation will not be deepened; but if evil (unbelief) is not removed at all, the revelation will not be seen. The solution is to remove evil, but gradually. Every form of

---

3. *Luke 15:11-24.*

unbelief and every degree of admixture of belief with unbelief must be allowed to come to expression in world history. Entire civilizations and cultures have manifested various forms of unbelief, and many have perished in unbelief. Yet unbelief is gradually being removed, and, in the conflict with belief, unbelief will eventually be fully removed. Through an age-long and agonizing conflict, good will gradually overcome evil. Every thought raised up against the knowledge of God will be taken captive. There will come a time, at the end of the conflict, when the earth will be full of the knowledge of God as the waters cover the sea. So, moral evil will be made to serve the good.

Application 2: Natural Evil Is a Final Call Back from Moral Evil

If moral evil is made to serve the good, why is there natural evil? Natural evil is imposed by God because of moral evil. But it is not punishment. It is a call back from moral evil. It is not the only call back, nor the first call back. There is the inner call back of conscience in the feeling of shame. There is the external call back to self-examination through the voice of others. Natural evil is the last, and final, call back. It assumes resistance to earlier call-backs. It serves to restrain, recall from, and remove moral evil. It is a call to stop and think, to overcome our disposition to neglect, avoid, resist, and deny reason in the presence of what is clear about God. Evil (unbelief) begins with neglect (not diligently seeking to know God, and the consequent failure to understand). But it is complicated by avoidance (self-deception regarding our seeking to know), and resistance (self-justification regarding our failure to know.) It ends with denying reason itself (shutting one's eyes) to avoid seeing God. It is these added barriers of self-deception and self-justification which must be penetrated by natural evil. Physical death, as a visible sign of spiritual death, is the final call to stop and think. Recognizing one's creaturely dependence in death is opposed to all self-sufficiency and pride. As a call back from moral evil, natural evil assumes the promise of redemption given by special revelation.

ASSUMPTIONS AND REFORMULATION:
The Ironic Solution

The assumptions of this solution to the problem of evil should be made plain: that if there is no clarity, then there is no inexcusability and no morality; that there is a clear general revelation concerning the existence and nature of God—that this clarity can actually be demonstrated; that there is no other way to deepen the revelation of the divine nature (justice and mercy)—that no book version of history or near substitute for experience can deepen it; that knowledge of God (not virtue or happiness) is the good. This last assumption is not only to be resolved abstractly, but existentially. To those who come to this knowledge through suffering, the objection to suffering ceases. Job's experience exemplifies this.[4]

The original problem of evil was understood as saying: because of all the evil in the world, I don't see how it is reasonable to say there is an all good and all powerful God. Given the nature of evil, which reverses the order of things, the problem of evil must now be reformulated: because of all the moral evil in me, I fail to understand good and evil: how evil serves the good, and how natural evil is a call back from moral evil. Because of my failure to use reason, because I have shut my eyes, I cannot see what is clear.

---

4. Surrendra Gangadean, *The Book of Job: Deepening the Revelation of God's Glory for All Time—An Ironic Theodicy* (Phoenix: Logos Papers Press, 2024).

13

ON THE NECESSITY FOR
NATURAL THEOLOGY

Paper delivered at the regional Society for Christian
Philosophy Conference, Grand Canyon University

Spring 2004

ABSTRACT

NATURAL THEOLOGY ATTEMPTS TO SHOW what can be known of God and man and good and evil from general revelation. Skepticism maintains this knowledge is not possible and fideism maintains that proof is not necessary. The failure of skepticism and fideism to preserve meaning makes natural theology necessary. In addition, historic Christian belief in creation–fall–redemption requires natural theology in order to be meaningfully believed. To show what is clear (about God) from general revelation requires a clearer understanding of reason and presuppositional thinking. A program of natural theology to engage internal and external objections to Christian theism is offered.

INTRODUCTION

Natural theology attempts to show what can be known of God and man and good and evil from general revelation. Skepticism in general maintains knowledge is not possible, hence natural theology is not possible. Fideism in general maintains that proof for one's first principles is not necessary, hence natural theology is not necessary. Before engaging in its program, natural theology must show why proof is necessary and how knowledge is possible. The possibility, necessity, and extent of the knowledge of God become more evident in historic Christian theism, which is based on the over-arching and under-girding themes of creation–fall–redemption.

SKEPTICISM

In the history of skepticism, from ancient to contemporary, the basis of skepticism has shifted. At times, it is grounded metaphysically in various formulations of the problem of the one and the many. At other times, it is grounded epistemologically in variations of empiricism and rationalism. Most recently, it has been grounded in hermeneutics, in issues related to interpreting experience and constructing worldviews. From time to time, it has been grounded in the nature of knowledge itself, whether knowledge is discursive, cognitive, and propositional, or whether it is relational, mystical, and a matter of encounter.

Metaphysical skepticism denies there is an object of knowledge. In the ancient world, this was done in two ways: either all is flux (becoming without being—Heraclitus, or all is *dukkha*, dependently co-arising—Buddhism), or all is permanent (being without becoming—Parmenides, or all is one, beyond all dualities—Shankara's *Advaita*). Where all is permanent, change is an illusion (*maya*). Where all is change, permanence is an illusion (no object, no self). Since knowledge of the world involves permanence and change (some change in permanence and some permanence in change), on the assumption that all is one (either change or permanence), knowledge is not possible. The dualism of Plato and Aristotle attempted to address the problem of permanence and change, but left significant problems unresolved.[1]

Epistemological skepticism reckons with the limits of experience and reason as they have been used in the modern period (Enlightenment). Experience may come through ordinary sense experience (common sense), or sense experience systematically pursued (science), or through inner experience (intuition). Ordinary experience gives appearance and not reality (Is the ocean blue? Does the sun rise?). Furthermore, through sense experience we cannot know there is an external world or material substance (Berkeley), nor causality or a self as

---

1. Gangadean, *History of Philosophy*, 87-105.

perceiver (Hume). Science does not attempt to show that the external world exists, or that all is matter, or that matter is eternal. Naturalism is the methodological assumption of science and empiricism, held on pragmatic grounds, with a tentativeness which disinvites philosophical criticism. Intuition admits of no corrective process. But neither are the deliverances of intuition self-certifying. Truth (or goodness) is not always connected with beauty, and, what is called enlightenment experience (nirvana, *samadhi*) becomes inescapably connected with interpretations which are irreconcilable.

Methodological doubt of ordinary (or extra-ordinary) experience led Descartes to what he took to be the first and indubitable truth of reason ("I think, therefore I am"), upon which he attempted to erect a superstructure of knowledge (foundationalism). But the *cogito* became doubted in light of monism (absolute idealism) along with the mind/body and subject/object distinctions. The existence of the self is no more self-evident than the existence of God ("We hold these truths to be self-evident, that all men are created equal"). Furthermore, the traditional proofs for the existence of God (ontological, cosmological, and teleological), taken separately, were found problematic at least, over a period of time. And reason seemed to present us with equally coherent and incommensurable worlds (Leibniz and Spinoza). Kant's synthesis of sense experience and reason left the world beyond appearance (the noumenal world) devoid of cognizable content and open to the speculation which followed. Reason, with its tendency to universalize, was seen as incapable of grasping the particulars of the real world (Nietzsche), or the concrete situation in which all exists (Kierkegaard).

Far from reason being a transcendent standard which gives knowledge of an objective world in which we exist, hermeneutical skepticism holds that reason (as well as science) is itself subject to the situation in which we find ourselves. We are always historically situated and cannot transcend our history. The world we live in is constructed on the basis of our identities and language grounded in our social context. There is no objective world in itself (anti-realism). The canons of rationality differ from one worldview to another. All is interpretation (Nietzsche). We are bound in a hermeneutical circle. Claims to objectivity are attempts to privilege one's own position for advantage over others. It is inevitably repressive of the other, in the name of common standard, defined by one's own meta-narrative. Since all things are understood within the confines of one's meta-narrative, one must recognize in-commensurability between worldviews, the reality of alterity, and the ultimacy of difference. This recognition is said to be the virtue of tolerance. Hermeneutical skepticism says our beliefs are inescapably without proof and should be recognized as such. Fideism acquiesces to this.

FIDEISM

Fideism applies to all interpretive belief systems which make no attempt to prove their first principles, especially in light of existing challenges to them. It applies to theism as well as to anti-theism, to science as well as to philosophy, to realism as well as to anti-realism, to foundationalism as well as to anti-foundationalism. It occurs whenever reasons given are not sufficient to rationally exclude competing views. While fideism applies to a wide range of views, most discussions have focused on theistic fideism, particularly on Christian fideism. Christians have attempted to give reasons for their beliefs, but, in light of the challenges of skepticism, Christian fideism has responded by maintaining either reason (proof) is not necessary for belief, or not sufficient for belief or not called for by Scripture.

That reason (proof) is not necessary for belief in God seems obvious, since many believe without proof. Many maintain that faith, by definition, is not sight (proof) and many have no idea of the proofs as they have been given historically. Some have argued that reason is not necessary since belief in God is properly basic, like belief in the external world, for which proof seems irrelevant. Properly basic beliefs occur naturally under certain conditions if one's cognitive faculties are properly functioning. Natural belief in God is warranted, without proof, although warrant may be weakened in the presence of objections if they are unanswered (Plantinga). Again, reason is said to be unnecessary for faith since faith is said to precede understanding and that we must believe in order that we might understand. Having first believed, faith then seeks to understand (Augustine). And again, reason is said to be unnecessary since faith is by grace and not a work of human reason (Barth).

Furthermore, reason is said to be insufficient for faith. The proofs do not seem to persuade most people to believe, nor does knowing move someone to act. People are said to know, deep down, the truth of

God's existence and yet suppress this truth, and to know what is right and yet do what is wrong. Reason is said to be finite and incapable of discovering or apprehending the mysteries of the faith, which remain paradoxes to the intellect, even after they are made known by revelation. If some are able to come to the truth of first things through dialectic, this is not available to most (Plato's Allegory of the Cave), and is accessible only to few minds which have been trained in metaphysics (Aquinas). Faith is said to be inaccessible to reason. The individual before God, in his unique particularity (Abraham called to sacrifice Isaac), has no guidance possible from reason, which deals in universals. Faith is a leap beyond reason (Kierkegaard). Reason is said to be fallen and fallible and its use, apart from revelation, leads man away from God. Reason is said to be conditioned by pre-theoretical commitments so that all proofs are in the end circular, reflecting one's presupposition. And lastly, reason itself is said to be not sufficient for justification, but is thought to itself require justification, which can be found only in God, specifically, in the Triune God of the Bible (Van Til/Bahnsen).

There are reasons offered for fideism based on appeal to Scripture. There are no proofs given in Scripture for the existence of God, so it is thought that no proof is necessary. This view assumes that everything needed by the believer is expressly given in Scripture, and in a form that does not require good and necessary consequences. This view affirms the sole authority of Scripture (*Sola Scriptura*) over against all other authorities, including reason and general revelation, not merely over all other appeals to special revelation and to persons as authorities. It is pointed out that there are warnings raised in Scripture against the wisdom of this world, and against vain philosophy (simpliciter). There is said to be in Scripture an exaltation of proclamation of things foolish in the eyes of the world, and this is understood in a way that excludes reasoning and persuasion. Furthermore, the fullness of blessing is said to be reserved for those faithful in this life who will, in life after death, see God face to face (beatific vision). The highest good, therefore, does not require and is not accessible to the life of reason.

THE NECESSITY FOR NATURAL THEOLOGY

One response to the pressing weight of skepticism and fideism is to make the point that the knowledge of God (and of the world) is not discursive, to be attained by reason and inference. It is more akin to knowledge by experience through acquaintance or encounter. It cannot be expressed in words or communicated to another through words. One must have the experience. This knowledge is non-cognitive (not a matter of true or false), and non-propositional (not to be argued for or against). It is immediate, direct, personal, relational, and mystical, like an embrace.

While it is true enough that thinking is not the same as or a substitute for experience, it is equally the case that experience is not the same as or a substitute for thinking. They are two distinct but inseparable aspects of human knowledge. We don't simply experience, but "experience as." An embrace has significance in light of assumptions about the other in the embrace, assumptions not derived from the experience itself, assumptions of which we may become more conscious and critical and perhaps change, so that the significance of the embrace may change or deepen over time in one and the same person. No experience is meaningful without interpretation. Any appeal to experience stripped of interpretation becomes meaningless. The shift to non-cognitivism in order to possess knowledge, without engaging with the objections of skepticism and fideism, and without engaging in natural theology, is in vain, since experience devoid of meaning is empty. A different strategy is required which can show the inadequacy of both skepticism and fideism, even as non-cognitivism is inadequate.

Skepticism has value. Its value is negative. Its lasting value is that it will not let fideism pass without identifying itself as such. Skepticism is aware of the arbitrariness of fideism when it claims to be objective and exclusive, and finds that arbitrariness self-destructive. But skepticism reaches an over-extended conclusion (that no knowledge is possible) by assuming it has considered all relevant assumptions. There are assumptions which skepticism has not considered. There are alternatives to the assumption of monism (either nothing is eternal or all is eternal). There are alternatives to ontological dualism (both matter and spirit are eternal). Theism, the view that only some (God the Creator) is eternal is an alternative to both monism and dualism. There are alternatives to rationalism and to empiricism and to the synthesis of the two, which recognize what is uncritically assumed in both. There are alternatives to science (pure facts without interpretation) and deconstruction (pure interpretation without facts). One can identify and distinguish pure experience/fact (for example, the embrace) from its significance, given by interpretation. If there were no alternatives to the assumptions it has considered, then skepticism would be granted. But if it were granted, and carried out consistently, skepticism would lead to nihilism, the destruction of all meaning by the destruction of all distinctions. Qualified skepticism ("this view is incoherent") is possible; total skepticism ("all views are incoherent") becomes self-referentially absurd.

Fideism, too, has value, and its value is positive. It recognizes the impossibility of nihilism to which skepticism leads, and the inadequacy of pragmatism to overcome self-conscious nihilism. Positions of fideism purport to offer its adherents a meaningful vision of the world. A more self-conscious fideism maintains its right to exist by an exclusivist claim to truth and meaning. But fideism wishes to make some distinction between faith and understanding. In the motto "faith seeking understanding," it is assumed that one can believe more than one understands. If it were possible to believe more than one understands, then one could believe what one did not understand. To open a gap between believing p to be true and understanding p, is to affirm p while emptying p of meaning. I believe p as far as I understand p. There is more to understand of p, and I seek to understand more of p, but I do not and cannot believe more than I understand. If "faith seeking understanding" means "understanding seeking more understanding," there is nothing controversial here. By faith, I believe p to be true; by reason, I understand the meaning of p. As truth is inseparable from meaning, so faith is inseparable from reason. It is not the case that faith is static and understanding grows in "faith seeking understanding." Faith grows as understanding grows; faith is tested as understanding is tested.

Faith, in the theistic sense, is directed to what is invisible. Faith is contrasted with sight, which is directed to the visible, but it is not contrasted with understanding, which is directed to what is invisible. Faith in Christian theism is being sure of what is hoped for and certain of what is not seen.[2] Since faith is inseparable from understanding, the certainty of faith is the certainty of understanding. The certainty of understanding in faith is not different from the certainty of understanding

---

2. *Hebrews 11.*

a proof for what is unseen. Fideism, therefore, insofar as it separates faith and understanding, empties faith of meaning and nullifies its purpose, which is to offer its adherents a meaningful vision of the world. But insofar as it does not separate faith and understanding, it has the certainty of proof in its understanding. So true faith, contrary to fideism, is inseparable from reason, understanding, certainty, and proof. Faith, without reason and proof, that is, fideism, is empty of meaning. Fideism fails in the same way that skepticism fails. Both fail to preserve meaning. Both failures make natural theology necessary.

There is a third set of reasons why natural theology is necessary. Historic Christianity is structured on the theme of creation–fall–redemption. The implications of each of these, when understood, requires natural theology.

1) Historic Christianity assumes the reality of sin. Since sin is a reality in Christianity, Christianity must give some account of sin. Unbelief is regarded as root sin. Unbelief is inexcusable because there is a clear general revelation of the existence and nature of God in the creation. "Since the creation of the world God's invisible qualities—his eternal power and divine nature—have been clearly seen, being understood from what is made, so that men are without excuse."[3] Men are without excuse for unbelief of what is clear. If there is no clarity of general revelation for which one is held accountable, there can be no sin. But if there is clarity of general revelation, then presumably one should be able to see what is clear. And since it is clear, one should be able to show what is clear, especially over against objections which would deny clarity. To see what is clear is to see why the denial of clarity fails. Christian theists, believing in the reality of sin, should be able to show what is clear. To do so would be to do natural theology.

2) Historic Christianity not only affirms the reality of sin, but it affirms divine judgment on sin. The wages of sin is death.[4] This death is present in unbelief in this life and in the life to come. This death is spiritual and is inherent in unbelief. It is the meaninglessness that is inherent in the failure to see what is clear at the most basic level of all of one's understanding. This death is also said to be everlasting. Everlasting death is maximal consequence. Maximal consequence requires

---

3. *Romans 1:20.*

4. *Romans 6:23.*

maximal inexcusability, which in turn requires maximal clarity. The contradiction of what is maximally clear is not logically possible. Maximal clarity can be avoided only by ceasing to think, that is, to give up or to deny reason itself. Natural theology in Christian theism must show maximal clarity.

3) Historic Christianity affirms redemption. Christ is the Lamb of God who takes away the sin of the world. If sense is to be made of the death of Christ by which sin and death are removed, then clarity and inexcusability must be shown by natural theology.

4) Historic Christianity has been exclusivist, believing that redemption is through Christ alone. It also believes that Christ's redemption is for all peoples. If people are called away from competing worldviews to the Christian worldview, reasons for the truth of its exclusive claims which do not beg the question must be given. This requires natural theology.

5) Historic Christianity holds up the highest good and the goal of life as the knowledge of God. Creation and history reveal God. Through an age-long and agonizing spiritual war, good will overcome evil. The earth shall be full of the knowledge of God as the waters cover the sea. If God's justice and mercy are to be understood, the inexcusability of unbelief must be understood. If we do not understand clarity, then we cannot understand inexcusability. But if we understand clarity, then we can show clarity. This is the work of natural theology.

WHAT IS REASON?

Some clarification in the understanding of reason is necessary in order to show more specifically how knowledge is possible. There are different senses of reason that must be kept clearly in mind whenever the term "reason" and its derivatives are used. There is first, reason in itself, to be distinguished from reason in its use and reason in us. There are different uses of reason and different aspects of reason in us.[5]

Reason in itself is the laws of thought. These laws are most basically the law of identity (*a* is *a*), the law of non-contradiction (not both *a* and *non-a*, at the same time and in the same respect), and the law of excluded middle (either *a* or *non-a*). These, minimally, have been

---

5. Gangadean, *Philosophical Foundation*, 10-15, 27-31.

commonly accepted in the history of philosophy as the laws of reason and the laws of thought. "Finite" and "fallen" may apply to human users of these laws, but not to the laws themselves. They may apply to the failure to use reason critically, rather than a failure of reason itself. When any of these laws are broken, reason is not being used and thinking ceases.

Reason is used to form concepts, judgments, and arguments, which are the forms of all thought. Reason is used critically as a test of meaning. Meaning is more basic than truth. We must know what a statement means before we can know if it is true. When a law of thought is violated, there is no meaning. Reason is used to interpret experience in light of one's basic beliefs. And reason is used constructively to construct a coherent world and life view. The constructive use of reason is not the same as the critical use. Reason should be used critically first, to test one's basic beliefs for meaning, before constructing a worldview upon them. Likewise, the interpretive use must be distinguished from the critical use. Much confusion in hermeneutical skepticism can be avoided by observing some of these distinctions.

Reason in us is natural, not conventional. It is universal, the same in all persons. It is a common ground between all worldviews. It is the source of coherence in constructing a worldview and in the test for meaning of its basic beliefs. It is the common ground by which thoughts (concepts, judgments, and arguments) are formed and that by which experience is interpreted in light of basic beliefs. Reason in us, as common ground, is not historically situated; it is universal. This prevents incommensurability between worldviews, even when basic beliefs in different worldviews are contradictory.

Reason is ontological. It applies to being as well as to thought. There are no square-circles, no uncaused events, no being from non-being. God is not both eternal and not eternal, at the same time and in the same respect. If reason did not apply to being, then statements could be true and not true, at the same time and in the same respect. If *a* could be *non-a*, then being could not be distinguished from non-being. All distinctions would lose meaning, and all meaning would be lost.

Reason is transcendental. It is authoritative. It is self-attesting, the highest authority. It cannot be questioned because it makes questioning possible. A statement which violates a law of reason is not meaningful and cannot be true, regardless of its source.

Reason is also fundamental. It is fundamental to other aspects of human personality. Thought supplies the belief concerning the good as the object of desire. And thought and desire move a person to act. It is knowing the truth that sets a person free.

Thinking is presuppositional. This follows from the nature of reason in itself, reason in its use, and reason in us. We think of what is less basic in light of what is more basic. We think of truth in light of meaning; we think of experience in light of basic belief; we think of conclusion in light of premises; we think of the temporal in light of the eternal, and the finite in light of the infinite. We must know what a statement means before we can know if it is true. If it violates a law of reason, it is not meaningful because reason, as the laws of thought, is transcendental—it is the test for meaning, and thus, of what can and cannot be true. If a statement is meaningless, it cannot be true because reason is ontological. If there is agreement on what is more basic (that reason is the laws of thought, universal, ontological, and transcendental), there can be agreement on what is less basic. If there is doubt that reason is ontological, disagreement is not even possible because skepticism here lapses into nihilism and the loss of meaning.

Since thinking is presuppositional, and reason, as the test for meaning, is most basic, this position can be described as Rational Presuppositionalism. It is a position distinct from empiricism, rationalism, and fideistic presuppositionalism.

THE FIRST APPLICATION OF RATIONAL PRESUPPOSITIONALISM:
Show There Must Be Something Eternal

The first act of reason is in forming concepts, and the most basic concept is about existence. Since existence is either temporal (with beginning) or eternal (without beginning), and since eternal is more basic than temporal, our most basic concept is about eternal existence. The possible judgments concerning what is eternal are four: all is eternal; none is eternal; some is eternal; and some is not eternal. Can we know if there is something eternal? The following is offered as proof that something must be eternal.

1. Contradictory statements cannot both be true and cannot both be false (at the same time and in the same respect).
2. The contradiction of "some is eternal" is "none is eternal."
3. If "none is eternal" then:

    All is temporal.

    All had a beginning.

    All came into being.
4. If all came into being, then being came into existence from non-being.
5. Being from non-being is not possible.
6. Therefore, the original "none is eternal" is not possible.
7. Therefore, its contradiction "some is eternal" must be true.[6]

Being comes from being alone. Non-being is the absence of being and of the power of being to cause to be. If being could come from non-being, then there would be no distinction between being and non-being (*a* could be *non-a*). Skepticism and nihilism are the result.

It is clear through reason, therefore, that something must be eternal. To doubt this, one must give up reason. To give up reason is to give up meaning. "There must be something eternal" is maximally clear. The opposite is not possible. To doubt what is maximally clear, one must give up reason. To give up reason is to deny one's nature as a rational being and so to bring upon oneself spiritual death, which is meaninglessness.

THE PROGRAM OF NATURAL THEOLOGY

The goal of natural theology is to show what is clear about God and man and good and evil from general revelation. It is to respond to all objections raised against the knowledge of God, proceeding from what is most basic in general revelation to what is equally basic in special revelation. It must show all that is clear from general revelation which is necessary for inexcusability, as well as respond to philosophical objections to the doctrines of special revelation. What follows is an outline

---

6. Gangadean, *Philosophical Foundation*, 61-63.

of the objectives by which this goal is to be achieved. The objectives state what must be done and indicate only in the most general way how this may be done.

1. Show that there must be something eternal.

Since eternal is our most basic concept and since God is eternal, it must be shown that there must be something eternal. This first step is necessary but not sufficient to prove the existence of God. This proof is a modification of the ontological argument: what cannot be logically conceived cannot exist.

2. Show that only some is eternal.[7]

Since God is Creator of all things, only some (God) is eternal. All else is temporal. This step uses the cosmological argument in a variety of ways.

  i. The material world is not eternal (vs. material monism). It is not self-maintaining in general (entropy), in its parts (sun and stars), and as a whole (the Big Bang oscillating universe or the inflationary universe).

  ii. The material world exists (vs. ordinary idealism—Berkeley). The cause of what I see is not my mind, or another mind, but outside all minds.

  iii. The soul exists—the mind is not the brain (vs. material monism). A neural impulse is not a mental image, nor does the mental image perceive itself.

  iv. The soul is not eternal (vs. ordinary dualism—Plato, and qualified non-dualism—Ramanuja). The soul goes through unique events in time (growth in knowledge, enlightenment, etc.).

  v. The soul exists (vs. absolute idealism, *Advaita*—Shankara). The soul is neither unreal, that is, an illusion/*maya*, nor real/eternal).

---

7. Gangadean, *Philosophical Foundation*, 71-137.

3. Respond to the problem of evil.[8]

If God is all good and all powerful, why is there evil? The teleological argument is used to respond to the problem of natural evil and moral evil.

   i. Natural evil (toil and strife, and old age, sickness, and death) is not necessary. Original creation was very good, without natural evil (vs. origin by evolution, natural or theistic).

  ii. Natural evil is due to moral evil. It is imposed, not as punishment, but as a call back from moral evil. Suffering is a call to stop and think.

 iii. Moral evil is permitted for a purpose. It is made to serve the good through deepening of the divine revelation.

 iv. There is an ironic solution to the problem of evil, requiring understanding the nature of evil in light of the clarity of general revelation.

4. Show the moral law from general revelation.[9]

If there is not a moral law which is clear from general revelation, then human responsibility and moral evil are not possible. This moral law must be clear, comprehensive, and critical.

   i. The moral law is clear because it is grounded in the fundamental features of human nature. It is grounded in the reality of choice, in the nature of thinking, in the natural unity of our being, in the work required to bring into being and sustain in being, in being born ignorant, in being born human, in being of a sexual union, in valuing and producing what is of value, in being born equal, and in being born changeable.

  ii. The moral law is comprehensive in that it applies to all choices and all aspects of human nature which come to expression in choice.

---

8. Gangadean, *Philosophical Foundation*, 156-161; In this work, see the essay: "The Problem of Evil: An Ironic Solution"

9. Gangadean, *Philosophical Foundation*, 171-284; Gangadean, *History of Philosophy*, 61-69; Gangadean, *The Westminster Catechisms*. See LCQ. 91-148.

iii. The moral law is critical. The consequence of observing the moral law is life, which is, obtaining the good; the consequence of not observing the law is spiritual death, both individual and corporate.

5. From deism to theism.[10]

Deism maintains that God creates but does not act in history. Theism (Judaism, Christianity, and Islam) maintains that God creates and acts providentially in history, including, specifically, in giving scriptures.

  i. God acts in history in imposing natural evil. Natural evil is not in the original creation and not inherent in moral evil.

  ii. Natural evil, as a call back from moral evil, requires redemptive revelation to show how God can be both just and merciful.

  iii. Special revelation must be consistent with general revelation, and must show how God is both just and merciful.

  iv. Biblical revelation only is consistent with general revelation and shows how God is both just and merciful.

6. The root of conflict among theists.[11]

Judaism, Christianity, and Islam profess to hold to some basic scriptures in common. Since scripture is redemptive revelation, the conflict between them is rooted in their understanding of the divine nature regarding how God is both just and merciful in redemption.

  i. Judaism and Christianity affirm that God is both just and merciful by nature, and that mercy must satisfy divine justice by atonement. Islam affirms that God has no nature by which he is bound; mercy can set aside divine justice—there is no need for atonement.

  ii. Biblical Judaism affirms the justice and mercy of God in vicarious atonement through the death of another, as seen in the Temple sacrifice on the Day of Atonement. Post-Biblical Judaism affirms that atonement is in and by oneself.

---

10. Gangadean, *Philosophical Foundation*, 190-191.

11. Gangadean, *Philosophical Foundation*, 191-194; Gangadean, "Paper No. 31: Divisions Among Theists: Sources and Response," "Paper No. 91: Christianity and Islam: The Difference," and "Paper No. 56: The Gospel: A Summary With Explanation—Repent: For the Kingdom of Heaven Is at Hand," in *The Logos Papers*.

iii. Christianity affirms the justice and mercy of God in vicarious atonement through human representation (Christ in the place of Adam). The lamb symbolically represented Christ, in whose death the reality of atonement is accomplished.

7. Rational challenges to doctrines of Christianity.

Non-theists and non-Christian theists have objected to ecumenical doctrines in Christianity. If Scripture is divine revelation, it must be shown that these doctrines, while not originating from human reasoning, are in accordance with reason, and are consistent with all that can be expected from both general and special revelation.

i. The doctrine of the Trinity requires an understanding of what is meant in saying "God is one."[12]

ii. The doctrine of the Incarnation requires an understanding of unity and diversity of natures in one person.[13]

iii. The doctrine of the Fall requires an understanding of the nature of moral evil (sin) and of representation.[14]

8. Philosophical questions in the continuing divisions within Christianity.

Redemptive revelation in Scripture assumes the reality of sin in the failure to understand clear general revelation. Understanding Scripture assumes the understanding of general revelation. Continuing divisions within Christianity reveal lack in understanding what is clear

---

12. Gangadean, *History of Philosophy*, 40; Gangadean, "Paper No. 16: The Historic Christian Faith: The Holy Spirit Guides the Church into All Truth," in *The Logos Papers*. See Part V; Gangadean, *The Westminster Catechisms*. See LCQ. 8-9.

13. Gangadean, "Paper No. 16: The Historic Christian Faith: The Holy Spirit Guides the Church into All Truth," in *The Logos Papers*. See Part VII.

14. Gangadean, "Paper No. 14: The Biblical Worldview: Creation–Fall–Redemption (Expanded Version)" and Papers No. 145–147 on The Biblical Worldview (Parts V–VII): The Fall, in *The Logos Papers*.

in general revelation. The perspicuity of Scripture rests on the clarity of general revelation.

    i. There is continuing division concerning the sufficiency of vicarious atonement (grace vs. works).[15]

    ii. There is continuing division concerning divine sovereignty in predestination and human freedom and responsibility.[16]

    iii. There is continuing division concerning hermeneutics: what is literal and what is contextual interpretation.[17]

    iv. There is continuing division concerning the good: is the knowledge of God gained through a direct vision of God in heaven, or is it the knowledge of God gained through the work of dominion on earth through history?[18]

CONCLUSION

Natural theology, I believe, is not only possible. It is necessary. The external and internal challenges to Christian theism have accumulated through the Enlightenment period, although they have roots going back into ancient history. The need for natural theology today is more urgent, if not acute, as ancient worldviews come face to face. All human beings need meaning, and neither skepticism nor fideism can provide that meaning for human beings as they become more epistemologically self-conscious and consistent. A deeper understanding of reason, leading to a deeper, clearer, and more consistent understanding of good and evil, can lead us out of our present impasse, to a unity and fullness we had not thought was possible.

---

15. Gangadean, *Philosophical Foundation*, 194-195.

16. Gangadean, "Paper No. 16: The Historic Christian Faith: The Holy Spirit Guides the Church into All Truth," See Part VIII; "Paper No: 18: Salvation by Grace: The Sovereignty of God in the Salvation of Man;" and "Paper No. 97: Freedom and Predestination: A Concise Critical Analysis," in *The Logos Papers*.

17. Gangadean, "Paper No. 15: Hermeneutics: Principles of Interpretation—Applied to General Revelation and to Scripture," in *The Logos Papers*.

18. Gangadean, "Paper No. 106: The Good and Heaven: The Good Is Not the Beatific Vision," in *The Logos Papers*; In this work, see the essay: "The Good and the Beatific Vision"

14

ON THE ORIGIN OF
THE MORAL LAW

Paper delivered for the Canyon Institute for Advanced Studies,
Grand Canyon University

Spring 2003

T HERE IS A MORAL LAW WHICH IS CLEAR, comprehensive, and critical. It is clear because it is grounded in human nature; it is comprehensive, applying to all aspects of human nature; and it is critical
because its consequence is a matter of spiritual life and death.

CLARITY

There are two reasons why we must speak of the moral law as clear.
First, philosophy is opposed to dogmatism, which is assertion without
rational justification. It is opposed in principle to dogmatic theism as
well as to dogmatic naturalism. The alternative to dogmatism is skepticism, which says that knowledge is not possible, that nothing is clear.
Consistent skepticism leads to nihilism, which is unlivable as well as
unthinkable. The only alternative to dogmatism and skepticism is to
show that some things are clear, that the basic things are clear, that the
basic things about God and man and good and evil are clear to reason.

Second, Christianity presupposes the clarity of general revelation.
Paul, in his letter to the Romans, said that what may be known of
God is clearly seen, being understood from what has been made, so

that men are without excuse.[1] If there is no clarity, there is no inexcusability, and therefore no sin, and no need for salvation. There would be no need for Christ as the Lamb of God who takes away the sin of the world, if there is no basis for the reality of sin. If there is no clarity and inexcusability, believers in Christ must explain why there is any need to speak of Christ. But if there is clarity, they must be prepared to show this clarity.

Clarity, then, is more than important. It is essential, both in philosophy and in Christian theism. The issue of clarity has often been neglected. We take our assumptions for granted, without trying to prove them, in contrast to alternative assumptions. When our dogmatism is challenged, we find ways to avoid having to show what is clear. If the challenge persists, we resist, often by quibbles, appeals to unknowns, and by begging the question. Finally, we may move to deny the validity of reason itself and retreat into skepticism. But the issue of clarity cannot, with integrity, be avoided. Even if we are unable to show, or if we fail to show, what is clear, we are still to be committed in principle to clarity. The alternatives leave no room to stand.

THE NECESSARY CONDITIONS FOR MORALITY

To be rationally justified, the moral law must satisfy the necessary conditions for morality. There must be a metaphysical absolute, that is, God. There must be personal immortality. There must be freedom. There must be clarity. And, there must be rationality. I will look at each very briefly, leaving room for questions later. First, God. Suppose there is no God. Then all is eternal in some form or other, whether all is matter or all is spirit or both matter and spirit are eternal. If all is eternal, if there is no creation, the distinction between good and evil might still be made, but it cannot be rationally justified. If all is nature, then all is natural. If all is one, then good and evil are one. If there is no personal immortality, if death ends it all, it cannot be rationally justified why I should do one thing rather than another. If all ends sooner or later, we may all do as we please. If there is no freedom, there is no rational way to hold a person accountable and, hence, no basis for morality. If there is not an objectively clear moral standard, again, we could

---

1. *Romans 1:20.*

not reasonably be held accountable for knowing it or for observing it. If there is no rationality, if reason as the laws of thought is not authoritative, or if reason does not apply to being as well as thought, then there is no basis for clarity and, hence, no basis for morality. In speaking about what is clear in this context, I can only be very brief. What is said here can be developed in discussions afterwards.[2]

THE GOOD

The most basic concept of ethics is the concept of the good. The good is the end in itself, chosen for its own sake and not for the sake of anything else. It is the source of unity in a person, in a group, and between groups. It is the highest value, the *summum bonum*. It is the goal of life, the meaning and purpose of existence, the source of happiness.

The good is to be distinguished from virtue and happiness. Virtue is the means to the good; it is not the good itself. There are different kinds of virtue: moral virtues, such as love, wisdom, and courage; natural virtues, such as talent, health, and environment; and instrumental virtues such as money, car, and house. Money is not the good because it is not and cannot be sought for its own sake. Love is not the good. If we love others, we seek the good for them. Survival is not the good. We do not survive merely for the sake of surviving.

Happiness is the effect of possessing what we believe is the good. It is not the good and is not sought directly apart from a belief about the good. Lasting happiness is the effect of possessing what truly is the good, in contrast to what is falsely thought to be the good.

Ethics therefore is teleological, that is, goal oriented, not deontological—in which virtue is considered the good, or consequential—in which happiness is considered the good. The greater part of disputes in ethics can be cleared up if the good is clearly distinguished from virtue and happiness.

MORAL LAW 1

Moral law 1 concerns the good and God. The good is grounded in human nature in the reality of choice. If choice of means and ends

---

2. Gangadean, *Philosophical Foundation: A Critical Analysis of Basic Beliefs,* Second Edition.

are real, then the good as the end in itself is real. If there is to be rational justification for the good, the good as a source of unity within each person must be one. That is, there is one and only one good for each person. If there were two distinct goods, there would be no rational way to decide between them and we would be frozen in inaction.

As a source of unity between persons, there is one and the same good for all persons. Good for a being is based on the nature of that being. Good for a horse is based on the nature of a horse. Good for a rabbit is based on the nature of a rabbit. Good for a man is based on the nature of man. Since good for man is based on human nature, and since there is one human nature, there is therefore one good for all human beings.

The good, based on human nature, must be easily knowable. It must be objectively clear, knowable by all who can be held morally responsible, apart from cultural background. While there is one good for all, there are many views of the good. One's view of the good is based on one's view of human nature, which in turn is based on one's view of what is real or eternal. That is to say, the moral absolute is based on the metaphysical absolute. If the good is objectively clear, it must also be clear what is eternal.

It will be argued here that it is clear that only some is eternal. By clear is meant clear to reason, as the laws of thought, that one has to deny reason to avoid what is clear. It is clear that there must be something eternal. The contradiction is that nothing is eternal. But if nothing is eternal, then all is temporal, all had a beginning, all came into being. And all would have come into being from non-being. Since being from non-being is impossible, the original "none is eternal" is impossible and the contradiction "some is eternal" must be true. This is a paradigm of what is clear to reason. We can see if there are nuanced understandings of "being from non-being" which are not merely quibbling, which could defeat this argument.[3]

It is clear that the material world exists. The cause of what I see is not my mind, nor some other mind, but is outside all minds. This is opposed to all forms of idealism. It is clear that the material universe is not eternal. The sun and the stars will burn out. The older, Big Bang, oscillating universe theory has significant objections. And the current inflationary theory either asserts that being came from non-being, or,

---

3. Gangadean, *Philosophical Foundation*, 293-309.

is blocked by dogmatic naturalism from saying that God created the original stuff of the universe *ex nihilo*.

It is clear that the soul exists—that the mind is not the brain. Thought cannot be reduced to motions of atoms in the brain. The brain may be necessary for thought in our present embodied state, but it is not sufficient for thought. A neural impulse in my brain, through which I perceive a table, is not identical with the mental image of the table. These are not identical because they have different sets of properties. Nor is the self, mind, or soul, which is the perceiver of the mental image, the same as the mental image.

It is clear that the soul is not eternal. It is not without beginning, although it is everlasting, without end. A soul, eternal in time, would have had infinite time. Apart from the problem inherent in applying infinite to time, the eternal soul would, in infinite time, have infinite knowledge. It is clear we do not have infinite knowledge. So, the soul is not eternal.

These arguments, if they are sound (and I believe they are, even to the fourth and fifth level objections), eliminate the various claims that all is eternal in some form or other. They eliminate the worldviews of material monism, spiritual monism, and dualism. Since there must be something eternal, it follows that only some is eternal, that is, some is eternal and some is not eternal. And since what is eternal did not come into being from non-being, it was brought into being or created by what is eternal. Hence, the Creator, or God, exists.

The first moral law is the most basic law. It is the basis of all other laws. It is about the metaphysical absolute and the moral absolute; it is about God and the good. The first moral law then is this: God, as creator of human nature, is the determiner of good and evil for man.

To understand this law is to understand the steps used in its derivation and their implications concerning what is opposed by this law. Some of these can be listed here with brief explanation.

1. Theism, which is belief in God the Creator, is opposed to all forms of non-theism. It is opposed to atheism, pantheism, polytheism, and shamanism. Philosophically, it is opposed to material monism, spiritual monism, and dualism.

2. Objective clarity, that only some is eternal, is opposed to all forms of skepticism and fideism or dogmatism.

3. Subjective clarity is opposed to the claim that knowledge is insufficient for morality. It is opposed to voluntarism, the view that the will can be opposed to the understanding; and to emotivism, the view that the feelings can be opposed to the understanding. It asserts that if you know the truth, the truth will set you free.

4. Theonomy, the view that God the Creator is the determiner of good and evil for man, is opposed to all forms of autonomy, that man, understanding himself apart from God, is the determiner of good and evil. It is opposed to all ethical theories based on autonomy. It is opposed to ethical egoism, utilitarianism, deontology, existentialism, naturalism, tradition, humanism, stoicism, and mysticism.

5. The moral law is opposed to heteronomy. God does not impose the moral law from without, apart from human nature. The law is knowable by reason from general revelation. It is not known only by special revelation.

6. The moral law is opposed to positivism or the divine command theory, in which the law is seen as arbitrary, apart from human nature.

7. Teleology is opposed to deontology and consequentialism. The good is not virtue or happiness.

The consequences of observing or not observing this law are critical, a matter of spiritual life or death. Moral evil is a denial of one's nature as a rational being. In moral evil, one neglects, avoids, resists, and denies reason in the presence of what is clear about God. In moral evil, man puts himself in the place of God to determine good and evil. The consequence of the denial of reason is spiritual death. Individually, it brings meaninglessness, boredom, and guilt. Corporately, it brings the death of relationships, institutions, and cultures. Spiritual death is present and inherent in moral evil; it is not imposed and future. On the other hand, to affirm what is clear about God brings a life full of meaning.

MORAL LAWS 2–10

The summary of moral laws 2-10 is intended to show how the law is clear, being grounded in human nature; how it is comprehensive, not bare and minimal; and how the law given in special revelation is knowable from general revelation.

Moral Law 2

The second moral law concerns the nature of thinking and the nature of God. It is concerned with divisions among theists. It deals with differences in how theists conceive the divine nature. By nature we think and by nature we think about God. Thinking is presuppositional. We are to think about the less basic in light of the more basic, not the more basic in light of the less basic. We are to think of man in light of God, not God in light of man. Man is the image of God; God is not the image of man. We are to think of the finite in light of the infinite, not the infinite in light of the finite. Specifically, we are to think of finite justice in light of infinite justice, not infinite justice in light of finite justice. If we think in this way about God's justice, the disputes between theists can be resolved.

The first dispute is between deism and theism. Deism says God creates but does not rule. Theism says that God creates and rules. Theism claims that God rules in justice and mercy and acts redemptively in history. The question universally asked is this: if God is all good and all powerful, why is there evil? One would naturally expect a world without natural evil, especially death. If God is infinitely powerful, he could create a world without physical death. If he is infinitely good, he would create such a world. Theists must agree with this but go further. If God could and would create a world without natural evil, then he must have; and if he must have, then he did. Original creation was without natural evil. Historic theism has affirmed the conclusion of this simple deduction. Original creation was very good. There was no physical death for man. Physical death was not original. It was imposed, not as punishment, but as a call back from moral evil. Natural evil is a call to stop and think, to see what is clear about God. As a call back, it requires special revelation to show how God can be both just and merciful to man in his sin. So, general revelation shows that God rules in history. God the Creator is not to be likened to the creature, who takes death as necessary and natural.

Thinking is presuppositional. The basic distinctions between theists, between Judaism, Christianity, and Islam, and within Christianity, are about what satisfies the infinite justice of God. Is there need for atonement? Is the suffering of natural evil and physical death atonement? Is atonement through one's own suffering or through another? Must this other be human? Is the suffering of this other sufficient? Theologically, it is asked: is Christ the Lamb of God who takes away the sin of the world? And many have asked: is punishment, as something future and imposed, consistent with the divine justice? Moral law 1 said the consequence of moral evil (not seeking, not understanding what is clear, and not doing what is right) is spiritual death, which is present and inherent in moral evil, not future and imposed.

Moral Law 3

Moral law 3 concerns integrity and knowledge. There is a natural unity in our being. To act according to this unity, we should act consistently. Integrity, as a concern for consistency, is opposed to hypocrisy. We should not say one thing and do another. To profess a concern to know and not see what is clear shows a lack of integrity. To make a vow, our most explicit profession, and not keep it, is a lack of integrity. All failure is not hypocrisy. Failure, with self-deception and self-justification, is. In hypocrisy, the name of God, or that by which he makes himself known, is taken in vain. The failure to see what is clear becomes hypocrisy when the failure is avoided by self-deception and resisted by self-justification.

Moral Law 4

Moral law 4 concerns the good and work and hope. To bring into being and to sustain in being requires work. Work is not an end in itself; it is a means to the good. What is this good and how is work a means to the good? Good for man is based on human nature. Good for man as a rational being is the use of reason to the fullest. Since reason is used to understand the nature of things, and the nature of things created reveal the nature of God, the good for man is the knowledge of God.

Knowledge and only knowledge satisfies the formal requirements for the good. The good must be continuing; it can continue from this life to the next. It is inexhaustible; it can grow and be pursued forever. It is comprehensive, including all aspects of human nature and activity. It is inalienable; it cannot be taken away from a person. It is corporate, requiring many to achieve it. It is cumulative, increasing through the ages. It is communal; it increases as it is shared. It is fulfilling; it is the source of satisfaction in everything that satisfies. It is ultimate; it reaches to what is infinite and eternal. And it is transformative; is has the power to transform our being.

The knowledge of God comes through the knowledge of creation. And the knowledge of creation comes through the work of dominion. In dominion, man develops all the powers latent in himself and the creation. As a result, in the words of Isaiah the Prophet, the earth will be filled with the knowledge of God as the waters cover the sea.[4] Is there hope that this will come about? The nature of the good and the nature of man require knowledge through dominion. The infinite goodness of God guarantees that good will overcome evil, that evil will be made to serve the good.

True hope, that the good will be achieved through the work of dominion, is opposed to false hope, that the good can be achieved without the work of dominion, and to no hope, that there is no connection between work and the good. True hope affirms that man, made in the image of God, will complete the work of dominion as God completed the work of creation. According to moral law 4, we should work for the good with true hope.

Moral Law 5

Moral law 5 concerns authority and insight. We are born ignorant and need to be taught the good and the means to the good. Our first, natural teachers in authority over us are our parents. Authority is rational, not personal. It is based on insight, not might. Insight is historically cumulative, not individual. Authority based on insight must be honored; authority without insight must be changed where possible. It is opposed to authority without insight in family, state, school, and

---

4. *Isaiah 11:9.*

church. It is opposed to institutional structures in which the philosophical does not lead the psychological and the practical. It is opposed to totalitarianism among institutions. No institution is total, over other institutions. All institutions are equally under the moral law according to their form and function. It is opposed to state over church, and to church over state. It is opposed to state over family and to family over state. In public education, the state, claiming religious neutrality, exercises illegitimate authority over the family. This law requires us to give the honor of authority to whom this honor is due.

Moral Law 6

Moral law 6 concerns human dignity and rationality. We are born human. Human dignity distinguishes us from the animals. Human dignity consists in the capacity to understand. We understand by reason, which is the same in all persons at all times. Human society is a society of rational beings, and participation in or separation from human society depends on the exercise of the capacity to understand. We are to affirm human dignity, that is, we are to treat others as having the capacity and the responsibility to understand. This affirmation is against the use of force in murder and war. Intellectual war against false ideology prevents physical war. It is opposed to racism and to gender wars. It is opposed to abortion, euthanasia, suicide, and intervention to preserve life which has lost the capacity to understand. It is opposed to psychotherapy which disregards responsibility for understanding. It is opposed to the view that temporal or final separation from rational human society is a denial of human dignity.

Moral Law 7

Moral law 7 concerns sex and love, and marriage and the good. We are all born of a sexual union. A person is a union of body and soul. A physical union is a natural sign of a spiritual union. Sex is the sign and seal of love. The physical is not to be separated from the spiritual; sex is not to be separated from love. Together they constitute a full union of persons, which is monogamous and lasting. A full union therefore is marriage. Love in marriage seeks the good for and with the other and for those we bring into being. Marriage, then, is to serve the good and is to be protected to this end. It is opposed to all that separates sex and love. The good for marriage is opposed to regarding the other as the good. Marriage is to be based on friendship, which is the effect of mutual commitment to the good. Ordinary infidelity is rooted in spiritual infidelity, which is a lack of commitment to the good.

Moral Law 8

Moral law 8 concerns value and talent. We naturally value things. No one values all things alike. Value is a function of supply and demand. Demand is a function of one's view of the good. Supply is a function of talent. Talent is an ability to achieve some aspect of the good. Talent is grounded in the uniqueness of our being. It is God given, to each, for all. It is developed by the efforts of others as well as one's own effort. It is fully developed in vision of the good. One is to develop one's talent in pursuit of the good in service of others. Failure to do so is to take from others what is of value that is intended for them. It is, morally, the most basic form of stealing. God as creator and giver of talent owns all absolutely. Man is a steward, not absolute owner. This is opposed to the view that man individually or collectively owns absolutely what is of value. It is opposed to the neglect or misuse of talent. It is opposed to social and economic policies which neglect or hinder the use of talent. The use of talent for the good increases the richness of life for all; its neglect and abuse increases the poverty of life for all.

Moral Law 9

Moral law 9 concerns truth and justice. We are born equal. In justice, equals are to be treated equally. Full social justice is both preventative and corrective. Truth is necessary and sufficient for justice. Full justice requires knowing and speaking the whole truth. We are to seek justice by knowing and speaking the truth. It is opposed to false worldviews which support oppression in societies. It is opposed to ignorance and fideism, which fail to see what is clear and to take false thoughts captive. It is opposed to privacy in decisions affecting public affairs. It is opposed to closed societies which restrict freedom of speech, and to the abuse of freedom of speech as the right to rational discourse. One who fails to witness to the truth shares in injustice and its consequence. A faithful witness brings about justice.

Moral Law 10

Moral law 10 concerns suffering and the good. We are born change-able. We can change in what we think about good and evil. Suffering arises when we think we cannot possess what we believe is the good. Since the good is inalienable, discontent and envy arises from a false view of the good. Moral evil is a failure to seek and to understand what is clear about God. Its inherent consequence is meaninglessness, bore-dom, and guilt. Natural evil of toil and strife, and old age, sickness, and death are a call back from moral evil. It is not a hindrance to the good, but is intended to serve the good. We are not to be discontent in pursuing our own view of the good, but to be content in pursuing what truly is the good. This is opposed to envy, stoicism, resentment, discouragement, self-indulgence, cynicism, and fatalistic resignation. To those who do not seek the good, suffering is avoided as meaning-less. To those who seek the good, all things are seen as working to-gether for the good.

If what has been said above can be supported as sound, then there is a moral law which is clear, comprehensive, and critical. It is a law that every human being can live with gladly, because it is in everyone, and because this law enables us together to achieve the good.

15

THE TASK OF
CHRISTIAN PHILOSOPHY

Paper delivered for the regional Society for Christian
Philosophy Conference, Grand Canyon University

Spring 2002

ABSTRACT

CHRISTIANITY PRESUPPOSES THE CLARITY of general revelation.
Clarity is the basis of inexcusability, and sin, as unbelief, is inexcusable. If there is no inexcusability, there is no sin and no need for
Christianity as redemptive revelation. There are many challenges to
theism in general and to Christian theism in particular. Responses to
these have not been based on the assumption of clarity and inexcusability. It is the task of Christian philosophy to respond to what challenges the clarity of general revelation. Knowing what is clear implies
being able to show that unbelief of what is clear is contrary to reason.
Christian philosophy must respond to skepticism and fideism, to various forms of non-theism (material monism, spiritual monism, and dualism), and to various forms of non-Christian theism (deism, Judaism,
and Islam). Christian philosophy must also respond to ethical views
which challenge the clarity of the moral law given in general revelation.

INTRODUCTION

Christianity presupposes the clarity of general revelation regarding the
existence and nature of God, and the moral law written in the heart of

man. Christian philosophy must respond to the internal and external challenges to what is presupposed in Christianity.

Christian philosophy must show that some things about God and man, and good and evil, are clear to reason, in contrast to all forms of skepticism and fideism. It must show that only some (God, the Creator) is eternal, in contrast to all forms of non-theism—nothing is eternal, or all is eternal. It must show that there is a moral law, grounded in human nature as created by God, in contrast to all forms of human autonomy. In addition, Christian philosophy must respond to the internal challenges of theism (deism, Islam, and Judaism) and to the divisions within Christianity which are grounded in uncritically held assumptions.

Christian philosophy must justify the Christian notion of sin and death and redemption by showing how sin (moral evil) is possible. It must show the connection between the clarity of general revelation and the inexcusability of unbelief. To show clarity, it must respond to the challenge of skepticism. There have been many responses to skepticism from Plato to Plantinga, by Augustine and Aquinas, by Descartes and Kant, by Nietzsche and Quine, by Wittgenstein and Derrida. Justification and warranted belief have been addressed, but the inexcusability of unbelief has not received sufficient attention.

Proofs for God's existence (if they succeed), or warrant for Christian belief, do not show clarity and inexcusability. Appeal to suppression of an instinctual knowledge of God does not show the inexcusability of unbelief. It does not show how alternatives to theism or to Christian theism are inexcusable (*anapologia*, without reason).

Christian philosophy must fully defeat skepticism. If some things are not clear, then general revelation is not clear, and unbelief is excusable. Skepticism rests on uncritically held assumptions. In attempts to achieve knowledge, rationalism and empiricism fail to recognize assumptions and are vulnerable to doubt. Descartes' *cogito* requires more work in order to establish the real existence of the self over against Vedantic idealism. Reid's Common Sense realism requires more work in order to establish the real existence of the world over against Berkeley's idealism.

To overcome skepticism requires getting to the most basic level of thought. Reason in itself is the laws of thought (identity, non-contradiction, excluded middle). The laws of thought make thought possible.

They cannot be questioned but make questioning possible. Reason in its critical use is a test for meaning. The meaning of a statement must be known before judging its truth. If a law of thought is violated, there is no meaning and there can be no truth. Hence, there are no square-circles, no uncaused events, no being from non-being. If we cannot know these things, nothing can be known. To avoid knowing some things, one has to deny reason itself. One cannot deny reason and retain any thought. Since we cannot avoid thought, we cannot deny reason. The attempt to deny reason to avoid what is clear is inexcusable.

The attempt to deny reason is an act contrary to human nature and is an act of self-destruction. To neglect, avoid, resist, or deny reason empties life of meaning, which leads to boredom and guilt, the state of spiritual death. A Christian can argue that reason is the life of the logos (the Word of God) in all men. To deny reason is to deny the life of God in man. The wages of sin is death.

Suppose we can know some very basic things by reason, can reason show the existence and nature of God? Can Christian philosophy answer the internal and external challenges to Christian theism? In light of the history of philosophy, is this not too daunting a task, foolhardy, an invitation to disaster? In reply, it can only be said there is no choice if inexcusability requires clarity. The survival of Christianity as a vital cultural force requires that thoughts raised up against the knowledge of God be taken captive. We can say "there are giants in the land" and wander in the wilderness until we die, or we can understand that the divine grace, which began redemption, is able to complete it. Christ is the Lamb of God who takes away the sin of the world. He is the Word of God who makes God known. The earth is to be filled with the knowledge of God. It isn't rash, therefore, to think that Christian philosophy must answer the challenges to Christian theism.

Christian philosophy must show that it is clear that God the Creator exists. It must show that only some (God) is eternal, that is, without beginning, that all else is temporal, that is, created, with beginning. Christian philosophy must show that there must be something eternal, that only God is eternal; that matter exists (vs. idealism) and that matter is not eternal (vs. material monism); that that soul (self, mind) exists and that the soul is not eternal. In doing so, Christian philosophy must use all three arguments for the existence of God, in combination, with some revision to each. The ontological argument shows there must be something eternal (whatever that may be); the cosmo-logical argument shows that only some is eternal; and the teleological argument shows that kinds are specially created, and that evil in the world is not an argument against the existence of an all good, all pow-erful, God, but that ironically, the reverse is true.

STEPS IN SHOWING THE CLARITY OF GENERAL REVELATION

I will outline below what I believe is necessary in order to show that it is clear that God the Creator exists. Showing the clarity of general revelation is necessary, because clarity is presupposed in the Christian concept of sin. If believers claim something is clear, they should be able and willing to show this clarity. The program for showing clarity proceeds in define stages, from the more basic to the less basic. If we understand what is more basic, we can understand what is less basic. If we agree on what is more basic, we can agree on what is less basic. Care is required to observe this simple principle in order to avoid need-less disputes. This epistemological method can be described as Rational Presuppositionalism. It recognizes that our set of beliefs form a system (a worldview) and that less basic beliefs presuppose, or are supported by, more basic beliefs. Rational Presuppositionalism is a form of foun-dationalism, but goes deeper than its classical form. Rational Presup-positionalism differs from fideistic presuppositionalism in that it not only uses reason to construct a coherent worldview from basic beliefs (taken for granted as true), but uses reason critically at the basic level as a test for meaning.

The Ontological Argument: There Must Be Something Eternal

Christian theism affirms God as Creator of all things. "In the begin-ning God created the heavens and the earth." God is eternal and all else is temporal. God created all things *ex nihilo*. From this idea of creation *ex nihilo*, the infinite wisdom and power of God are derived. Plato's divine maker is neither creator of matter nor of the soul. The Demiurge is not infinite. To show it is clear that God exists, it must be shown first that there is an eternal being, and secondly that all else is temporal. To show there must be something eternal it must be shown that the contradiction "nothing is eternal" implies being would have to come from non-being, which is impossible.[1]

This form of ontological argument—from the concept of an eternal being to the necessary existence of an eternal being or substance—does not prove the existence of God, as Anselm's argument purports to. It argues that, if anything exists, something exists eternally. It does not show that something exists necessarily. That something exists is taken as assumed by all in any discussion.

The value of beginning with this argument is that it makes explicit a process of argument which, if not agreed upon, prevents further discussion which would be fruitless. If there is no agreement on what is more basic, there can be no agreement on what is less basic. It is a paradigm of what is clear to reason. If it is clear and not agreed to, it shows how one must deny reason to avoid what is clear. It shows inexcusability.

The Cosmological Argument: Only Some Is Eternal

If something must be eternal, is it that all is eternal in some form or other, or is only some (God, the Creator) eternal? If all is eternal, is it matter only (material monism), or spirit only (spiritual monism), or matter and spirit (dualism)? In the history of worldviews, as alternatives to theism, no other kind of being has been asserted to exist. If there are forms, or numbers, or laws, they are neither material nor efficient causes, needed to explain change in the world. Perhaps one could attempt to construct a logically possible world (assuming there is no appeal to an unknown at the basic level) in which there are other substances or dimensions or time and space relations, but those have not yet been put forward so as to merit serious attention. We can safely focus on actual worldviews, held historically, until other worldviews are presented. Since matter (extended and non-conscious) and spirit (conscious and non-extended) are mutually exclusive and exhaustive, by the law of excluded middle, there is no reason for expecting other views to come along.

---

1. Gangadean, *Philosophical Foundation*, 61-68.

Material Monism

Traditionally, metaphysics has been concerned with just three alternatives to theism, and historically, just three views have been exemplified: material monism in western science, spiritual monism in eastern mysticism, and dualism in Greek philosophy. It is appropriate to begin with material monism, which has been the most prevalent form of anti-theism in the West recently. Material monism asserts that all is matter in some form or other. There is no non-physical reality; there is no God; there is no soul. All processes can be explained in natural terms only, including the origin of the cosmos, the existence of thought and perception, and the origin of all life forms.

What Christian philosophy must show is that the material world is not eternal and that it is not the only kind of reality. It must show that the material world is not self-maintaining in general, or in its parts (sun, stars), or as a whole (the Big Bang oscillating universe, or inflationary universes). It must also show that thought cannot be accounted for by motion of atoms in the brain, and that in perception, a mental image is not identical with the neural impulse (*a* is not *non-a*). Mental state terms cannot be analyzed without remainder into statements containing only behavioral terms. The structure and process (change) in the cosmos cannot be accounted for in natural/physical processes alone, neither in the starry heavens above, nor in human consciousness within. These are outlines of cosmological arguments against material monism.[2]

The Natural Teleological Argument: Order in the World Is by Special Creation, Not Evolution

There are teleological arguments, based on natural design, against the evolutionary implications of material monism. The longstanding dispute between science and religion is due to uncritically held assumptions on the part of both. There are three issues in this dispute: first, is the dispute a matter of science or religion or philosophy; second, which assumption (uniformity or non-uniformity) best explains the data; and third, is a compromise position, theistic evolution, possible? Science assumes methodological naturalism in assuming only natural

---

2. Gangadean, *Philosophical Foundation*, 71-86.

causes operate and that all knowledge is from sense experience. Religion assumes the existence of God and scripture. Neither side argues for its assumption, but interprets the data in light of their first principle. The dispute resting on first principles belongs in the realm of philosophy, which must critically examine basic beliefs for meaning.[3]

After this dispute is resolved, the question becomes which assumption (uniformity or its alternative, non-uniformity) best interprets the data in the fields of geology, biology, and astronomy. In geology, the data of fossil beds, coal beds, sedimentary strata, mountain ranges, volcanic plateaus, ocean depths, and meteorological changes, can best be explained by non-uniformity.

In biology, there are several stages in macro-evolution (amoeba to man). Can randomness and natural law account for each stage? How reasonable are the probabilities that life arose from non-life by chance and not by design? Is there a purely natural explanation in going from life to more complex life? Are there transitional forms from more complex life to hominids, or must we go to punctuated equilibrium? Can the path of ascent from hominid to human be agreed upon, given the methods of research and reconstruction, given the relation of language and thought, and given the distinction of mind and brain? There are problems of logical gaps in each stage, not merely an exploiting of empirical gaps in favor of non-naturalism.[4]

Is there a third alternative? Theistic evolution attempts to mediate the dispute between historic theism and scientific naturalism. Is this third position possible without compromising fundamental features of both alternatives? Theistic evolution requires, over against historic theism, a revision of the concept of the soul as something infused into an already living being. The concept of creation as continuing in theistic evolution implies no unity of human nature and a reduction of differences in kind to differences of degree. Theistic evolution requires a revision in the concept of God in order to have natural evil compatible with the goodness of God in creation. Over against scientific naturalism, theistic evolution requires God to guide the mechanism of the

---

3. Gangadean, *Philosophical Foundation*, 87–89.

4. Gangadean, *Philosophical Foundation*, 90–96.

process of evolution (random micro-mutations), which would involve an intolerable degree of interference by non-natural causes.[5]

In the dispute between naturalistic science and special creation, the claim of incompatibility of the age of the heavens and the age of the earth rests upon the assumption of uniformity (vs. relativity) of time. Given current understanding of the relation of gravity and time and an expanding universe, this source of dispute must be re-evaluated.[6]

The arguments against material monism and reflections on the dispute between science and religion show it is by no means clear that naturalism overcomes theism. Rather, naturalism must show that it does not deny reason in the meaning of its assertions. The objections to material monism are fundamentally logical, from the nature of things, not merely empirical.

The Cosmological Argument Continued

Spiritual Monism

Spiritual monism is the second major alternative and objection to theism. It asserts, in contrast to material monism, that reality is fundamentally spiritual, and it explains the physical as a manifestation of the spiritual. Epistemologically, it is a more radical form of empiricism, appealing to an inner experience of enlightenment or awakening as a self-certifying source of truth. In various forms of Hindu (Vedantic) thought, and Buddhism, it begins with reincarnation and seeks release from the cycle of rebirth through an immediate awareness of what is taken to be ultimate reality. From the point of view of enlightened consciousness, reincarnation itself is seen as illusory (*maya*) or, that all distinctions of intellect vanish, including the distinction between enlightened and unenlightened consciousness.

Reincarnation assumes the eternal pre-existence of the soul in contrast to theism, in which the soul is created. It is argued for on the basis of certain experiences (*déjà vu*, recollections from past lives, and manifestations of special powers not acquired by experience in this life). Other explanations besides pre-existence are available, in addition to contrary evidence. The philosophical reasons for reincarnation have

---

5. Gangadean, *Philosophical Foundation*, 98-100.

6. Gangadean, *Philosophical Foundation*, 96-97.

defeaters. There are other (better?) alternatives to no afterlife besides reincarnation. The karma theory of explanation, by explaining any and every possible event ad hoc, has no predictive power and hence explains nothing. Suffering for one's own karma is said to be fair, but it does not explain how suffering through innumerable rebirths without clarity of general revelation can be fair, and, if it is clear, why is there a need for many lives to achieve this knowledge? If we have not learned through innumerable past lives, is reincarnation hopeful? And, is it possible to be finally released from rebirth if there has already been an infinite time in which to find release?[7]

Recourse is made to the illusory nature of the world (*samsara*) and the need for enlightenment to realize this. But appeal to experience, including the experience of awakening, must be interpreted to be meaningful, and has been interpreted differently in various traditions. A valid interpretation must be internally consistent, and the interpretation of *Advaita* (absolute non-dualism of Shankara) and *Dvaita* (qualified non-dualism of Ramanuja) are admittedly incoherent in many ways.[8]

For Shankara, it cannot be explained in whose mind the illusion resides, or how illusion concerning self-consciousness is possible, or how the world can be neither a thing nor a thought, or how the world can be neither real (eternal) nor non-existent. Instead of giving up the assumption that "all is one" for belief in the temporal reality of the world as created, Shankara moves to give up reason. The giving up of reason to avoid what is clear about God is inexcusable and results in the spiritual death of meaninglessness.

The claim by Ramanuja that the many selves are part of the one God encounters equal difficulties. Is the infinitude of God the sum of finite parts? Can the soul be finite and eternal? If all the parts are infinite, then each is complete in itself and not a part of another. And if some parts are finite (and temporal) and other parts are infinite and eternal, why is this not creation and theism, rather than pantheism?

Dualism

A third major alternative to theism has been dualism—matter and spirit are both eternal. Christian theism encountered the Greek dualism of

---

7. Gangadean, *Philosophical Foundation*, 103-105.

8. Gangadean, *Philosophical Foundation*, 110-115.

Plato and Aristotle as its first major challenge outside of Judaism. The clarity of general revelation, in opposition to dualism, has not been pressed, and aspects of ontological and ethical dualism have lingered in the Christian worldview. Augustine allowed a degree of Platonic thought, and Aquinas did the same for Aristotle. Christian philosophy must show that matter is neither eternal and independent of spirit as in Platonic dualism, nor eternal and dependent on spirit (Prime Mover/pure actuality) as pure potentiality.[9] The dualistic explanation of evil as the opposition of the body to the soul must be shown to be incoherent in itself and inconsistent with the goodness of creation in theism.[10]

Theism: The Nature of God and Preliminary Problems

At this point, the incoherence of the three major forms of "all is eternal" has been brought to attention. But theism itself has been challenged as being incoherent. These challenges must be met if the clarity of general revelation is to be upheld. The nature of God, knowable from general revelation, must be clarified to begin with, in contrast to sub-theistic views of pantheism, dualism, polytheism, and panentheism. In addition, some preliminary difficulties must be addressed. How is creation *ex nihilo* different from being from non-being? How is creation of matter and spirit (other than God) possible? How is creation not a unique event in time? And why did God create, as against not create, or, why did God create this world instead of some other world?[11]

The Moral Teleological Argument: Both Moral and Natural Evil Serve the Good

The major problem facing theism historically has been the problem of evil. If God is all good and all powerful, why is there evil? David Hume's *Dialogues Concerning Natural Religion* explores several solutions which are unsatisfactory: that God's goodness is perfect but incomprehensible; that the answer will be known in the afterlife; that there is more good than evil; that God is finitely powerful; that God is

---

9. Gangadean, *Philosophical Foundation*, 131-134.

10. Gangadean, *Philosophical Foundation*, 129-131.

11. Gangadean, *Philosophical Foundation*, 139-144.

morally indifferent. In the end, we are left with Philo's argument that natural evil in many forms is not necessary.[12]

Theists have appealed to free will as a solution to the problem of evil. They have generally accepted that natural evil is not necessary. Natural evil is due to moral evil; moral evil is due to free will; and free will is necessary for human dignity. But there are objections. Free will makes moral evil possible, not actual. If it is actual, that does not show that evil is necessary. Free will does not have to make moral evil possible (God is free without the possibility of evil, and man, in his final blessedness, is free without the possibility of evil). Furthermore, one can pass from innocence to virtue without any moral evil.[13]

Theism has a serious problem, at least, with explaining the existence of evil. To maintain clarity of general revelation, more is needed than saying the problem is not a contradiction, or, that there is a reason, known to God but not to man, why there is evil in the world. An alternative solution is needed, an ironic solution to an ironic problem. To outline an ironic solution employing Rational Presuppositionalism, Christian philosophy must clarify the meaning of basic terms in the argument. Good and evil must be defined in relation to human nature as rational, and in light of the inexcusability of unbelief. In this solution, moral evil, understood as unbelief, is permitted for a purpose. Moral evil serves to obscure the revelation to the person in unbelief, as well as to deepen the revelation of the divine nature for all to see. If moral evil is removed abruptly, the revelation will not be deepened. And if unbelief is not removed, the revelation will not be seen. Moral evil (unbelief) in every form and degree of admixture with belief is allowed to come to expression in world history, and, in history, good (belief) gradually overcomes unbelief.[14]

Natural evil was not original in the creation, but was imposed by God to restrain, recall from, and remove moral evil. In this way, evil is made to serve the good. The assumptions of this solution must be scrutinized. Is there a clear general revelation (so as to make unbelief inexcusable)? Is there any other way to deepen the revelation apart from

---

12. Gangadean, *Philosophical Foundation*, 145–154.

13. Gangadean, *Philosophical Foundation*, 154–156.

14. Gangadean, *Philosophical Foundation*, 156–161; In this work, see the essay: "The Problem of Evil: An Ironic Solution;" Gangadean, *The Book of Job: Deepening the Revelation of God's Glory for All Time—An Ironic Theodicy* (Phoenix: Logos Papers Press, 2024).

actual evil? Does the good (the knowledge of God) justify the existence of evil, without denying its nature as evil?

By understanding good and evil more consistently, and by applying it to one's self, the irony of the solution can be seen.

1. If God is all good and all powerful, why is there evil in the world?
2. Because of all the evil in the world, I cannot see how God is all good and all powerful.
3. Because of all the unbelief in the world, I cannot see how God is all good and all powerful.
4. Because of all the unbelief in me, I cannot see how God is all good and all powerful.
5. Because I have turned off my reason, I cannot see how God is all good and all powerful.

We can call this solution the Ironic Solution, consistent with the nature of evil as presupposed by Christian theism, from the start.

There Is a Moral Law Which Is Clear, Comprehensive, and Critical

Christian philosophy must address two final steps in showing the clarity of general revelation. It must answer the question of ethics and show the transition from general to special revelation.

Ethics is concerned with giving a rational justification for an answer to the question, "what is the good?" Both skepticism and non-theistic alternatives challenge clarity. Christian philosophy must show there is a moral law which is *clear* (because it is grounded in human nature), *comprehensive* (applied to all choice and all aspects of human nature), and *critical* (its consequence is a matter of life or death). Christian philosophy, consistent with Rational Presuppositionalism, must begin with what is most basic in ethics. The good (the end in itself, the highest value, the source of unity) is assumed in all choice. It is distinct from virtue (the means to the end in itself) and from happiness (the effect of possessing what one believes to be the good). The good is grounded in human nature, which is grounded in one's view of what is real. Since it is clear that only some (God, the Creator) is eternal, God as creator of human nature is the determiner of good and evil for man.

God as determiner is opposed to man, understanding himself apart from God, as the determiner of good and evil. This is sufficient to rule out ethical egoism and utilitarianism, deontology and existentialism, as well as other forms of human autonomy.[15]

The moral law must address divisions among theists concerning the nature of God, based on the nature of thinking (the less basic in light of the more basic). It must address divisions within a person (lack of integrity) based on the unity of our nature. Work, as necessary for the good, requires hope that the good will be achieved. We are born ignorant and must be taught the good and the means to the good. Those in authority must have insight into the good. We are born human, having the capacity to understand, and must be treated as having the capacity and responsibility for understanding. We are born of a sexual union, a natural sign of love and the commitment required by love. We naturally value things, and, by possession of talent, are obligated to create what is of lasting value, in service to others. We are born equal as persons and we have a natural obligation to do justice (to treat equals equally). Therefore, we are to know and speak the truth in order to achieve justice. We are born changeable and can misconceive the good. We are not to turn from the good in discontent due to such misconception or because of natural evil, which is a call to stop and think.[16]

The moral law, knowable from general revelation, is the same in content as the moral law given in special revelation. It is universal and perpetual and the means to the good. It is not the means to redemption, but makes manifest the need for redemption. And one is enabled, by redemption, to seek the good through the way of life given in the moral law.

General Revelation Is Necessary for and Requires Special Revelation

The need for redemption and for redemptive revelation can be seen in understanding the existence and nature of natural evil. Deism denies the necessity for special revelation by failing to understand the origin of natural evil (physical death). Physical death is not original

---

15. Gangadean, *Philosophical Foundation*, 171-183. In this work, see the essay: "The Good and the Beatific Vision"

16. Gangadean, *Philosophical Foundation*, 185-284.

in creation. God, as all powerful and all good, could, would, must have, and therefore did, create mankind without physical death (not to speak of other forms of natural evil). Physical death is not inherent in moral evil. The inherent consequence of moral evil is spiritual, not physical, death. Physical death, therefore, is imposed by God, because of moral evil, as a call back from moral evil. A call back, as mercy, requires redemptive revelation to show how God can be both just and merciful. Mercy does not set aside divine justice, but satisfies it. What would count as redemptive revelation must be consistent with what is clear from general revelation, and must show how God is both just and merciful to man in sin. Biblical revelation, with its teaching on vicarious atonement, and the Christian interpretation which finds both justice and mercy in Christ's atonement, satisfies the requirement for special revelation. Other scriptures and other interpretations do not meet the requirements.

Response to Past and Continuing Challenges

If Christian philosophy can get this far, many of the external challenges by non-theism would have been met. Yet challenges remain to show Christian theism in contrast to non-Christian forms of theism (Judaism and Islam); to settle longstanding disputes within Christian theism (e.g. free will vs. predestination); to answer objections put forward by Kant and Nietzsche and Marx and Freud to popular distortions of Christianity (pietism, fideism, and otherworldliness); to avoid reconstructions of Christian theism put forward by Kant, Schleiermacher, Hegel, and Ritschl, which fail to reckon with the clarity of general revelation.[17]

Serve All Areas of Dominion: Foundation for the Glory of God

Finally, Christian philosophy must serve the good, not only negatively, but positively. If eternal life is knowing God, and if through dominion the earth shall be full of the knowledge of God, Christian philosophy must serve all areas of dominion by helping to establish the philosophical foundations of the various academic disciplines on

---

17. Gangadean, *The Logos Papers: To Make the Logos Known*; *History of Philosophy: A Critical Analysis of Unresolved Disputes*; *Philosophical Foundation: A Critical Analysis of Basic Beliefs*; *Theological Foundation: A Critical Analysis of Christian Belief*; *The Westminster Confession of Faith: A Doxological Understanding*.

which each discipline must build. Philosophy of Art (aesthetics), Philosophy of Literature (hermeneutics), Philosophy of science (natural and social), Philosophy of Law, Philosophy of History, as well as other areas, must be worked out. If Christian philosophy is to be relevant and regarded, it must enable others in the interpretation of personal and communal experience in ways that further the knowledge of God. Christian philosophy, therefore, has a task which is as necessary and demanding as it is rewarding.

16

THE BIBLICAL WORLDVIEW
Creation, Fall, Redemption

Small speaking engagement, Grand Canyon University

2002

T HE APPEARANCE OF CHRISTIANITY MARKS the beginning of a new
era in world history. Christians believe God had acted in history
in a unique and definitive way. The long-awaited messiah, promised
to all mankind, had come. The assumptions of this belief were radi-
cally distinct from all other beliefs. God had created the heavens and
the earth. All mankind had turned away from God into sin and death.
And Christ, the Word of God incarnate, had brought grace and truth
to all mankind. Christianity is distinct from non-biblical religions
and philosophies in affirming the creation of the world and the fall of
mankind, and it is distinct from the other biblical religions of Judaism and Islam in affirming redemption in the incarnation, death, and
resurrection of Christ.

Creation, fall, and redemption—these are the basic themes of biblical revelation. The latter assumes the former and is unintelligible without understanding the former. Redemptive revelation in the Scriptures
assumes the existence of clear general revelation in the creation, as well
as the existence of moral evil in the denial of clear general revelation.
The movement in history is from good to evil to a restoration to what
is good. The restoration from evil to good is gradual. Evil affects the understanding of good and evil itself, and only gradually, through much
conflict, do we overcome our denial of what is clear, and come to understand the true nature of good and evil. The redemptive restoration

to what is good, through long, intense conflict with evil, serves only to deepen the good, in a way otherwise impossible. Good does not merely overcome evil, but causes evil to serve the good.

The themes of creation, fall, and redemption are best introduced from the first three chapters of Genesis, with the following caveats. First, the reading of any text will reflect the assumptions of the reader. This is as it should be. What is needed is a critical awareness of one's assumptions. To say that there are many different interpretations is not the end of all discussion, but an invitation to begin critical philosophical reflection on the different interpretive frameworks. The less basic assumes the more basic; special revelation assumes general revelation. If there is agreement on general revelation, there will be agreement on special revelation. Second, there are many degrees of the use of reason and of understanding among those who broadly agree on general and special revelation. Popular levels of understanding do not reflect what has been achieved in the historical process of creedal definition of doctrine—what the best minds agree upon after much discussion. And historical/creedal understanding does not reflect some of the philosophical responses to challenges made since the last period of creedal definition, a period sometimes lasting for centuries.

What follows is a philosophical development of historical/creedal interpretations of the text of the first three chapters of Genesis. Reason is being used to understand general revelation, and reason and general revelation are being used to understand the text.

CREATION

In the Beginning

Original creation is *ex nihilo*. There is no preexisting substance from which the creation is formed; matter and spirit are created by God from nothing. They are other than God and not a part of God. This is in opposition to naturalism—which claims matter is eternal, to dualism—which claims that both matter and souls are eternal, to pantheism—which claims that all is part of God, and to spiritual monism—which claims that the physical universe is non-existent.

Subsequent creation is by forming original creation and filling the earth that has been formed with living beings. Original creation does not form itself into the present cosmos without a creative act. What is formed is by acts of separation. And life does not appear each after its kind by natural processes, but by the act of creation. Special creation by the act of God is opposed to naturalistic or theistic evolutionary explanations of the origin of the cosmos and of the kinds of living beings.

Creation and Revelation

Creation is revelation. Creation is revelation *necessarily*. The act of a being is according to the nature of the being and reveals the nature of the being; the visible reveals the invisible. The revelation is *intentional*. Creation *ex nihilo* assumes infinite power and knowledge. There are no unintentional effects in creation. The effect of revelation is intended. There are no external limitations on the divine power. What is created is declared good. It came to be as it was intended. And while acts necessarily reveals one's nature, which acts are done are by intention. The revelation is by creation, *exclusively*. There is no revelation apart from the creation. Special revelation is set in the theater of creation. To attempt to know God directly apart from creation is to attempt to know unmanifest being apart from manifestation in act.

The revelation in creation is full, not bare or minimal. To be full is not to be infinite. Creation does not exhaust the infinitude of God. The creation in all its vast array reveals the divine glory. The uniqueness of each person as this unfolds in their life story reveals something unique about God as a person. While creation is not exhaustive of God's infinitude, the fullness of creation cannot be exhausted by man.

The revelation in creation is clear. It is objectively clear by reason to those who seek to know God. The eternal power and divine nature are clearly revealed so that unbelief is without excuse.[1] The clarity is such that one has to deny one's reason to avoid seeing God. Moral evil cannot be understood apart from understanding the clarity of general revelation.

Man: The Image of God

Man is made in the image of God. Human nature is multi-dimensional. In its broadest aspect, human beings have the attributes of God

---

1. *Romans 1:20.*

such as wisdom, power, justice, and goodness, but in a finite, temporal, and changeable way. Man is the image of God, not of nature, or of animals. Man is the image of God and is not God or divine. Man, the finite creature, is to be understood in light of the infinite creator and not the creator in light of the creature. Man, as made in the image of God, reveals God more fully than all else in the creation. Man is a body/soul unity in which the body visibly and symbolically reveals the soul. Self-knowledge and the knowledge of God, therefore, are intimately connected.

Man is to manifest his bearing the image of God by being like God in a creaturely way. Man is to exercise rule in the creation even as God ruled in the creation of heaven and earth. The creative work given to man is to exercise dominion over the works of creation. His naming the creation reveals his understanding of the nature of each kind of created being. In dominion, man is to creatively form the creation and fill it in a way that accomplishes God's purpose in creating. Man is to develop the powers latent in the creation so as to make manifest the true nature of things. This includes developing the powers of talent latent in human beings.

Because the creation is vast in diversity and deep in complexity, dominion requires a great number of human beings acting cooperatively over a long time to accomplish dominion. The result of the human effort of dominion is increase in knowledge of the nature of the creation, including the nature of man, who makes the effort. Since the nature of the creation reveals the nature of God, through dominion, the earth is to be filled with the knowledge of God. Thus, man's highest good, the knowledge of God, is achieved corporately through dominion over creation, which is intended by God to be self-revelation.

The Choice of Good and Evil

There are two ways before man, always: the way of good resulting in life, and the way of evil resulting in death. These two ways are exhaustive and mutually exclusive. Good for man is determined by his nature, which has been determined by God through creation. Man, the image of God, knows himself to be different from the animals. He is distinguished from them by his capacity to understand, by his rationality. Good for man as a rational being is the use of his reason the fullest.

Since reason is used to grasp the nature of things, and the meaning of the nature of things is what they reveal of God, good for man is the knowledge of God. Evil, on the other hand, is the failure to use reason; it is the failure to know God. It results in the failure to find meaning in the world. The lack of meaning is the inherent consequence of failure to use reason or of the denial of one's reason. This meaninglessness, and, with it, boredom and guilt, is spiritual death, and is the necessary consequence of the denial of one's nature as a rational being. It is an act of self-destruction.

In Genesis, the two ways are represented in the two trees—the tree of life and the tree of the knowledge of good and evil. Man is forbidden to eat the fruit of the tree of the knowledge of good and evil, for in the day that he eats, he will surely die. The names of the trees reveal their significance. They represent the way of life and the way of death, the choice between good and evil. The forbidden tree does not forbid the knowledge of good and evil, since this is presupposed in the command concerning the tree. What is forbidden is not knowledge of good and evil by discovery, but knowledge of good and evil by determination from oneself understood independently of God. What is forbidden is human autonomy to determine good and evil, the denial of one's creatureliness, and thereby the declaration of independence from God who, as creator of human nature, is the determiner of good and evil for man. The pursuit of the good requires knowledge of the existence and the nature of God, and understanding oneself and all things in light of God, so as to ever increase in the knowledge of God. The choice to seek the knowledge of God as the good or something other than this, which man autonomously determines to be good, remains before all men, always. The choice is structured into human nature by creation. In all he does, man can either love self above God or love God above self.

Work and Hope

Man is given the task of ruling the creation. Ruling is made necessary by the demands of his nature as a body/soul unity. To provide for material needs requires knowledge and control of the environment. To provide for spiritual needs requires truth, beauty, and goodness, or knowledge, holiness, and righteousness. For the former needs, knowledge as wisdom is pursued as a virtue, in order to achieve other ends. For the latter needs, knowledge of what is ultimate is pursued as an end in itself, for its own sake. Because man is a unity of body and soul, and not merely a soul that happens for a while to be in a body, these two forms of knowledge are not independent, but very intimately connected. The knowledge of the infinite God requires knowledge of the finite creature, which reveals God. The fullness of the knowledge of God requires filling the earth with image bearers of God, whose lives lived out under innumerable varied conditions of understanding good and evil are part of the revelation of God which man is called to understand. The goal of dominion requires the corporate effort of many over a long period of time.

This goal and the hope of achieving it is kept before man in perpetual remembrance by the institution of the Sabbath day. The Sabbath is a reminder to man of his origin, his purpose, and the hope of achieving that purpose. Man is the image of God, created by God. As God worked and completed his work on the seventh day, man is to work and complete his work. As God's work of creation is revelation, so man's work of dominion is to gain knowledge of this revelation. As the earth is filled with the glory of God in all its vast array, the vast host of the human race is to fill the earth with the knowledge of the glory of God as the waters cover the sea.[2] Man is to work to this end for six days in each week. On the seventh day, he is to look at his work as God looked at his work and see if all things done are very good. He is also to rest in anticipation that the work to be done will one day be completed, and that he will enjoy the works of his hands, the enjoyment that comes from possessing the good in the knowledge of God.

The Institution of Marriage and Family

By creation, the original human institution is the family, which begins with marriage. By the union of male and female, all human beings, after creation, have their origin. The goal of marriage is to fill the earth and to rule over it in order to attain the knowledge of God. Companionship in marriage is an effect of pursuing the good together.

---

2. *Isaiah 11:9.*

Children are brought into the world and nurtured in order that they might achieve, possess, and enjoy the good.

The origin of marriage is in the unity of the diversity of male and female. Man is made in the image of God, and male and female reflect the nature of God, but in diverse aspects. Male and female are first spiritual characteristics, which are mirrored in biological characteristics. The characteristics of male and female, both spiritual and biological, do not override other more basic aspects of human nature. The same is true for other characteristics arising from one's nurture and from the uniqueness of one's personhood. The characteristics of male and female, which are united in one being, become expressed in two persons, who in turn unite in marriage.

Marriage is a full union of two persons, each of whom is a union of body and soul. The union of marriage is not only physical and not only spiritual, but both physical and spiritual. The union of marriage is a voluntary giving of oneself and taking of the other. The physical union is a sign and seal of the spiritual union of love for one's complement. To separate the sign from the reality desecrates the sign and denies the body/soul union of a person. As a full union of two persons, marriage is a monogamous relationship that is lifelong. The union of marriage is the beginning of a new family unit, with freedom from all claims which might threaten its integrity.

The Unity of Mankind

By creation, mankind was bound in unity. There is a unity of origin, place, task, and responsibility. All share the same biological origin in the first human pair and kinship bonds continue through the generations. There is one human race; later ethnic diversity is secondary to and grows out of this primary unity. All life began in one place. There is a geographical center and geographical continuity is assured by the rivers which flow from this one place. There is a common goal which binds all in a cultural unity and which can be achieved only by a functional unity of all. The generations are bound one to another in a covenantal unity. Parents act on behalf of their children. Their act affects all succeeding generations. The act of the first man uniquely has consequences reaching to all mankind.

The Goodness of Creation

The original state of the creation was very good. Each thing created was good; together, all was very good. Originally, there was no moral or natural evil. This was so because of the infinite power, knowledge, and goodness of God. God has the power to bring about what he intends. By his knowledge and power, he is able to bring about a world without moral or natural evil. By his goodness, he wills to bring about such a world. Therefore, the world came to be in a state that was very good. Later, moral evil began by the act of man, who by nature is changeable. Because of moral evil, natural evil was imposed on the creation. No thing by nature is evil, but evil is a denial of a thing's nature. Evil does not alter the divine goodness, but the divine goodness causes evil to serve the good.

THE FALL

The fall of man is the beginning of evil in the world. It introduces radical discontinuity and division in the creation at all levels. It introduces disorder into the world by reversing the order of being, and thereby destroys being. It puts the less basic in place of the more basic, the finite in place of the infinite, the creature in place of the Creator. Evil in a person obscures the nature of all things to that person, including the origin, existence, and nature of evil. Individuals struggle through decades and cultures struggle through centuries to understand good and evil. Outside of where God's rule is acknowledged, evil rules in a hopeless disorder and chaos, intellectually, psychologically, and socially. The understanding of evil in Genesis sets this worldview apart from all others.

The account of the origin of evil has three parts: temptation, sin, and death. In understanding the temptation, its purpose, source, and content must be noticed. In understanding sin, its several levels must be observed. In understanding death, its inherent characteristics must be recognized.

Temptation

Temptation is a trial of faith, a test of one's understanding of good and evil. In itself, a temptation is not evil nor intended to cause evil. Its purpose is to reveal to the persons tested where they are in their pursuit of the good. Since persons in moral evil can be in self-deception and denial of their condition, testing is necessary to make them aware of their condition. The test must have results that are visibly manifest so that evil cannot obscure the result. Temptation reveals what is already present, it does not bring about any change in the moral condition of a person except knowledge of that condition. Temptations, trials, or tests are therefore necessary; they are not gratuitously permitted. And temptations are not the cause of evil, but the revealer of evil, if evil is present.

Temptation requires circumstances in which one's moral condition can be explicitly manifested. Circumstance can vary indefinitely. In the Garden, the two trees made the manifestation of obedience explicit. The test will always seem sudden to those who are not prepared, and take by surprise those who are not watchful. Even with warning, to the self-confident, awareness of temptation arises after the fact, when one's condition has been revealed. While the primary cause of temptation, as a test of understanding, is God, and the proximate cause may be an external agent, the immediate cause of temptation, when one is tempted to evil, is from within the person who is tempted.

The content of temptation concerns the understanding of good and evil and the use of the means to having this understanding. It concerns also the pursuit of the good, since understanding increases with pursuit and decreases with failure to pursue the good. The good for man is the knowledge of God. And it is by the Word of God that God is known. The Word of God comes to man from within the nature of man as reason, from around man in the nature of creation as general revelation, and from God as special revelation. In the temptation, man's response to the Word of God in all three forms is tested. The question in the temptation is: has man understood the good as the knowledge of God, and has man used reason to understand the revelation of God?

Sin

Sin occurs at the more basic level before it occurs at the less basic level. Root sin occurs before fruit sin, the invisible before the visible. If reflects all dimensions of man's being. Man fails to do what is right in the outward act of eating of the tree of the knowledge of good and evil. But first, he fails to understand the nature of good and evil, the nature of sin and death, and the nature of God and man. And he fails to understand these things because he has not continued to seek God. In desire, thought, and act, man has turned aside. He has turned aside from God and the Word of God to self. How did this turning from the Word of God occur?

When questioned about the Word of God ("Has God said . . .?"[3]), the answer reveals knowledge of what God said. When this word is denied ("You will not surely die. For God knows that in the day you eat of it your eyes will be opened, and you will be like God, knowing good and evil."[4]), the denial and the reason for the denial are believed by man, and this leads to the act of eating. Before the outward act, there is unbelief; before unbelief, there is misunderstanding; before misunderstanding, there has been the failure to seek understanding. What is it that is not understood and believed?

Man disbelieves the Word of God: "For in the day that you eat of it [the tree of the knowledge of good and evil] you shall surely die."[5] He disbelieves this by believing the denial of it: "You will not surely die." The necessary connection between sin and death is denied. But since understanding the nature of sin implies understanding death, to disconnect the two shows that neither is being understood. There is in this the failure to understand the significance of the name of the tree and how eating of this tree signifies partaking of the way represented by the tree. And since the understanding of good and evil are necessarily connected, failure to understand evil or sin shows failure to understand the good. In addition, to believe that what God said is not true is to believe that God is mistaken or lying, neither of which can properly be said about a being who is infinite in knowledge and goodness. So, to believe, "you will not surely die," is to deny the existence of God as such by failing to understand his nature.

The depth of unbelief and misunderstanding is further revealed by considering the implications of believing the reason given in support of, "You will not surely die." The reason given is: "you will be like God,

---

3. *Genesis 3:1.*

4. *Genesis 3:4.*

5. *Genesis 2:17.*

knowing good and evil."[6] This requires an understanding of the nature of good and evil, of how God knows good and evil, and of whether we can know good and evil as God does. Good, for a being, is based on the nature of the being. Evil, for a being, is the denial of the nature of that being. Since the nature of a being is determined by God who created the being with that nature, it is God who determines what is good and evil for that being. God knows good and evil, not by discovery after the fact of a being's existence, but by determination through creation. Since man is self-evidently finite and cannot create the nature of things, man cannot know good and evil in the same way that God does. To misunderstand and blur the radical distinction between the finite creature and the infinite Creator, in believing "You will be like God, knowing good and evil," requires the abandonment of reason, and with it a denial of human nature.

If man had been pursuing his task of naming the creation, if he had been pursuing the good as the knowledge of God through dominion, he would have been growing in his understanding of himself and of God. When tested, it proved that he had turned from this view of the good to another view based on a misunderstanding of self and God. Man viewed himself as independent of God, and wanted to be like God, in knowing good and evil. He put himself in the place of God as the determiner of good and evil. The outward (evil) act of eating of the tree of the knowledge of good and evil revealed the inward (evil) reality of having put himself in the place of God, to know good and evil as the determiner of the meaning of things.

Moral evil, then, in its origin, has several different aspects. There is the evil of not seeking the knowledge of God as the good. There is the evil of not understanding and believing the clear revelation of man as finite creature and God as infinite Creator. There is the evil of not understanding and believing the clear revelation of the nature of good and evil and the relation of sin and death. There is the evil of the act of eating what is explicitly forbidden. There is the evil of denying reason, the Word of God in man, in order to deny the clear difference between the infinite God and finite man. There is the evil of denying one's nature as a rational being, which denial is the act of self-destruction. There is the evil of putting oneself in the place of God, to

---

6. *Genesis 3:4.*

act autonomously to determine good and evil. This root of evil bears fruit in every form of evil. The fruits of evil cannot be removed without removing the root.

Death

The inherent consequence of sin is death. Divine justice is revealed in the necessary connection between sin and death. Death, which is inherent in sin, is present where sin is present, not future and imposed. Popular conceptions of future punishments fail to see the necessary connection of sin and death, and unavoidably distort divine justice. How are sin and death necessarily connected? To deny reason is to shut one's eyes. It brings spiritual blindness, necessarily, and with it, the darkness of mind in misunderstanding, and unbelief. Since reason understands the meaning of the creation in light of the Creator, to deny reason brings meaninglessness, in two ways, necessarily. To deny reason is to deny the possibility of thought itself, and to deny God as Creator is to deny the possibility of understanding the meaning of creation. All explanations of the origin of creation apart from God fall apart. Meaninglessness is *death to the intellect*.

From meaninglessness arises boredom. Since no object of desire can be valued as more significant than any other in a meaningless world, there is none worth pursuing above another. A sort of anomie or listlessness results. Attempts to escape boredom by pursuing any desire, even to excess, fail, since no finite object of desire can be a substitute for the infinite. In a world without meaning, a person is caught between desirelessness and the burning of desires which cannot be satisfied, which increases desirelessness, and from which there is no escape. Boredom is a state of *death to the emotions*.

It is difficult to take responsibility for bringing this condition on oneself. There are continuing attempts to avoid awareness of one's true condition. We multiply our distractions. Where exposure cannot be avoided, self-justification begins. The endlessness of self-justification reveals the unceasing torment of guilt. An attempt to give a reason where there is no reason, because reason has been denied, reveals the hopelessness of trying to justify oneself. Guilt strips the guilty of all moral worth. The sense of worthlessness paralyzes one's will to seek the good for oneself and is *death to the will*.

Thus, meaninglessness, boredom, and guilt are inherent in the sin of denying what is clear. As sin occurs in thought, desire, and will, so death is present in all these aspects of a person. In scriptural categories, sin involves turning from seeking God in holiness to seeking self in unholiness; turning from knowledge with understanding to unbelief with misunderstanding; turning from righteousness in obedience to unrighteousness in disobedience. The death that occurred in the day he ate is spiritual, not physical death. By divine justice, meaninglessness, boredom, and guilt begins with sin, and deepens as sin deepens, without end. There are no consequences of sin, in this life or beyond, besides spiritual death.

REDEMPTION

Redemption is the purpose of God to restore man from sin and death to righteousness and life, yet in such a way that evil serves to deepen the original divine purpose of self-revelation in the creation. Evil objectively reveals the nature of the creation and of God in ways not otherwise disclosed without evil. Evil is allowed to come to full expression in human history, in every form and degree of conflict and admixture with the good. In this conflict, good gradually, fully, and finally overcomes evil. Man's original rule is enlarged by evil to include rule over evil in himself and others.

Redemption begins with God's call of man to repentance. Although resisted at first, this call persists and deepens. When man responds to this call in repentance and faith, he is forgiven and justified by God in a way that frees him from guilt and self-justification. And man is restored to his divine purpose by a gradual process of sanctification, in which he learns to overcome evil in himself and in the world. In doing so, mankind comes to know God and to fill the earth with the knowledge of God as the waters cover the sea.

The Call to Repentance

1. Shame and Self-deception

The first call to repentance is an inner call from the feeling of shame. When man's inner sin is exposed by the outward act of disobedience, he experiences shame. He stands naked. His physical nakedness becomes a sign of his spiritual nakedness. Man is ashamed of himself in his fallen condition. He does not want to see himself or be seen in this condition. Instead of acknowledging his sin and the shame which calls him back, he avoids it by covering it up from himself and others. Both the intent to cover up and the act of covering up requires self-deception about one's true condition. Man wishes to think of himself as a seeker after truth, although he has placed himself in the position of determiner of truth on the basis of what is pleasing to self. In self-deception, he convinces himself that he seeks truth, even the truth about God. He is convinced that it is not clear. He would be ashamed to admit it is not clear because he determines truth by what is pleasing to self.

2. The Question and Self-justification

After resistance to the inward call, the second call to repentance is an outward call, from another, in the form of a question: "Where are you?"[7] The question is not a call for information, but for self-examination. Although one's condition may be concealed from oneself, it is not concealed to the one who sees what is clear. When what is concealed is brought to the light ("Have you eaten . . . ?"[8]), blame is shifted to others in order to justify oneself. Man's rational nature demands of him an accounting. We are required by reason to give a reason for our conduct. Anything short of rational justification is mere self-justification, seen for what it is by reason, and rejected. In his fallen condition, man resists responsibility and accountability to others, and would even accuse others in order to excuse himself ("The woman you gave me . . ."[9]). The accused accuses the accuser. Man accuses God in a desperate attempt to justify himself ("You did not give me enough evidence"). Resistance to the outward call has reached its limits.

3. The Curse and the Promise

In the face of man's deepened resistance, a third call to repentance is made. It is a pervasive, continuing, and final call, reaching to the depths of man's being. It is unrelenting in its increase, penetrating in its effect,

---

7. *Genesis 3:9.*

8. *Genesis 3:11.*

9. *Genesis 3:12.*

and inescapable in its reach. Man is called back by God through the curse. Its purpose is man's good, a call back from evil, and it is made with a promise of redemption. In the curse, the suffering of natural evil is imposed upon man to make him stop and think about his condition. The original goodness of creation is changed. The ground is cursed, along with plants, and animals; their fruitfulness is greatly decreased, so that only by toil can man eat bread. The pains of child-bearing are greatly increased; with sin and autonomy entering with all who are born comes increase of alienation and strife. Toil and strife continue all the days of man's life until the curse comes to full expression through old age, sickness, and death.

Physical death is the final expression of the curse. It is the end of man's call back. There is no call back after death. Physical death is not punishment for sin. It is a natural evil imposed on man for a gracious purpose, and must be distinguished from spiritual death, which is inherent in sin, and which goes on with sin forever. Physical death mirrors and reminds man of spiritual death. Natural evil is imposed on man because of moral evil and serves various purposes. It *restrains* man from going as far as he might into moral evil; it *recalls* man from moral evil; and it serves to *remove* moral evil from those who have turned back.

To restrain the general level of moral evil reached in human history, the general level of natural evil has increased. Human lifespan has greatly decreased; cultural divisions of mankind and strife have greatly increased; the fertility of the earth has greatly decreased. Periodically, natural evil increases with moral evil to the level of famine, war, and plague. Natural evil may increase for both the just and the unjust, serving different purposes in each, according to the need for restraining, recalling from, or removing moral evil. As moral evil is removed, natural evil will be removed. As natural evil is imposed by God, so it will be removed by God. The removal of death and the reunion of soul and body will occur when man completes the work of dominion and fills the earth with the knowledge of God.

The sorrows of the curse are relieved only by the hope of the promise, and the promise can be known only by special revelation. Special revelation is redemptive revelation. It declares God's will to restore man from sin and death to righteousness and life, and tells how this will be accomplished. Although man's call back through natural evil gives him reason to hope for divine mercy, man cannot know how God can be both just and merciful to him in his sin. Justice requires payment of debt. Mercy would forgive the debt. Only special revelation reveals how both justice and mercy are possible at the same time, without one violating the other, thus making special revelation necessary. Special revelation is organic. Although its basic features are all present from the beginning, it becomes fuller and clearer in detail as history progresses.

What are the basic features of the promise made in redemptive revelation? The first concerns the reversal of the Fall by spiritual war; the second concerns the seed of the woman who will accomplish redemption; and the third concerns the final outcome of the struggle. Man was seduced to do evil by believing a lie: "You will be like God, knowing good and evil." All who believe the lie are children of the liar. Man's alliance with evil will be broken and reversed: "I will put enmity between you and the woman, between your seed and her seed."[10] There will be a spiritual war between those who love self more than God and those who love God more than self. The war will be age-long, through all succeeding generations. And it will be agonizing, as each seeks to destroy the other. The enmity between good and evil will endure; there will not be peace through compromise and tolerance. But there will come one, the seed of the woman, who will fully destroy evil spiritually ("he will crush your head"), though evil will strike back physically ("you will strike his heel"). Man is given hope that good will overcome evil through one who is to come, the promised seed.

Repentance and Faith

How is man to respond to this third, final, and continuing call to repentance? How is he to respond to human suffering of toil and strife, and old age, sickness, and death? On the one hand, he can continue his autonomy and with it his resistance to God's call back to repentance, and make sense of his world as he pleases, apart from God. One may see death as natural, as original and not imposed, because there is no God who creates and rules the world. One may even see human suffering as evidence that there is no God who is all good and all powerful. One may regard suffering as absurd, not considering it to be a call back from evil, and reject life under the curse. On the other hand,

---

10. *Genesis 3:15.*

one may acknowledge one's condition of sin and death, one's need for divine mercy, and embrace the provision of redemption from God.

At the beginning of human history, man comes to repentance and faith. He sees his condition as one of death due to sin, and repents of it. By faith, he chooses to live under the curse as God's call back, and embraces the promise of redemption through the seed of the woman: "Adam named his wife Eve, because she would become the mother of all the living."[11] As he considers all future generations in this act of naming, the future implications of the curse and the promise become clear. The curse will be upon all who are yet to come because of the sin of the first man. They too will have sin from which they will be called back by the curse. There will be strife and spiritual war in the generations yet unborn. He cannot avert that. Yet from one to be born will come redemption from sin and death for all men.

Justification

Upon repentance and faith, man receives forgiveness of sin. Forgiveness is revealed in a way that deepens his understanding of sin and grace: "The Lord God made garments of skin for Adam and his wife and clothed them."[12] Man's lack of righteousness is covered, not by his own effort, but by God, through the death of another. Wearing the garments of skin constantly reminds man of his need and of God's provision. Both the atonement of sin, through the death of another, and the provision of the covering of righteousness, through the life of that other, are symbolically displayed in the sacrificed animal. The symbol points to the reality of the one to come who will redeem man from sin. By his repentance and faith, man affirms and declares both the justice and mercy of God in dealing with his sin. Man no longer has to try to justify himself in his sin; he is justified by God, who in justice and in mercy covers his sin.

Sanctification

Although man is forgiven the penalty of sin and is regarded as righteous through the work of another, the power of sin remains in him.

---

11. *Genesis 3:20.*
12. *Genesis 3:21.*

He is still characteristically autonomous, even though this is concealed from himself and others by self-deception and self-justification. Without the compulsion of suffering, which strips from him every secondary good, man does not seek the knowledge of God as his highest good. He must live under the curse and learn of good and evil through suffering: "So the Lord God banished him from the Garden of Eden to work the ground from which he had been taken."[13] There will be no life apart from the knowledge of God, and no knowledge of God without dominion through suffering. Man clings to a distant memory of original goodness and innocence, but is required by suffering in the present to extend his rule over sin. The way to life is guarded by "cherubim and a flaming sword."[14] Man longs for Eden, but cannot return without dealing with his sin. He seeks a quick and easy return, but finds the way long and difficult. Ever recurring romantic and utopian ideals, which fail to recognize the reality of sin, are doomed to failure. There is no life for man apart from the knowledge of God.

---

13. *Genesis 3:23.*
14. *Genesis 3:24.*

17

ROMANS 1

*The Biblical Doctrine of
Clarity and Inexcusability*

Round table discussion with several pastors in Phoenix, Arizona

1996

N O INTELLIGENT CHRISTIAN WILL ARGUE THAT unregenerate sinners are without excuse for their unbelief. Paul makes this all too
abundantly clear in Romans 1:20. However, debate does exist about
the basis of inexcusability. The majority of Protestants, Arminian and
Reformed, presuppositional and evidential, believe that inexcusability
rests fundamentally in the truth that all sinners willingly suppress the
knowledge of God within themselves, sinning, in effect, against their
better knowledge. Mired in destructive self-deception, what the unbeliever knows of God and will not accept, he knowingly rejects.

In opposition to the idea that unbelievers know God deep down inside and suppress that truth in sinful rebellion, is the idea that unbelievers in spiritual death do not seek after the clear truth of God and,
therefore, do not know God deep down inside. In other words, the objective revelation of God is never subjectively realized—it fails to "get
through." Here, inexcusability is not a matter of knowledge knowingly
suppressed, or repressed, but is a matter of clear and present truth un-
acknowledged. In effect, sinners in unbelief are primarily accountable
for not understanding and not believing what is clearly revealed of God.

The doctrines of both clarity and inexcusability do not first surface
with Romans 1:18-21, but spring from the beginning of redemptive

revelation, in Genesis chapter 3. It is from within this context, as well as the rest of Scripture that follows, that we must eventually come to and uncover the coherent meaning of Romans 1:18-21. From Genesis chapter 3, we see that God's testing of Adam in the Garden was designed to reveal where Adam was in his seeking the clear truth of God. Was he seeking the good, the knowledge of God, or was he seeking to determine the good for himself in autonomous rebellion? From the beginning, the serpent's temptation was directed at the heart of what Adam understood to be true regarding the nature of God and himself. In directly contradicting God's command that both Adam and Eve would surely die upon eating of the forbidden fruit, the serpent tactfully insinuated that God is either ignorant or a liar, both of which God clearly cannot be. The crux of the matter is whether Adam ate the fruit of the tree because he wanted to be autonomous and repress what he deep down knew to be true of God, or whether he, in spiritual death, had not sought after the knowledge of God and, thus, did not know what is clear of God, or at least had neglected what perhaps he did at one time know to be true of God. When we do not diligently seek to know God, our knowledge of him can be missed or lost all together. Therefore, we need not insist that Adam paradoxically knew deep down that God could not lie or be ignorant, yet still agreed with the serpent's appeal, as though the test was a heart matter and not a head one. Furthermore, the serpent's temptation also incorporated a suggestion that both Adam and Eve, though created, could be like God knowing good and evil. As both Adam and Eve were responsible to know that God cannot lie or be ignorant, both were likewise responsible to know the clear truth that, as finite beings, they could not be as God, who is eternal. Likewise, because God is eternal, he alone determines good and evil. He does not discover it, as Adam and Eve would have had to if the serpent's lie were the truth. Moreover, clear thinking on the part of both husband and wife would also have kept them from trying to hide from an omniscient and omnipresent God, which showed yet an even greater deficiency in their understanding of the nature of God. If Adam and his wife had been seeking to know the clear truth concerning the nature of God and man, they would have rejected the serpent's lie; they would have seen the temptation as complete nonsense, an impossible suggestion.

The original sin of our first parents, the sin of not seeking to know what is clear of God and his creation, is with all of us today, both believers and unbelievers. The idea that inexcusability assumes clarity, rather than a suppressed knowledge of God, coherently demonstrates how unbelievers and believers sin alike; sin is fundamentally not seeking to know God as he has revealed himself, both generally and specially. Paul speaks to this in Romans: "As it is written: 'There is no one righteous, not even one; there is no one who understands, no one who seeks God.'"[1] Regarding how Paul's analysis relates to sin in both the believer and the unbeliever, is shown in how Peter, though clearly regenerate, insisted that Jesus as Messiah could not be made to suffer. Peter's attempted suppression of the truth of Christ's mission stemmed from a false assumption that was born of not seeking what God had clearly revealed of his redemptive plan in Scripture. Shall we assume that Peter was rebelliously suppressing an innate understanding that the Messiah had to suffer, or shall we instead assume that Peter wrongly believed that the atonement for sin would come without the shedding of the Messiah's blood? Though Peter came to see the error of his uncritically held assumptions, unbelievers are forever unwilling to seek after and acknowledge the clear truth of God. Both the Old and New Testaments speak to this matter. Isaiah writes, "They know nothing, they understand nothing; their eyes are plastered over so they cannot see, and their minds closed so they cannot understand."[2] Clearly, this verse is best interpreted to mean that God's objective revelation is not subjectively realized by the unbeliever. This same sentiment is mirrored by St. Paul in 2 Corinthians 4:3. Paul writes, "And even if our gospel is veiled, it is veiled to those who are perishing. The god of this age has blinded the minds of unbelievers, so they cannot see the light of the gospel of the glory of Christ, who is the image of God." We see an example of Paul's above emphasis nowhere better than with the teachers of the law. These individuals were operating from age-old assumptions about the nature of the Messiah that ran in direct contrast with the life and teachings of Christ. Their problem was that in light of their own entrenched assumptions, they would not and could not see the truth and consistency of Christ's claims. They hated Christ

---

1. *Romans 3:10-11.*

2. *Isaiah 44:18.*

not because they knew he spoke the truth and could not stomach it;
they hated him because what he preached did not align with their beliefs (Messianic and otherwise) and also because he brilliantly exposed
their illegitimate authority. We should expect the spiritually blind to
be unwilling to seek after and understand spiritual truths—resorting
instead to blind authoritarianism and militant self-justification. Continuing with his general point about not seeking and not understanding, Paul writes in 1 Corinthians 2:14, "The man without the Spirit
does not accept the things that come from the Spirit of God, for they
are foolishness to him, and he cannot understand them, because they
are spiritually discerned." What is foolishness to those in unbelief is
such because they have not understood it, and they have not understood it because they have not sought the clear truths of God. This notion, that unbelieving man in spiritual death is unwilling and unable
to know God, is not entirely foreign to Hebrew thought. While not of
canonical authority, the apocryphal book of Wisdom states in chapter 13, verse 1, "For all men were by nature foolish who were in ignorance of God, and who from the good things seen did not succeed in
knowing him who is, and from studying the works did not discern the
artisan." Concerning his own life in sinful unbelief, Paul writes in 1
Timothy 1:13, "Even though I was once a blasphemer and a persecu-
tor and a violent man, I was shown mercy because I acted in ignorance
and unbelief." Clearly, ignorance is a matter of not knowing what is
true—not a matter of suppressing what is true. One who knowingly
suppresses the truth cannot also be suppressing the truth ignorantly.

Though what St. Paul stresses must not be overlooked, we cannot help
but see that Jesus himself confronts the sinner as ignorant and unwilling
to know the truths of God. Christ speaks in Matthew 13:14-15:

> 'You will be ever hearing but never understanding; you will be ever
> seeing but never perceiving. For this people's heart has become cal-
> loused; they hardly hear with their ears, and they have closed their
> eyes. Otherwise they might see with their eyes, hear with their ears,
> understand with their hearts and turn, and I would heal them.'

The emphasis of Christ's words here seems to reveal a problem with the
cognition of the truth and not a willful rejection of it. Furthermore, in
Luke 23:34, Jesus declares, "Father, forgive them; for they know not

what they do." Here we see that the greatest rebellion against God is not chalked up to the willful suppression of the truth, but to culpable ignorance. This flows perfectly with how Jesus' apologetic efforts were consistently aimed at showing where the assumptions of others were clearly at fault and how they were responsible for their obstinacy in not seeking and not knowing the clear truths of God. When Christ asked whether John's baptism was of God or of man, and who David's Lord was in Psalm 110, he knew that the questions he raised would serve to expose and demolish the uncritically held assumptions of those in authority, those who were in positions of instruction in the faith. In fact, many of Christ's debates ended in silence, revealing that the truth is clear and that sinful man must turn off his mind not to see it. Time and time again, the gospels reveal a Christ who taught people what they did not already know or realize, yet ought to have. Luke writes, "And beginning with Moses and all the Prophets, he explained to them what was said in all the Scriptures concerning himself,"[3] and, "Then he opened their minds so they could understand the Scriptures."[4] The gospels reveal the same psychological effect of regeneration time and time again—coming to see the truth of what had not before been understood because of a lack of seeking to know the truth of God. Even in everyday life it is common that when believers come to the Lord, they do so through a process of realizing that their past assumptions and basic beliefs no longer make any sense in the light of God's clear and compelling truth. What Nicodemus did not understand about regeneration is the effect of having not diligently sought out the clear truth of God and cannot be attributed to any type of suppressed knowledge. Furthermore, time and time again, we see Christ admonishing his followers for being of dull mind and slow in understanding, but never do we see Christ admonishing them for anything that can be categorized as willful suppression of the truth. Never do we see Christ appealing to suppressed knowledge, but always to the blindness of unbelief and the unwillingness of sinful man to seek after the clear truth of God. In John 8:43, Christ speaks to this, "Why is my language not clear to you? Because you are unable to hear what I say." What else could our Lord have said to make himself any clearer?

---

3. *Luke 24:27.*

4. *Luke 24:45.*

It is now appropriate to give an interpretation of Romans 1:18-21 in light of the above analysis that men are without excuse for not understanding and believing in what God has clearly revealed of himself.

Romans 1:18 says, "The wrath of God is being revealed from heaven against all the godlessness and wickedness of men who suppress the truth by their wickedness." We need not assume here that unbelievers suppress the truth while at the same time knowing it, but instead, suppress and hinder the truth of God principally by the mountain of lies and falsehood they concoct out of their darkened and ignorant minds. Paul's emphasis is to set up the idea that the truth of God, both specially and generally revealed, has been systematically suppressed, hindered, and held down by false assumptions and lies. Helmut Thielicke remarks:

> The fact that the divine majesty is objectively presented in the works of creation (Rom. 1:18 ff.) by no means implies a corresponding capacity in man to lay hold of this presentation and, as it were, put it to fruitful effect. It is quite possible for God's revelation to be objectively given while it is subjectively obstructed. Hence the revealing of revelation takes place only in the miracle of the Holy Spirit.[5]

In connection with Thielicke's last point, a robust Reformed apologetic must never be willing to grant too much to the unregenerate mind in terms of what it knows to be true of God. If it is the case that the unregenerate does not seek and does not understand God's revelation,[6] why ought we to insist that they know the truth of God? After all, the Holy Spirit not only regenerates our deadened minds so that we may confess belief in Christ, he also must first work in opening our minds to seek and understand what we before did not comprehend about the truths of the Spirit, as Paul speaks about in 1 Corinthians.[7]

Romans 1:19 says, "since what may be known about God is plain to them, because God has made it plain to them." God's wrath against unbelief is made all the more understandable in light of the fact that the truth of God is and has been clearly manifested to all persons, universally in the form of general revelation and non-universally in the

---

5. Helmut Thielicke, *Theological Ethics, Volume 1: Foundations* (Grand Rapids: Eerdmans, 1979), 164.

6. *Romans 3:10.*

7. *1 Corinthians 2:6-16.*

form of special revelation. Regardless of the particular mode of God's revelation, it has been made clear and intelligible.

Romans 1:20 says, "For since the creation of the world God's invisible qualities—his eternal power and divine nature—have been clearly seen, being understood from what has been made, so that men are without excuse." This verse can be understood as emphasizing the general or universal manifestation of God's clear revelation of himself. Since the beginning of history up until this present day, God's clear universal revelation of himself has been manifested to all rational persons. Not only is it clear that God exists, it is clear that all opposing beliefs are incoherent and false. The Christian must be able to demonstrate the substantial incoherence of all ideas raised up against the knowledge of God. From what is clear generally, the Christian is called to silence the spiritual monist, as well as the material monist. It is our task to rout the Mormon and completely demolish the strongholds of Islam. The truth of God is clear, and the Church's apologetic must be reinvigorated in that truth. As Christ our Lord took all thoughts captive and did not appeal to a repressed knowledge within the unbeliever, so too must we fight.

Romans 1:21 says, "For although they knew God, they neither glorified him as God nor gave thanks to him, but their thinking became futile and their foolish hearts were darkened." Undoubtedly, Romans 1:21 is the *locus classicus* for those who assert that all persons in unbelief willingly suppress what they know to be true of God as their Creator. Upon first impression, this passage appears to say as much and nothing less. What alternate interpretation can be given that does not unnecessarily twist the immediate sense of the verse, yet still makes room for the assumption that the unbeliever does not know God deep down inside? To begin, while Paul uses Romans 1:20 to speak of that clear universal revelation of God that holds all men without excuse to this very day, verse 21 can be understood as documenting how God's clear special revelation has undergone an unmistakable pattern of generational decay in what people knew to be true of God and of his commands. In short, since none seek and none understand, what God has specially revealed of himself has been just as neglected from the beginning as has his general revelation. Starting from a truly Biblical framework, the reader of Romans 1:21 would have to admit that all persons descended from Adam, and that there was a slow, but

progressive neglecting, distortion, and dissolution of God's special revelation originally transmitted to our first father. While it is demonstrably
true that God has not manifested himself specially to all persons, the
entire human race does spring from an original historical point that
was saturated with God's special revelation. For example, because of
the effects of spiritual death (not seeking, not understanding), what
Cain learned from his father concerning God quickly became something less than glorifying to God. While Cain knew enough to bring
sacrifice, he did not care enough to understand, in contrast to Abel,
who understood the tremendous significance of the bloody sacrifice.
More or less, this generational pattern of revelation decay carried all the
way to the Flood, where only Noah and his sons were left with God's
original and undistorted special revelation. As also occurred with the
immediate descendants of Adam, from this post-Flood historical point
the generations of men slowly moved further and further away from
what Noah and his sons had preserved of God's special revelation. On
this matter, Henry M. Morris comments:

> Accordingly, we are on solid ground when we adopt Genesis 1–11
> as the true framework of ancient history. When we take our stand
> on this fundamental premise, we find that all the phenomena of
> mythology and all the discoveries of archaeology and geology cor-
> relate with each other and with the Bible in a most satisfying way.
> These data, when carefully examined, all point to a world where the
> people first knew the true God, then rapidly corrupted that knowl-
> edge into pantheism, polytheism, occultism, and idolatry, with all
> the evil practices these encourage. This was true in the primeval
> world and then again in the postdiluvian world.[8]

While it is true that an Aztec warrior could not be held personally accountable for what Ham and his descendants once knew of God, he is
held accountable for failing to know of what God has clearly revealed
of himself generally. What Paul says in Romans 1 concerning the de-
basing practices of mind and body committed by those of darkened intellect can be easily interpreted as a pre- and post-Flood indictment of
how sinful man slowly but surely dissolves the truth of God, turning

---

8. Henry M. Morris, *The Long War Against God: The History and Impact of the Creation/Evolu-
tion Conflict* (Grand Rapids: Baker, 1989), 263.

it into a detestable and distorted lie. The history of Israel shows time and time again that although they knew of God as a nation and as individuals, they consistently failed to seek after the knowledge of God, wherein the truth dissolved into gross idolatry. Whereas all persons are responsible to see what is clear of God from general revelation, there are those specifically who are under special indictment for their failure to seek after and understand God's special revelation as well. The generational decay in the Book of Judges is a perfect example of how special revelation can be both known and disregarded because of a lack of seeking God earnestly. Judges 2:10-12 reads:

> After that whole generation had been gathered to their fathers, another generation grew up, who knew neither the Lord nor what he had done for Israel. Then the Israelites did evil in the eyes of the Lord and served the Baals. They forsook the Lord, the God of their fathers, who had brought them out of Egypt. They followed and worshiped various gods of the peoples around them.

Furthermore, Hosea 4:6-7 reads:

> My people are destroyed from a lack of knowledge. 'Because you have rejected knowledge, I also reject you as my priests; because you have ignored the law of your God, I also will ignore your children. The more the priests increased, the more they sinned against me; they exchanged their Glory for something disgraceful.'

And lastly, Jeremiah 2:11 reads, "Has a nation ever changed its gods? (Yet they are not gods at all.) But my people have exchanged their Glory for worthless idols." One may neglect or distort what they have been taught of God, not so much because they rebelliously loathe its content, but because in spiritual death they have not uncovered its true significance and, thus, cannot discern its meaningfulness for their lives. One can see a pattern emerge in the Bible regarding complacency and pseudo-religiosity in the life of God's people that inevitably leads to a defective reinterpretation of God's revealed will. From the history of Israel alone, the reader of Romans 1:21 need not assume that Paul is speaking about first century Gentiles who willingly suppress an innate knowledge of God. Instead, one need only assume that Paul is alluding to God's historical special revelation, which, though clearly given to the race of man at times, has been systematically debased and forgotten by generation after generation.

Along with verse 21, the final verse of chapter 1, verse 32, "Although they know God's righteous decree that those who do such things deserve death, they not only continue to do these very things but also approve of those who practice them," has been used to help substantiate the theory that unbelievers willingly suppress what they know to be true of God. From a different angle, this verse can be understood as seamlessly pointing ahead to the general idea expressed in 2:14-15 concerning the law of God written on the hearts of all men. Nowhere does verse 32 allude to the idea of man possessing a formal and specific knowledge of God; for it is quite easy to see how man can have the law of God in the very structure of their being and have no understanding of God specifically as Creator. Though nearly all societies demonstrate a universal law code, and all men act against their consciences, it is not the same thing to suggest that all men willingly suppress a formal and immediate knowledge of God within them.

There are four principal benefits in assuming that unbelievers in spiritual death do not know God. One, the Christian is not stuck with the ugly paradox of the unbelieving believer. Because of this awkward predicament, Cornelius Van Til, the great presuppositional apologist, spoke of Romans 1:18-22 as "this most difficult passage." It need not be. The perspicuity of Scripture demands that such a crucial issue as this be relatively easy to comprehend, as opposed to being intrinsically enigmatic. Two, this position is consistent with the whole of Scripture, and is not primarily founded on one particular verse. Moreover, there is nothing heretical in this position that makes it immediately less appealing than the assumption that unbelievers knowingly reject the truth of God. Three, as opposed to the assumption that unbelievers resist the truth of what they know about God, this position carries with it no voluntaristic baggage—the will warring against the intellect.[9] The issue is an intellectual one, not a moral one. And fourth, this position upholds the cultural mandate, whereby we master the lies that suppress the truth and expose the incoherence of those thoughts raised up against the knowledge of God.

---

9. Gangadean, "Paper No. 120: Contra Voluntarism: The Will Is Not Independent of the Intellect," in *The Logos Papers*.

———

18

WHY I LEFT THE CHARISMATIC MOVEMENT

Published in Covenanter Witness[1]

Volume 93, No. 10

May 18, 1977

THE CHARISMATIC MOVEMENT IS SEEKING to appeal to all groups of Christians promising a deeper life in God through the baptism of the Holy Spirit. I was in this movement for several years. I realized after some years that its distinctive doctrines were unscriptural and its practices harmful to the growth of Christians and the advancement of Christ's kingdom. I am sharing some of the reasons I broke with the movement in the hope that those who find themselves attracted to it will take a closer look at its doctrines and practices.

While there is a great variety of beliefs and practices on the periphery of the Charismatic movement, the further one goes into it, the clearer its distinctive features appear. Among them are the following: the baptism of the Holy Spirit is distinct from conversion; many who are converted do not have the baptism of the Holy Spirit; this baptism is necessary if one is to live the victorious Christian life; the baptism has been lacking in the Church because of the widespread unbelief among its leaders.

Charismatics argue that because baptism was a separate experience from conversion for some, it is a distinct experience and that tongues

---

1. See: reformedpresbyterianarchives.com/the-covenanter-witness

is the normal, some say necessary, sign of baptism. The disciples in the upper room had a separate experience. They had to wait for the Spirit[2] and received it sometime later.[3] Here they spoke in tongues. Likewise, it was separate in Samaria,[4] though there is no explicit mention of tongues here. Cornelius is taken to be a non-believer and his experience is conversion and baptism at the same time. And they spoke in tongues.[5] The disciples at Ephesus who had the baptism of John had a separate experience and they spoke in tongues.[6]

This argument fails to notice what is unique to the transition between the Old and New Testament. The Holy Spirit was not given in the Old Testament as he was after Christ's death. So, one could be saved (converted) in the Old Testament without the baptism of the Spirit. Those who were saved under the Old Testament administration and also lived in the New Testament dispensation *had to have* a separate experience. In this way, they were unique, and a case for baptism as a separate experience cannot be made from them. Clearly, the apostles were saved as were the Ephesian disciples under the Old Testament economy. Cornelius was a God-fearer with all his house, a status assigned to non-Jews who were converted. The Samaritans likewise were not strangers to the covenants. Thus, speaking in tongues has to be examined in light of the unique circumstances of those who received it being in the transition period and receiving it from the apostles, as an indication of the apostles' unique authority to speak God's Word.

Furthermore, the numerous instances of conversions in the Book of Acts where there is no record of a separate experience, or of speaking in tongues, ought to be enumerated and weighed in getting the whole picture. Notice must also be made of the effect of the separate experience on those first disciples who would continue in Christ. Could the one whom the apostles would preach be Christ if he had not fulfilled the prophecy of Joel,[7] *all* authority being indeed his? The reading of the Book of Acts out of its context in the history of redemption is chiefly

---

2. *Acts 1:4.*

3. *Acts 2:4.*

4. *Acts 8:14-17.*

5. *Acts 10:44-48.*

6. *Acts 19:6.*

7. *Acts 2:33.*

responsible for the exemplary use of Acts with its consequent error in the doctrine of baptism as a separate experience. Thus, failure to apply the *Sola Scriptura* principle (all the Scripture and only the Scripture in interpreting Scripture) has produced this error.

Thus, those who are in Christ are baptized with the Spirit. They do not require a second experience. To seek a second experience is in vain. It can only lead to deception. And to promise the baptism to those who have it is foolish. Furthermore, to promise victory through this "second" blessing is more than misleading. It also follows that since the baptism has not been lacking in the Church, there was no widespread unbelief as such that was the cause of it being lacking.

The Charismatic, at this point, may want to go back and show from Scripture that it is a separate experience. Well and good. Or he may appeal to his own experience and the testimony of others and speak much of its benefits. It is unscriptural to appeal to one's experience to establish a doctrine. The experience must be brought to Scripture to be interpreted and evaluated. In doing so, a very different meaning of the experience might emerge.

The Charismatic claims that there can and ought to be and are miracles today, appealing to passages as Mark 16:17 and 1 Corinthians 12:28-29. Miracles done by *men in the Bible* are signs of the authority of the speaker who brings new revelation from God.[8] No one need doubt that God may work sovereignly to do miracles today. But Charismatics claim *men today* work such miracles. Men have the gifts today. Along with the "gifts" come new revelations of the Spirit. Although the disclaimer is often made that their word is not Scripture, the natural connection in the Bible between miracles and authoritative revelations moves the mind of their followers to give heed to their word as if it were Scripture. And often the new revelations are practically more important than the Scripture in guiding their lives from day to day.

The Mark 16 passage is not in some of the early New Testament manuscripts. And the 1 Corinthians 12:28 passage, if applied normatively, would mean there are apostles today, just as in the New Testament, who speak just as authoritatively. Some Charismatics hedge at this point and try to give a new sense to the word "apostle." But there is no warrant for a "new sense" from Scripture. As far as the miracles

8. *John 3:2; 2 Corinthians 12:12.*

they perform, one often has to stretch and coax the experience into being a miracle. And then add qualifiers where the "healings" do not last or are not complete—such as a deficiency of faith in the person healed. These qualifications absolutely kill it as being a New Testament miracle. Desperate men and women are often drawn out to extremities hoping for a miracle. Some have died believing all the while that God would heal. This is a pitiful condition. The simple believe every word of the reports of healing. I have never myself witnessed a single miraculous healing done by men claiming to have gifts, though I have often heard them claim a miracle done in my presence. The claim to know things supernaturally is a phenomena present in other religions and by itself should not be taken as support of the other teachings of the person, no matter how sincere and pious the person may be.

A claim that is woven into much of the Charismatic is that God speaks to a person directly in his spirit, apart from his understanding. Appeal is made to passages like 1 Corinthians 14:14 (my spirit prays, my understanding is unfruitful) and 1 Thessalonians 5:23 (your whole spirit and soul and body be preserved blameless). This is the highway to knowing God—direct communion with one's spirit above, apart and even against one's rational faculty. But 1 Corinthians 2:9-16 speaks of the spirit of man knowing the *words* of God. So, no absolute appeal can be made to man's spirit as a non-rational faculty. "Spirit" is also used to refer to the affections of man (blessed are the poor in spirit). Care must be taken to determine the meaning of "spirit" by the context in which it is used. The appeal to one's spirit as an irrational faculty, through which God speaks directly to the believer, leads to reliance on impressions, intuition, and imagination. So again, the authority of Scripture is practically bypassed.

There are a number of broad and significant, though not distinctive, features of the Charismatic movement which are an integral part of its foundation. The Charismatics could not get off the ground without these.

1. It is anthropocentric. In its worship and service, the needs of men are more prominent than the glory of God, much the way the crowds thronged Jesus for his miracles.

2. It is antinomian. There is much celebration of being free from the law and little delighting in the law of God. The law is conceived of negatively and narrowly, rather than as a guide in service to God in every aspect of life.

3. It is Arminian. It is one's act of faith that makes the final difference in conversion, perseverance, and all accomplishment, not God's unconditional election and irresistible grace.

4. It is perfectionistic. Because of its failure to grasp the breadth and depth of the law of God, and because of its trust in human ability, it is thought possible to live without sin in this life, at least while "walking in the Spirit." With such a view of sinlessness, it is hardly possible to grow in sanctification.

5. It is individualistic. Everyone is to go back to the New Testament directly, without using or even being aware of the work of the Holy Spirit through the pastor-teachers in history. Thus, the stated means of grace[9] are neglected. It is their common teaching that the historic churches have doctrine without life, so it is no use looking to them. This estimate locates the problem incorrectly. It is not that doctrine is not enough and you need the Spirit. The Spirit and the Word cannot be so separated. One can never truly have the Word without the Spirit or the Spirit without the Word. The problem is rather that many historic churches have departed from the sound doctrine they once had, and others profess the doctrine without believing it or without understanding its implications.

6. It is subjective. Sin is equated with "known sin;" Scripture is often interpreted in light of one's experience; Scripture passages are often allegorized or used as pegs on which to hang a message on the speaker's mind; the object of faith is often a "special word from the Lord;" appeal is made more to the emotions than to one's understanding, in order to deepen faith and obedience. It would be well to compare a Charismatic interpretation of a passage with what some Reformed commentaries say on it, in order to see the subjectivism more clearly.

---

9. *Ephesians 4:11-16.*

7. It is pietistic. It lacks a world and life view. It battles worldliness by otherworldliness instead of a proper view of the cultural mandate to subdue the earth, so as to fill the earth with the knowledge of the glory of God.

8. It is pessimistic. There is little or no faith that Christ's kingdom is now growing and will continue to grow by the present means of grace until all nations are discipled.

In short, its greatest claim—deeper life in God—is its greatest failure. Its distinctive doctrine, a second experience baptism of the Spirit, is unscriptural. Had it made proper use of the stated means of grace, the work of the pastor-teachers as summarized in the great creeds of the Church, such as the Westminster Confession, it could have avoided building on the wrong foundation of Arminianism, antinomianism, and its resultant perfectionism. The Reformed churches, however, share a great part of the responsibility, for our unbelief has become the occasion of our Charismatic brothers' stumbling. There is no room here for anyone to boast. All of us need to repent.[10]

---

10. For further critical analysis of the Charismatic distinctive, see: Gangadean, "Paper No. 122: Contra Charismatic Distinctive," in *The Logos Papers*.

19

—

THE GROWTH OF THE
KINGDOM OF GOD

Published in Blue Banner Faith and Life[1]

Volume 31, No. 2

April 19, 1976

THE REVEREND J. G. VOS BELIEVES THAT THE kingdom of God and the kingdom of Satan grow side by side until the end, according to the parable of the wheat and the tares. The former is not going to conquer the latter in this age. As a matter of fact, things are going to get worse, for Antichrist and his armies are yet to appear, and his appearance "will indicate to watchful Christians that the Lord's coming is very near."[2] Contrary to this, I believe that the kingdom of God is now growing to its fullness, displacing Satan's kingdom. The nations will be converted to Christ through the preaching of the gospel of the kingdom before he returns. Many Reformed Christians today would side with Rev. Vos's amillennial view. Few consider postmillennialism seriously. Is this difference important and, if so, which view, if either, is correct?

Some say the whole issue is not too important because the future has little bearing on what we ought to do. Expectation does not or need not affect program. But this is true only if we can live effectively with split personalities, so that we may try to disciple the nations

---

1. See: reformedpresbyterianarchives.com/blue-banner-faith-life

2. Johannes G. Vos, "The Signs Preceding the Second Coming of Christ," *Blue Banner Faith and Life*, July-September, 1974, 12.

while expecting to fail or expecting the Church to decline further. What happens, in fact, is that our program is adjusted to our expectation. Soon we begin to say we are to *witness* to the nations, not *disciple* the nations. We seek personal salvation, not the reconciliation of all things to Christ. And where we don't succeed, we say this age is an age of conflict, not one of conquest; after all, evil men and seducers are getting worse. We can't live very long with split personalities. Expectation affects program. They are organically one.

Some say the issue is not too important because it does not affect salvation. And salvation is the important thing. This view is especially harmful because, under the feeling of piety, it robs God of his glory. It is man-centered, not God-centered. It makes salvation the end, rather than the means to the end. It leads men into the fundamentalist camp, which selects out certain doctrines as important because they are necessary for salvation, rather than saying all Scripture is necessary if we are to be thoroughly equipped for every good work by which God is glorified.[3] If all Scripture is necessary, then Scripture about our expectation is necessary and, therefore, important.

Some say the issue is not too important because it is not too clear, and, it is not too clear because if it were, the Church would have been able to agree on it. But the Church has had to fight for every "clear" doctrine, including the deity of Christ. When the pastor-teachers, who are supposed to lead the saints into the unity of the faith, adopt this skeptical stance, it is a virtual surrender. Especially so when the skeptical stance is taken without being aware of the works of previous pastor-teachers on the subject. Arminians live as if the Synod of Dort never occurred. Kierkegaard wrote on the Incarnation as if the Council of Chalcedon never occurred. This is distressing. The same is true in eschatology. We have a special obligation to look closely at the earlier postmillennial arguments and answer them before adopting a new position. But this has not been done. Arguments used against postmillennialism have usually been against secondary points, or against straw men, or just question-begging or special pleading.

Some who say the doctrine of the kingdom is central in Scripture say eschatology is not too important. But the kingdom is an eschatological kingdom. Dispensationalists, pre-mils, a-mils, and post-mils

---

3. *2 Timothy 3:16.*

all have differing views on the nature, the goal, and the growth of the kingdom. Eschatology and the doctrine of the kingdom are inseparable. And if the one is important, so is the other. When we realize how the Jewish expectation led to the rejection of Christ, how Roman Catholic expectation led to empire-building, and how current evangelical expectation led to cultural retreat, we should conclude that our expectation is crucially important. The Church will continue to perish until we recover the vision of the kingdom by which God's glory is made known.

While my reasoning here is directed against Dr. Vos's view, some will say that unless you can deal with other views, your words have no weight, since you both may be wrong. I will try to speak to this. Dispensationalists like C. I. Scofield or Hal Lindsey say the kingdom is not present or spiritual, but future and Jewish (literally from Jerusalem). Some premillennialists like G. E. Ladd and J. O. Buswell attempt to maintain the kingdom is present and future, but seem to put the greater emphasis on the future rule from Jerusalem coming suddenly with Christ's return. If it can be shown the kingdom is present and spiritual, then dispensationalism is not true. And if the kingdom is present, spiritual, and growing to its fullness, then premillennialism is mistaken. Some amillennialists may say that the kingdom is present and spiritual, but how far it will grow is an open question. If it can be shown that the kingdom will grow to its fullness, this objection will be answered. Furthermore, if it can be shown that the kingdom of God cannot grow without displacing Satan's kingdom, then one of the major pillars of Mr. Vos's argument will be destroyed. And if this notion of growth is unequivocal, whereas his interpretation of certain passages as speaking of increasing evil or side by side growth can be interpreted consistently with the concept of growth, then his position will have no support at all. Because of the limitation of space, the arguments can be stated here only in a very compact form.

First of all, the kingdom is in spiritual reality, not the type and shadow of the Old Testament economy. The tabernacle and priestly ministry were an example and shadow of heavenly things.[4] So were the sacrifices.[5] So were the observing of times and the festivals.[6] They spoke of

---

4. *Hebrews 8:1-5.*

5. *Hebrews 10:1.*

6. *Colossians 2:17.*

the person and work of Christ. When Christ came, these were fulfilled. So also, was the life of Israel a type.[7] They were promised a land that flowed with milk and honey. When future blessings were promised, they were promised in material terms, things to eat and to drink and houses.[8] But the kingdom of God is not meat and drink, but righteousness and peace and joy in the Holy Ghost.[9] Christ said, seek first the kingdom of God and his righteousness and all these things (meat and drink) shall be added.[10] The promised land of milk and honey (of meat and drink) is not the kingdom of God, but is a shadow and type of the kingdom. Old Testament warfare, in possessing and keeping the land, is likewise typical. While they fought with a carnal sword, we fight with spiritual weapons.[11] Revelation 19:15, 21 is not a carnal warfare, but a spiritual one. The sword that proceeds from the mouth is the Word of God. The battle is pictured in Old Testament terminology because their warfare was typical of our spiritual warfare. Once the typical nature of the whole Old Testament economy is seen, we are in a position to properly translate unfulfilled prophecy. The rebuilding of the Tabernacle of David is seen in the Gentiles coming to Christ.[12] Only special pleading can hold out for a double fulfillment, here, one spiritual and the other literal or carnal, or one typical and the other antitypical.

Secondly, the kingdom is present. Being present and being spiritual are mutually entailing. If it is present then it is spiritual, and if it is spiritual then it is present. Although we have argued for its spiritual character above, we shall argue independently and not by implication for its presence. Scofield says we are in the church age and the kingdom is still future. But all those who are born again are in the kingdom.[13] The Gentiles at Colossae were in the kingdom,[14] not merely in the Church. The kingdom was not withdrawn, but was being preached

---

7. *1 Corinthians 10:6, 11.*

8. *Isaiah 65:21-22; 66:10-12.*

9. *Romans 14:17.*

10. *Matthew 6:33.*

11. *2 Corinthians 10:4-5; Ephesians 6:17.*

12. *Acts 15:13-18*; For a critique of Dispensational application of the rebuilding exclusively to the future, see: O. T. Allis, *Prophecy and the Church* (Philadelphia: P&R Publishing, 1945), 145-150.

13. *John 3:3, 5.*

14. *Colossians 1:13.*

throughout the Book of Acts: to the Samaritans;[15] to the Gentiles in Lystra, Iconium, and Antioch;[16] to the Jews at Ephesus;[17] to the Gentiles at Ephesus;[18] to the Jews at Rome;[19] to the Gentiles at Rome.[20] The Thessalonians were in the kingdom.[21] Dispensationalists who deny the kingdom is present must preach another gospel than Paul's and, if so, they invite the anathema he pronounced upon themselves.

Thirdly, the kingdom is growing from a small beginning. In the parable of the mustard seed:

> The kingdom of heaven is like a mustard seed, which a man took and planted in his field. Though it is the smallest of all your seeds, yet when it grows, it is the largest of garden plants and becomes a tree, so that the birds of the air come and perch in its branches.[22]

Or again: "The kingdom of heaven is like yeast that a woman took and mixed into a large amount of flour until it worked all through the dough."[23] It is impossible to get around the notion of the kingdom as a growing entity, starting from a small beginning. The dispensational and pre-mil kingdom does not grow; it comes in one fell swoop. Again, the stone in Daniel's dream that breaks up the image grows; it "became a great mountain and filled the whole earth."[24] Also, Christ is now ruling and will continue to rule until all his enemies be made his footstool, the last enemy to be destroyed is death.[25] The subjugation of his enemies is now taking place. It is a continuous and progressive activity and will continue until the last enemy remains. Christ wars through the Church; believers wrestle not against flesh and blood, but against

---

15. *Acts 8:12.*
16. *Acts 14:22.*
17. *Acts 19:8.*
18. *Acts 20:24-25.*
19. *Acts 28:23.*
20. *Acts 28:31.*
21. *1 Thessalonians 2:12.*
22. *Matthew 13:32.*
23. *Matthew 13:33.*
24. *Daniel 2:35, 44.*
25. *1 Corinthians 15:25-26.*

principalities and powers.[26] The last enemy, death, is destroyed by the personal return of Christ when the dead are resurrected.

Fourthly, the kingdom is growing to its fullness. In each of the above references, the growth continues to its natural end. The seed grows to a tree, it is not cut off as a sapling. The leaven leavens the whole lump, not just a part. The stone grows till it fills the whole earth, its natural end. Christ's rule continues until all his enemies be made his footstool. In each case, the end is reached by the process now in operation. The growth is not an indefinite growth, but a growth until it reaches its end. If we want to get an idea of what the growth of Christ's kingdom to its fullness might mean, we can consider the kingdom of Satan at its fullness in the days of Noah or in the days of Christ. The whole world was in darkness. When Christ's kingdom grows to its fullness, the earth shall be full of the knowledge of God as the waters cover the sea.[27]

The growth of the kingdom is throughout history, not the personal maturity of believers in each age. It is a common fallacy to take the growth of the part for the growth of the whole. If every believer in Paul's day, or in our day, were mature, it would not mean that the kingdom was mature. Again, the growth is not a simply numerical increase of believers throughout all time, although it is true that the end will come when the last elect is effectually called. The error here is in identifying the kingdom with the invisible Church, rather than with the visible Church, as the Westminster Confession rightly does.[28] If it were the former, then just one believer may be on earth when the kingdom would have reached its fullness. But the effect of growth is cumulative in the present. The mustard tree is fully present at the end of its growth.

Mr. Vos has made a distinction between relative and absolute fulfillment of prophecy. He applies this distinction to the prophecy that the earth shall be full of the knowledge of God as the waters cover the sea.[29] He uses this distinction to refer this prophecy to eternity and not to history. This allows him to maintain a relative fulfillment of it

---

26. *Ephesians 6:12.*

27. *Isaiah 11:9.*

28. *WCF 25.2.*

29. Johannes G. Vos, "Prophecy, Time and Eternity," *Blue Banner Faith and Life*, July-September, 1974, 34.

in history without having to commit himself to the nations being converted to Christ. Since he believes that the signs preceding the second
coming of Christ "were of such a nature that they might all appear in
any one generation of the world's history,"[30] a relative fulfillment of
this prophecy could have occurred in Paul's day or in our day. This
means that the mustard seed, leaven, stone, etc., that is, the kingdom,
could have grown to fullness in Paul's day, even with less than one or
five percent of the world's population as Christians. The mistake here
is to confuse relative and absolute *fulfillment* of prophecy with relative
and absolute *fullness* of knowledge. The darkness did cover the earth
without each and every person being in darkness.[31] So, the knowledge
of God may cover the earth without each and every person being converted. The extent of knowledge (every one or nearly all), the depth
of knowledge (compare Calvin and a new convert), the manner of the
knowledge (everyone knowing without everyone believing, as in some
churches), and the scope of knowledge (every thought showing forth
the glory of God), must be considered before concluding this prophecy can't have a fulfillment in history. While relative fulfillment may
occur with one percent converted, relative fullness of the knowledge
of God would be much closer to one hundred percent.

It may be that Mr. Vos feels constrained to adopt the position he
does because of his interpretation of the parable of the wheat and tares.[32]
He says "the field is not the church but the world" and, "according to
this parable, the population of the world will be mixed, of righteous
and wicked persons, throughout the present age . . ." He believes this
parable to be "decisive against postmillennialism, which . . . presupposes the conversion of practically the entire population of the world . . ."
He takes the tares to be non-Christians in general, not non-Christians
in the visible Church who "profess the true religion,"[33] but do not really believe it. There is an ambiguity here in the term "world." Is it the
earth or is it the ungodly world? If it is the earth, then the Church is
planted worldwide. After the wheat is planted, tares are sown among

30. Vos, "The Signs Preceding the Second Coming of Christ," 13.

31. *Isaiah 60:2.*

32. Johannes G. Vos, "The Second Coming of Christ and the Kingdom of God," *Blue Banner
    Faith and Life*, July-September, 1974, 19-20.

33. *WCF 25.2.*

the wheat. The tares resemble the wheat, making their appearance as tares when wheat and tares bring forth fruit. It is by their fruits that we can recognize false prophets as such. For the place of church discipline, here I find Calvin's exposition of this parable very sensible. This interpretation makes a lot of sense and is perfectly compatible with the belief that "practically the entire population of the earth" will be converted. If the field is the world of non-Christians, then the wheat is sown beside or among the tares and the question "from whence then hath it tares?" would be nonsensical. This parable is not decisive at all against the conversion of the world as Mr. Vos says. It is possible for everyone to be in the visible Church, i.e., profess the true religion, without denying the tares grow beside the wheat till the end.

Once it is granted that the kingdom of God grows to its fullness, it should be plain that this involves the conversion of the nations. Since the kingdom of Christ and the kingdom of Satan contend for the same human hearts, and for expression in the same spheres of culture, one cannot increase without the other decreasing. It should be reiterated that the kingdom of God spoken of here is his visible Church, sometimes called the kingdom of grace,[34] and not his rule over the remainder of the creation, sometimes called the kingdom of his power.[35] Christ's kingdom of grace is spoken of as having universal sway: Psalm 2:8; 22:27; 72:7-11, 17, 19; 86:9; 110:1; Isaiah 2:2-3; Amos 9:11-12; Acts 2:34-35; 15:17; etc. Since Mr. Vos has often espoused his father Geerhardus Vos's position, mention should be made of how the latter treats 1 Corinthians 15:25-26. In *The Pauline Eschatology*, he says, the "progressive subjugation of enemies . . . moves in the super-terrestrial sphere of the world of spirits, so that it can scarcely be counted among the prognostics of the approaching crisis; it consists of happenings unobservable by men."[36] We cannot agree that this conquest is unobservable by men, at least as far as its results are concerned. Christ came to destroy the works of the devil, which are very manifest here on earth. To think that the enemies are being conquered with men continuing in sin is incongruous. Furthermore, the enemies are not being destroyed by Christ apart from the Church, but by Christ

---

34. *SCQ. 102.*
35. *LCQ. 191.*
36. Geerhardus Vos, *The Pauline Eschatology* (Grand Rapids: Eerdmans, 1952), 91.

THE GROWTH OF THE KINGDOM OF GOD

through the Church. We pull down, by spiritual weapons, everything that exalts itself against the knowledge of God, and bring into captivity every thought to the obedience of Christ.[37] We wrestle against the rulers of the darkness when we contend with men, even as they fight against God when they fight with us.[38]

Mr. Vos has argued for evil increasing in the world, referring much of Matthew 24 literally to the future.[39] He notes J. Marcellus Kik's exposition of Matthew 24, but cites Rev. Arthur W. Kuschke Jr. for an alternative reading. Mr. Kik has responded to Mr. Kuschke's reading,[40] but Mr. Vos has not noted this in his remarks here. It is also left unclear which line of argument he wishes to take, whether parts of Matthew 24 refer primarily to the destruction of Jerusalem and others primarily to the second coming (in which case he does not specify here which parts refer to which event), or whether the whole of Matthew 24 applies to both events, to one as type, to the other as anti-type. Until these omissions are corrected, I believe Mr. Kik's exposition is still valid. In passing, it should be noted that Mr. Kik, who was an ardent advocate of postmillennialism, did not regard the millennium as still future, but refers it to the period between the two comings. In this, he represents the view of others who believe that this age is one of conquest and victory, not merely one of conflict.[41] Mr. Vos likewise speaks of the man of sin and of the Antichrist. We fail to find any attempt to rebut B. B. Warfield's discussion of these subjects.[42] For him, they did not conflict with the postmillennialism which he advocated.

Mr. Vos has argued against postmillennialism that in putting Christ's coming after a long period of time, it removes the reason for watchfulness.[43] However, he himself grants that Christ won't come until the

---

37. *2 Corinthians 10:4-5.*

38. *Acts 5:39.*

39. Vos, "The Second Coming of Christ and the Kingdom of God," 17. See point 3; Vos, "The Signs Preceding the Second Coming of Christ," 11. See point 3 on signs immediately preceding the second coming.

40. J. Marcellus Kik, *An Eschatology of Victory* (Phillipsburg: P&R Publishing, 1974), 65.

41. Kik, *An Eschatology of Victory*, 205.

42. J. E. Meeter, ed., *Selected Shorter Writings of Benjamin B. Warfield*, Vol. 1 (Nutley, NJ: P&R Publishing, 1970), 356; S. G. Craig, ed., *Biblical and Theological Studies* (Philadelphia: P&R Publishing, 1952), 463-475.

43. Vos, "The Second Coming of Christ and the Kingdom of God," 17.

gospel is preached in the whole world for a testimony.[44] The argument carries no weight therefore. Furthermore, watchfulness is not tied to the second coming only or primarily. Loraine Boettner has pointed out eight senses of the coming of Christ, some for which believers in every age must be watchful.[45]

Mr. Vos has argued that "postmillennialism represents the kingdom of God as coming gradually through the operation of forces now at work in the world, whereas the Scriptures represent it as coming in its final form suddenly and at a definite time, the second coming of Christ".[46] The argument is based on a non-sequitur which fails to notice that postmillennialism distinguishes between the kingdom of grace, which comes by growing gradually, and the kingdom of glory, which comes suddenly by the return of Christ—this failure is the basis of several of the criticisms brought against postmillennialism. For example, "Postmillennialism teaches a kingdom in which men are still in their natural bodies and still capable of committing sin."[47] This is true because postmillennialists recognize both the kingdom of grace in which believers now live, and the kingdom of glory, which is the consummated state of the kingdom of grace. They pray "that the kingdom of grace may be advanced, ourselves and others brought into it, and kept in it; and that the kingdom of glory may be hastened."[48] They do not identify the kingdom of God with the kingdom of glory only. Mr. Vos says, "Even if every individual in the whole world could be converted to Christianity, and every human institution 'Christianized,' still the final kingdom of God would not be here . . ."[49] I am not sure against whom this argument is directed, since no person is quoted as saying so. But postmillennialists do look for the world as such being converted to Christ, and every human institution being Christianized, before the kingdom of grace is consummated by the return of Christ and the destruction of all remaining sin, curse, and death.

---

44. Vos, "The Signs Preceding the Second Coming of Christ," 12.

45. Loraine Boettner, *The Millennium* (Phillipsburg: P&R Publishing, 1984), 248-262.

46. Vos, "The Second Coming of Christ and the Kingdom of God," 17.

47. Vos, "The Second Coming of Christ and the Kingdom of God," 17.

48. *SCQ. 102.*

49. Johannes G. Vos, "The Second Coming of Christ and Social Reform," *Blue Banner Faith and Life*, July-September, 1974, 25.

20

CAN UNBELIEVERS
DO GOOD?

Published in Covenanter Witness[1]

Volume 91, No. 1

January 1, 1975

C AN UNBELIEVERS DO GOOD? THERE ARE SEVERAL ways in which this question may be taken. If the question is reformulated to remove possible ambiguity, the answer is not difficult. "Can the unregenerate do anything to merit salvation?" Obviously not. Man's total depravity makes this impossible. Man is justified by faith without the works of the law. Most self-conscious Protestants are aware of this. But there are other aspects to the question that have puzzled many believers. For example, "Can the unregenerate believe the gospel and so be saved?" Again, no.

Regeneration is necessary before one can believe. This is central to Reformed theology. Another persistent question is: "What are we to think of the splendid humanitarian efforts of many who do not call on the name of the Lord?" If there is none that does good, if all our righteousnesses are as filthy rags, if the plowing of the wicked is sin, what are we to think of their efforts? The problem is felt most acutely when the unregenerate are leading the Christians in many aspects of our culture.

---

1. See: reformedpresbyterianarchives.com/the-covenanter-witness

It is at this point that many Christians, puzzled by these texts, conclude wrongly that not only are the works of the non-Christians inadequate, but the whole field of culture is held under suspicion as belonging peculiarly to the realm of darkness or to a neutral area, so that in any case the efforts of the non-Christians cannot be called good in any vital sense of the word. The realm of the good is restricted to Church activity so as to exclude all non-Christian efforts which lie outside the Church.

It is true that in one sense the good works of non-Christians are not good, but why specifically they are not good isn't often appreciated. Since the unregenerate are without Christ and therefore without God, their thoughts and actions are not and cannot be motivated by love for God. And since love is the fulfilling of the law, the unregenerate cannot fulfill the law. They cannot do good works in the manner that God requires of man. In other words, the unbeliever may refrain from killing and may do much to protect human life, all of which is formally in keeping with the law and of good use to himself and others. But since these works do not proceed out of love for God, they are not pleasing to God. That is why the plowing of the wicked is sin, because it is part of a life lived to glorify and enjoy self, rather than to glorify and enjoy God. When any man uses egotistically motivated good works to justify himself, he is wrapping himself in filthy rags in God's sight. Yet the neglect of good works because they cannot merit God's grace is more sinful and displeasing to God. To sum up then, the work of the unregenerate, inasmuch as it is not motivated by love for God, is evil. But insofar as it is formally in keeping with the law of God, it is good.[2]

Here another puzzle arises. According to Scripture, the tree is to be called good and its fruits good, or be called evil and its fruits evil. How then can we even in the latter sense say that the work of the unregenerate is formally good? If we recall that total depravity means that all our faculties have been turned away from God by the Fall, rather than that fallen man is corrupted to the fullest degree, we might understand how formally good works may proceed from the unregenerate man.

Fallen man has, in Adam, cut himself off from the life of God by which only he can do good. Recall the vine-branch discourse in John 15. But God has not purposed that fallen man here and now will be

---

2. *WCF 16.*

totally without his life. There remains in the unregenerate, even in the most extreme degree of corruption, some remnant of the original Edenic nature sparked by the life of God. This Edenic nature, sometimes conceived of as the image of God in the narrower sense, consisted of true righteousness, holiness, and knowledge. The mixed state of the nature of the unregenerate may be compared to the mixed state of the nature of the regenerate. In believers there remains some of the old nature, in this case the fallen nature. While believers will grow in righteousness, there will remain with them in this life, even at their best state, some remnant of the old nature. So it is with the unregenerate. There is parallel progress of believers and unbelievers as righteousness reigns unto life in the former, and sin reigns unto death in the latter. So, having located in the nature of the unregenerate the basis of formally good works, we can begin to properly understand and respond to their good works. As the believer progresses in the good by God's sovereign grace, called special or saving grace, so the unbeliever is kept from progress in evil by God's sovereign grace, called common grace. Romans 1 reveals God's giving up the unregenerate in judgment to the desires of their own hearts as they continue to suppress the truth of God. Every good done by man, therefore, is immediately attributable to the grace of God, God's life in man. Instead of grudgingly recognizing splendid gifts and efforts in the unregenerate as a threat to the truth of God's Word, we rather should find matter that affords praise to God, the God of all grace.

Left at this stage of explanation the matter is still unsatisfactory, for we do not yet fully appreciate the value of the works of the unregenerate. I am speaking of their good works, not the superabundance of their efforts that are contrary to the law of God. This is principally due to the fact that Christians have not understood the good works unto which they have been created and recreated. This requires an understanding of God's purpose in history, the nature of the kingdom of God, and the full significance of the law of God.

In creation, God purposes to manifest his own glory in, by, unto and, upon all his creatures.[3] In that purpose, man has a central role. Made in the image of God, man is to exercise dominion as God's ordained prophet, priest, and king in the creation. Thereby the earth is

---

3. *WCF* 2.2.

to be covered with the knowledge of the glory of God as the waters cover the sea. This we are commanded in the first commandment: know and acknowledge God. This we pray for in praying: hallowed be thy name. The advancement of this purpose is by the growth of the kingdom of God. Man's task consisted in filling the earth with God's image-bearers and together they progressively would fill the earth with the knowledge of the glory of God. Moved by devotion to God's glory, man would interpret in light of God the revelation God made of himself in his work of creation and rule in the creation so as to ever increase in knowledge, righteousness, and holiness.

Had Adam passed the probation in the Garden, success in his task would have been guaranteed. He and all in him would have been made perfect in righteousness forever. Adam's failure introduced sin and death into the world. God's purpose to reveal his glory in, to, upon, and by his creatures is not cancelled by the Fall; rather it is deepened. God purposed to order the Fall to his own glory.[4] Instead of Adam, Christ will head up all things. His task of exercising dominion is deepened, for he and those in him must now exercise dominion over sin while functioning as God's prophet, priest, and king. Further, God's new work of redemption serves to reveal the glory of his eternal attributes in an even greater way over and above the work of creation.

Now, how does this affect our appreciation of the good works of the unregenerate or for that matter of their works in general? Are they totally outside the task of subduing the earth? Does subduing involve settling the earth, developing sciences, arts, communications? Do we sit here now and communicate with each other apart from the efforts of millions of unregenerate men and women over the centuries? In how many ways have unbelievers contributed to the cultural mandate? How many believers owe their existence and nurture to unregenerate parents? Yet this is to look at the matter after the fact. Because the unregenerate have contributed to our culture, we cannot thereby justify our continued subjection to their leadership in the culture. For in many ways, their leadership slows and ultimately perverts our task to interpret, devote, and rule the creation to the glory of God. A positive comprehensive view of what Christians should be doing now would help us to understand the real significance of the ability of the non-Christian

---

4. WCF 6.1.

to do good works. Their ability to do good works is not self-sustained, but is sustained by the growth of God's kingdom in their midst, and must be understood in that context. And since the law is foundational to the kingdom, we must look at the law.

The whole duty which God requires of man is summed up in the Decalogue. Although delivered to Israel at Sinai on the tablets of stone, the law is revealed elsewhere in other forms. The law is in-created in every man. The works of the law are written in their hearts so that men are inexcusable for their sin.[5] This fact has major significance for evangelism and for structuring the institutions in which Christians and non-Christians live a common life. The law is also given to us in the great commandment to love the Lord our God with all our heart and our neighbor as ourselves. We can deduce from this that the law of God is universal (for all men and known of all men), perpetual (for all time—there never was any other standard), total (for every aspect of our lives), and spiritual (there cannot be a more perfect standard). It follows from this that, necessarily, we cannot understand what is required of us and forbidden to us, what are good works and evil works—in short, what is sin and righteousness—apart from the law of God. It also follows that because the law is comprehensive in scope, to understand it, we must meditate in the law day and night. Our understanding is improved as we build on the understanding God has given to the Church by its teachers over the centuries.

The law of God written in the heart of the unbeliever serves to restrain him from evil and guides to an extent his moral decisions. Ordinarily he would suppress this knowledge. As Christians properly interpret and apply God's law to all their dealings with fellow Christians and non-Christians, the knowledge of the law is renewed in their thoughts and the law does its convicting, restraining, and guiding work in their lives. Witness the effect of the principle of separation of church and state as institutions. This principle has had a liberating effect in many countries where state religion once oppressed people. Now, non-Christians support this principle and so do a good work. But Christians have not seen as clearly the need for separation of state and family, particularly in their task of education. They have not fought for the right of parents to educate their children, because they have

---

5. *Romans 2.*

not taken seriously their duty to educate their children to think, feel, and work as citizens of God's kingdom. When Christians begin to take seriously the reciprocal obligation they have to their children in the fifth commandment, in the context of seeking God's kingdom and glory, there will be a revolution of the first magnitude. The far-reaching changes would be hard to imagine when control of education passes into the rightful hands of parents. Then secular humanism is dis-established. If Christians would take God's law seriously and seek God's kingdom, they could soon recapture leadership in the culture. And instead of being led by non-Christians, they would lead non-Christians to do good works. Christians seeking to promote every law of God in a manner appropriate to the God-ordained end of every institution of which they are a part would restructure these institutions and thus influence non-Christians to good works. The alternative to this is that non-Christian thoughts, feelings, and actions will lead and influence Christians to build the humanist kingdom in institutions structured to ungodly ends. Christians and non-Christians must often live together in common institutions in this life. God's grace present in the non-Christians' ability to do good works makes their life bearable and makes our life with them possible. Where Christians are in cultural contact with non-Christians, God ordinarily channels many aspects of his common grace to the non-Christians through the Christians.

Insofar as Christians obey God's Word, they are the light of the world and the salt of the earth through the cultural expression of their corporate life. But where Christians, through disobedience, lose their salt and hide their light and become incapable of leading the non-Christians to good works, they are finding themselves cast out by the non-Christians and trodden under their feet. Here we see the mercy and justice of God over all men in the peculiar manner in which the unregenerate can do good works.

BIBLIOGRAPHY

Allis, O. T. *Prophecy and the Church*. Philadelphia: Presbyterian and Reformed Publishing, 1945.

Boettner, Loraine. *The Millennium*. Phillipsburg: Presbyterian and Reformed Publishing, 1984.

Burton, Kelly Fitzsimmons. *Retrieving Knowledge: A Socratic Response to Skepticism*. Phoenix: Public Philosophy Press, 2018.

Craig, S. G., ed. *Biblical and Theological Studies*. Philadelphia: Presbyterian and Reformed Publishing, 1952.

Gangadean, Surrendra. *The Book of Job: Deepening the Revelation of God's Glory for All Time—An Ironic Theodicy*. Phoenix: Logos Papers Press, 2024.

———. *The Book of Revelation: What Must Soon Take Place—Doxological Postmillennialism*. Phoenix: Logos Papers Press, 2023.

———. *History of Philosophy: A Critical Analysis of Unresolved Disputes*. Phoenix: Public Philosophy Press, 2022.

———. *The Logos Papers: To Make the Logos Known*. Phoenix: Logos Papers Press, 2022.

———. *Philosophical Foundation: A Critical Analysis of Basic Beliefs*. Phoenix: Public Philosophy Press, 2022.

———. *Theological Foundation: A Critical Analysis of Christian Belief*. Phoenix: Logos Papers Press, 2023.

———. *The Westminster Confession of Faith: A Doxological Understanding*. Phoenix: Logos Papers Press, 2023.

———. *The Westminster Shorter and Larger Catechisms: A Doxological Understanding*. Phoenix: Logos Papers Press, 2023.

Kik, J. Marcellus. *An Eschatology of Victory*. Phillipsburg: Presbyterian and Reformed Publishing, 1974.

Meeter, J. E., ed. *Selected Shorter Writings of Benjamin B. Warfield*, 2 Vols. Nutley, NJ: Presbyterian and Reformed Publishing, 1970.

Morris, Henry M. *The Long War Against God: The History and Impact of the Creation/Evolution Conflict*. Grand Rapids: Baker, 1989.

Thielicke, Helmut. *Theological Ethics, Volume 1: Foundations.* Grand Rapids: Eerdmans, 1979.

Toynbee, Arnold, and David Churchill Sommervell. *A Study of History.* New York: Oxford University Press, 1987.

Tussing, Rodney W. *Religion and Science: Deconstructing a Modern Paradigm.* Phoenix: Public Philosophy Press, 2019.

Vos, Geerhardus. *The Pauline Eschatology.* Grand Rapids: Eerdmans, 1952.

Vos, Johannes G. "Prophecy, Time and Eternity." *Blue Banner Faith and Life,* July-September, 1974.

———. "The Second Coming of Christ and Social Reform." *Blue Banner Faith and Life,* July-September, 1974.

———. "The Second Coming of Christ and the Kingdom of God." *Blue Banner Faith and Life,* July-September, 1974.

———. "The Signs Preceding the Second Coming of Christ." *Blue Banner Faith and Life,* July-September, 1974.

INDEX

ABOUT THE AUTHOR

DR. SURRENDRA GANGADEAN (1943–2022) was a professor of Philosophy at Phoenix College and at Paradise Valley Community College for forty-five years. Additionally, he taught from the pulpit at Westminster Fellowship for almost 30 years and taught courses at Logos Theological Seminary for over 25 years. Courses he taught include Introduction to Philosophy, Logic, Ethics, Philosophy of Religion, Eastern Religions, World Religions, Introduction to Christianity, Introduction to Humanities, Philosophy of Art, The Great Books, Philosophical Theology, Biblical Worldview, Biblical History, Church History, Systematic Theology, Biblical Hermeneutics, and Existential Hermeneutics. He received an M.A. degree in Literature from Arizona State University, an M.A. degree in Philosophy from the University of Arizona, and a Ph.D. in Natural Theology from Reformed International Theological Seminary. He presented academic papers and public lectures on Natural Theology and the Moral Law. Dr. Gangadean was the organizing President of The Logos Foundation, which serves academic education in Liberal Arts and Theology.